T0330084

The Dynamics of Knowledge Externalities

To Anna, Paolo, Emanuele and Francesco

To Maria Claudia, Bianca, Costanza and Filippo

The Dynamics
of Knowledge
Externalities
Localized Technological Change in Italy

Cristiano Antonelli

Department of Economics, University of Torino and Collegio Carlo Alberto, Italy

Federico Barbiellini Amidei

Research Department, Bank of Italy

Edward Elgar

Cheltenham, UK • Northampton, MA, USA

Published by
Edward Elgar Publishing Limited
The Lypiatts
15 Lansdown Road
Cheltenham
Glos GL50 2JA
UK

Edward Elgar Publishing, Inc.
William Pratt House
9 Dewey Court
Northampton
Massachusetts 01060
USA

A catalogue record for this book
is available from the British Library

Library of Congress Control Number: 2010939192

ISBN 978 1 84844 105 7

Typeset by Servis Filmsetting Ltd, Stockport, Cheshire
Printed and bound by MPG Books Group, UK

Contents

Acknowledgements   vii

1 Technological change and Italian growth 1950–1992:
   an intriguing puzzle   1

PART I   THE LOCALIZED GENERATION AND
         EXPLOITATION OF TECHNOLOGICAL
         KNOWLEDGE AND INNOVATION

2 The general framework   9
3 The localized generation of technological knowledge 15
4 The role of external factors in the localized generation
   of technological knowledge   19
5 The role of external factors in the localized
   exploitation of technological knowledge: localized
   appropriability and directed technological innovation 34
6 The emergence and decline of innovation systems   41
7 A model of localized technological change cum
   pecuniary knowledge externalities   51

PART II   THE ITALIAN EVIDENCE

8 Technological change in a distributed innovation
   system   75
9 The measures of innovative activity in Italy   91
10 Structural change and the building of systemic
   interdependence: the emergence of a distributed
   innovation system   124
11 Knowledge exploitation strategies and the direction of
   technological change   139
12 Knowledge generation and vertical dynamic
   interdependence within industrial filieres: econometric
   evidence on total factor productivity growth   162

13   A distributed system of innovation: the Italian
     evidence in the second part of the twentieth century   180

References   186
Index   201

Acknowledgements

This study is the result of a long-term research project designed and implemented by the Research Department of the Bank of Italy. The research has been made possible by the complementary support of the BRICK (Bureau of Research on Innovation, Complexity and Knowledge) of the Collegio Carlo Alberto. The views expressed in this book are those of the authors and do not necessarily reflect those of the affiliated institutions.

The authors gratefully acknowledge the comments and suggestions of Mario Amendola, Fabrizio Barca, Marcello de Cecco, John Cantwell, Paul David, Luisa Dolza, Jan Fagerberg, Alfredo Gigliobianco, Roberto Marchionatti, Fabrizio Onida, Raffaele Paci, Mario Pianta, Francesco Quatraro, Salvatore Rossi, Fabiano Schivardi, Alessandro Sterlacchini, Vera Zamagni, as well as of other participants at seminars and workshops in various locations, and, in particular, to all the participants of the Session 'Innovation systems and economic performance: Past leaders, catch-up countries and new late comers (20th–21st centuries)' at the XVth World Economic History Congress, Utrecht, 5 August 2009, where preliminary results of this research were presented.

The authors thank Federico Bonaglia, Irene Bonafine, Claire Giordano, Ferdinando Giugliano, Roberto Golinelli, Matteo Gomellini, Susanna Mantegazza for generously providing data or help in various forms, and Paolo Parisi for allowing us to show his artwork on the cover page.

1. Technological change and Italian growth 1950–1992: an intriguing puzzle

The economic growth of the Italian economy in the second part of the twentieth century provides large and systematic evidence about fast rates of growth of output and especially total factor productivity, and yet a lack of effort in the formalized generation of technological knowledge, as measured by traditional indicators such as expenses in research and development (R&D) activities or patents.

Since the 1990s, a wealth of case study evidence regarding sectors, firms and regions 'discovered' the relevance and complexity of the innovative processes at work during the 50 post-war years. This evidence shows that the Italian economy experienced, up to the early 1990s, fast and intensive growth, mainly driven by the increase of total factor productivity engendered by the widespread introduction of technological and organizational innovations. So far, the Italian case provides puzzling evidence of the growth of an industrial economy characterized by low levels of R&D expenditure and yet high levels of growth of total factor productivity. The solution to the puzzle can be found in the systemic congruence that has emerged in the Italian economy between the organization of the generation of technological knowledge and the traditional characteristics of the economic and industrial structure.

This book aims to draw attention to the relevance and uniqueness of the dynamics of technological change that characterized the industrial system in Italy. Identifying and framing in a structured and coherent interpretative context the significant established and novel elements of empirical evidence, the book shows how, contrary to current opinion, the Italian economic system had a notable capability to innovate, producing relevant technological change both with regard to its rate and direction. By focusing attention on total factor productivity, it is possible to concentrate on the uniqueness

1

of the technological change that characterized the fast and deep economic development and growth, and the radical structural transformation of the Italian economic system, during the second half of the twentieth century. The innovative ability of Italian firms was based upon the systematic valorization of user–producer interactions between upstream producers of capital goods and downstream producers of consumer goods, within industrial districts, and the systematic development of localized learning rather than on the traditional 'corporate model' based upon mechanisms of formal research funded and performed internally by large firms, as revealed by statistics regarding R&D and measured by indicators such as patents and publications.

From this point of view, the forms, the determinants and the effects of the technological change characterizing Italian economic growth were highly original and call for a specific interpretive model. The central assumption on which this study is based is that technological and organizational change, based upon qualified vertical and horizontal interactions among firms, and characterized by strong directionality towards the introduction of capital-intensive process innovations engendered by the same system of vertical relations, played a central role and it is indispensable to understanding the characteristics, the rhythms, the determinants and the weaknesses of Italian economic growth during the second half of the twentieth century.

This book is the result of an attempt to provide a systematic interpretative framework into which the emerging case study evidence can be framed. The aim is to elaborate an exhaustive and complete picture of Italian economic growth able to account for the characteristics of the process of generation and exploitation of localized technological knowledge and the ensuing introduction of localized technological change, as relevant aspects of Italian economic growth, which have been neglected for a long time and whose relevance has been underestimated. In so doing, this book contrasts the view shared by the main Italian economic history studies in the second half of the twentieth century, that do not give any importance to technological change and, more generally, to the extraordinary growth of output engendered by the substantial increase of total factor productivity up to the early 1990s. In order to provide an interpretative frame able to support the specific characteristics of these dynamics, the first part of the book elaborates the localized technological change approach, so as to appreciate and stress the role of the external context of the innovation process. It elaborates upon the notion of pecuniary externalities and shows how pecuniary knowledge externalities matter in explaining the dynamic capability of an economic system.

The book relies upon the large volume of literature that considers technological change endogenous to economic activity and actually constitutes its qualifying aspect, but integrates it with an in-depth analysis of the generation and exploitation of technological knowledge. In fact, it is possible to consider technological change as the result of a specific form of economic activity, which consists of the ability to accumulate and generate technological knowledge and expertise, and to draw on this stimulus and potential to introduce specific technological and organizational innovations. In the analysis of the particular process that leads to the introduction of innovation, it is necessary to consider not only the formalized innovative activities, proxied by classical indicators such as patents registered both in Italy and abroad and the expenditures on R&D, but also the more general fabric of technological knowledge, including knowledge interactions and knowledge externalities.

The focus on the localized technological change approach implemented by the notion of pecuniary knowledge externalities enables us to grasp the key role played by the specific character of the organization of the generation of technological knowledge in the Italian economy. In these decades, the organization of the production of knowledge in Italy takes place along two lines. On one hand, the group of large firms that had emerged at the beginning of the century, many under the control of the State, adopts the 'corporate' model. The corporate model was traditionally based upon the pivotal role of the large corporation able to perform intramuros R&D activities. The few Italian corporations in this period are more and more active in funding the generation of new knowledge and play an important role in the performance of these activities.

Next to the imitation and adaptation of the 'corporate' model, however, a second process takes place: one where small firms play an important role. Their efforts in the generation of technological knowledge are seldom identified by statistical measures as they rely on the accumulation and valorization of tacit knowledge, based both on internal learning and mainly upon the collective creation and implementation of external pools of knowledge. The systematic and systemic usage of external technological knowledge into the generation of new technological knowledge plays a key role in this context. This second part of the Italian economy is able to implement an original 'distributed' model for the organization of the generation, exploitation and dissemination of technological knowledge. Knowledge interactions among small and larger firms within horizontal and vertical network structures, such as industrial districts and technological filieres, provided access to emerging pools of collective knowledge and favoured the introduction of technological and organizational innovations by a broad array of firms. Such innovations, in turn, affected the structure of the system feeding, for quite a long stretch of time that apparently lasted until the early 1990s, a self-sustained and virtuous process of economic growth and structural change.

The empirical analysis shows how total factor productivity experienced a fast increase, not only in the so-called modern (or high-tech) industries but also, and mainly, in the traditional sectors. The rejuvenation of the traditional industries clustered within industrial districts together with the systematic increase in the quality content of their output appears to be one of the key characteristics of the process. In this context, the emergence of key sectors specializing in the supply of specialized machinery and intermediate goods was, at the same time, an input and an output of the process, leading to the creation of technological filieres where systematic user–producer interactions implemented internal learning processes.

As a result, at the aggregate level, the system exhibits a rapid shift away from the corporate model established in the twentieth century in the United States, towards a new distributed model based upon structured interactions among learning agents that share and barter technological know-how horizontally within industrial districts and vertically along filieres. In so doing, an original model of generation of knowledge emerged in Italy along lines that differ both from the established corporate model and the so-called open innovation model that has developed in recent years.

The new open innovation model is characterized by systematic outsourcing of knowledge generation activities and it is increasingly based upon actual knowledge transactions implemented by research contracts assigned by corporations to knowledge-intensive organizations, mainly based in the academic system, and upon the new venture capitalism. Here, the emergence of new surrogate markets for knowledge intensive property rights, resulting from the merging of financial markets and the markets for knowledge, is crucial. Corporations are experiencing a declining role in the performance of R&D activities while they remain active in funding the generation of new knowledge and its eventual purchase and exploitation, often in the form of mergers and acquisitions of new innovative small firms (Chesbrough, 2003; Chesbrough, Vanhaverbeke and West, 2006; Antonelli and Teubal, 2010).

In the Italian distributed model, the generation of knowledge is the result of enhanced social interactions that rely upon, and at the same time implement, qualified long-term transactions along vertical filieres among upstream suppliers of capital goods and downstream users. Repeated transactions in the markets for intermediary goods provide the opportunity to implement knowledge interactions that are fruitful both for the customers and the vendors of tangible goods. Such qualified user–producer interactions are the result of the implementation of coherent technological filieres that act as effective communication channels for the bilateral exchange of tacit knowledge. Here the emergence of the intermediary markets for machinery and intermediate inputs characterized by low transaction costs and high intensity of knowledge interactions is crucial. Such markets became increasingly articulated and sophisticated by stretching the chains of specialized suppliers by means of processes of vertical disintegration, the birth of new specialized firms and increased division of labour.

Intense market interactions along the chains of specialized suppliers, co-localized within industrial districts, favoured systematic knowledge interactions between users and producers, provided the opportunity to enhance the recombination of dispersed knowledge possessed by different agents and eventually led to the diffused generation of new technological knowledge. Italian small firms, as a result, were able to achieve higher rates of growth, as they were able to make systematic use of external knowledge, that is knowledge generated by other firms, including the corporate part of the economy, the technology generated in other countries and, to a large extent, the pool of collective knowledge implemented within industrial districts and technological filieres, as a key input into the generation of new technological knowledge.

The Italian innovative process was crucially conditioned: by a creative reaction, pulled by the sharp increase in the aggregate demand that Italian firms could take advantage of, via the participation of the Italian economy into the European markets; and by creative adoption, that is, by the systematic effort to reshape and adapt accessible technologies to their specific needs, providing key feedbacks to the upstream sectors that could, in turn, further improve their product innovations so as to increase their technological congruence with respect to the characteristics of the adopters. The emergence of such an original distributed model of generation, dissemination and exploitation of technological knowledge, with high levels of systemic and organizational congruence with the intrinsic characteristics of the Italian industrial system, played a crucial role in this context.

The emergence of a particular form of organizational and technological congruence is closely tied to the emergence of a specific form of innovative capacity. Thus, the Italian case can be considered an important reference to appreciate the extent to which a country's ability to introduce technological innovations and increase the levels of total factor productivity, that is, to enter and remain on an innovative path, crucially depends on its capacity to adapt the organization of the generation and exploitation of technological knowledge to the specific structural characteristics of its system (Abramovitz, 1956, 1989).

PART I

The localized generation and exploitation of technological knowledge and innovation

2.   The general framework

2.1   INTRODUCTION

This part of the book elaborates a microeconomic framework at the crossroad of the Schumpeterian and Marshallian traditions of analysis to explain economic growth based upon the role of technological change (Schumpeter, 1911 [1934]). While much of the economics of growth impinges upon an equilibrium approach at the aggregate level, this book uses the Marshallian analysis of partial equilibrium to elaborate a microeconomic Schumpeterian approach that analyses innovation as the consequence and the cause of self-organizing out-of-equilibrium processes. In so doing, it presents a methodological update of the localized technological change approach, stressing the systemic role of pecuniary knowledge externalities. Such externalities become available within qualified systemic conditions such as industrial districts and technological filieres providing abundant and cheap access to external knowledge, an essential input into the recombination and generation of new technological knowledge. This approach is relevant as it provides an interpretation of the Italian puzzle of very low levels of expenditure in R&D and yet high levels of total factor productivity growth.

Our basic argument is that unexpected changes in product and factor markets induced myopic firms, constrained by substantial irreversibility of production factors, to try to innovate. Their localization into (sub-) systems characterized by qualified mechanisms of knowledge governance and hence access to external knowledge at costs that were below equilibrium levels, made their reaction creative as opposed to adaptive. Such localization paved the way to the successful generation of technological knowledge and the eventual introduction of localized technological changes by firms, embedded in the fabric of knowledge networks. Good mechanisms of knowledge governance and effective mechanisms of user–producer interactions along vertical filieres and within industrial districts, made the creative reaction possible and enabled firms to actually introduce productivity enhancing capital-intensive process innovations.

This part of the book presents a generalized account of the localized technological change approach. In so doing, it provides the frame into which a detailed analysis of the key role of the external knowledge can be implemented. The appreciation of the role of the external context of action into which firms are embedded, both in terms of the features of the endowments and the access conditions to the pools of collective knowledge, provides the opportunity to grasp the features of the Italian innovation system and to implement the localized technological change approach.

2.2   LOCALIZED TECHNOLOGICAL CHANGE AS CREATIVE REACTION

According to Schumpeter (1947) innovation is the result of a particular form of reaction triggered by conditions of disequilibrium and favoured by specific and qualified conditions of access to external knowledge. The reaction, in fact, can be either adaptive or creative: the quality of the context into which firms are embedded is crucial to determine whether their reaction will eventually lead to the actual introduction of technological innovations or will consist in traditional adjustments along the existing isoquants, that is, technical changes. A quote from a key text seems appropriate here:

> What has not been adequately appreciated among theorists is the distinction between different kinds of reaction to changes in 'condition'. Whenever an economy or a sector of an economy adapts itself to a change in its data in the way that traditional theory describes, whenever, that is, an economy reacts to an increase in population by simply adding the new brains and hands to the working force in the existing employment, or an industry reacts to a protective duty by the expansion within its existing practice, we may speak of the development as an adaptive response. And whenever the economy or an industry or some firms in an industry do something else, something that is outside of the range of existing practice, we may speak of creative response. Creative response has at least three essential characteristics. First, from the standpoint of the observer who is in full possession of all relevant facts, it can always be understood ex post; but it can practically never be understood ex ante; that is to say, it cannot be predicted by applying the ordinary rules of inference from the pre-existing facts. This is why the 'how' in what has

been called the 'mechanisms' must be investigated in each case. Secondly, creative response shapes the whole course of subsequent events and their 'long-run' outcome. It is not true that both types of responses dominate only what the economist loves to call 'transitions', leaving the ultimate outcome to be determined by the initial data. Creative response changes social and economic situations for good, or, to put it differently, it creates situations from which there is no bridge to those situations that might have emerged in the absence. This is why creative response is an essential element in the historical process; no deterministic credo avails against this. Thirdly, creative response – the frequency of its occurrence in a group, its intensity and success or failure – has obviously something, be that much or little, to do (a) with quality of the personnel available in a society, (b) with relative quality of personnel, that is, with quality available to a particular field of activity relative to the quality available, at the same time, to others, and (c) with individual decisions, actions, and patterns of behavior. (Schumpeter, 1947:149–150).

In the localized technological change approach, innovation is induced by changes in the relative prices of factors and changes in the demand for goods that push the firm out-of-equilibrium. Firms are induced to innovate because they must respond to unexpected changes of the product and factor markets that alter their operational conditions. Adjustment to such changes and, more generally, to all unexpected events, often turns out to be difficult and, in most cases, costly. Substantial irreversibility of production factors qualify the production process and all changes, both in terms of substitution, when the relative prices of inputs change, and in terms of sheer quantities, when the expected levels of demand are not met by actual product market conditions, require some adjustment costs. In order to face the unexpected changes in product and factor markets, and because of the constraints imposed by the irreversibility of production factors, firms are induced to consider the possibility of changing their technology instead of their techniques (and hence the combination of their inputs). In order for the reaction to become creative, the given historical context in which it occurs plays a central causal role. Firms are induced to try to innovate by the changing conditions of product and factor markets through the economic cycle, but they are localized in the technical, productive, product, geographic and organizational areas in which they are rooted by the learning process and by the irreversibility of production processes and interaction networks. Innovative activity is first of all a form of localized creative reaction that takes place only when the systemic conditions into which firms are embedded are conducive. The context of localization is crucial in defining the specific form and content that induced innovation assumes (Antonelli, 1995, 1999, 2001, 2003 and 2008b).

This approach finds its roots in well-established lines of analysis. Marx (1867 [1976]) argued that increased labour costs determined by the rising phase of the cycle and by the contraction of unemployment were at the origin of the introduction of new technology and increased capital intensity. More precisely, Marx argued that an increase in wages caused firms to identify and appropriate the tacit knowledge accumulated in the learning processes matured in the course of productive activity and, on this basis, firms would innovate by introducing capital-intensive technologies that would enable them to substitute labour and hence increase unemployment and reduce wages. Innovation according to Marx was, above all, unidirectional: it was impossible for new technology not to be increasingly capital-intensive. The effects of an increase in the overall efficiency of the productive process are added to the effects of substituting capital for labour and together determine new levels of employment and wages. This interpretative approach has been proposed again and again. Particularly effective was John Hicks' line of analysis, in which the pressure of factor markets is the key factor determining both the rate and the direction of technological change.

Also, changes on the demand side exert a strong 'pull' effect. According to Kaldor (1972) and Schmookler (1966) growth in aggregate demand leads firms to introduce technological innovations in order to face the continuous pressure of rising levels of demand for their output in product markets. In the demand pull approach, however, little attention is paid to the generation of technological knowledge. As a matter of fact, Kaldor stresses more the effects of the demand pull in terms of increased investments and hence faster rates of adoption of new vintages of capital goods that incorporate 'automatically' better technologies, rather than in terms of the actual generation of the new technologies. Much demand pull analysis seems based upon a theory of diffusion of technological innovations rather than a theory of generation of technological innovations.

Our approach shares the endogenous understanding of technological change that is at the base of both the inducement and demand pull mechanisms, but pays much more attention to the mechanisms underlying the generation of technological knowledge. In particular, the analysis of the conditions of access to external knowledge plays a key role in our approach. The reaction of firms constrained by the irreversibility of their inputs may lead to the actual generation of new and superior technological knowledge and eventually to the introduction of productivity enhancing technological changes localized in the specific conditions of the production process, of product and factor markets, only if and when pecuniary knowledge externalities provide firms with access to external knowledge under specific and qualified conditions that make its search, purchasing and absorption costs much lower than in equilibrium levels.

When the structure of the system is such that knowledge externalities are not available or are outweighed by significant transaction, search and communication costs, when congestion and limited appropriability impede the use of external knowledge and the architecture of interactions limits knowledge interactions, single innovations may occasionally take place, but remain isolated acts of a minority of individual firms with little systemic effect. When the competitive threat to the established market position is weak and hence creative social reactions are not solicited, inferior technologies are likely to be resilient. Adaptive responses, as opposed to creative exaptive ones, are likely to occur when firms have no access to knowledge interactions and the generation of knowledge only relies upon internal sources. In such conditions, firms are not able to introduce new localized, productivity-enhancing technologies and can only switch, that is, change their techniques within the existing maps of isoquants. When the access of firms to external knowledge is costly, if not prohibitive, and adaptive responses, as opposed to creative ones, prevail, no technological change takes place and hence the structures of the system do not change.

The reaction of firms can be creative as opposed to adaptive and engender the actual introduction of successful, productivity-enhancing innovations, when and if the interactions and feedbacks shaped by the structure of the system provide access to external knowledge and external learning opportunities. The intensity and the effects of interactions are shaped by the structure of the system and, specifically, by the network topology of agents distributed in the multidimensional space, at each point in time. The distribution of agents in the multidimensional space is itself the endogenous result of agents' past locational strategies. Clearly knowledge externalities are internal to the system: they depend upon the specific combination of activities and channels of communication in place among them. Knowledge externalities depend upon the structure of the system. The organization and composition of the structure of the system into which firms are localized exerts a key role in shaping the dynamics both at the aggregate and the individual level.

Let us explore more systematically the role of technological knowledge in the localized technological change approach.

3. The localized generation of technological knowledge

The localized approach can be stretched so as to implement a broader understanding of what ignites and conditions the generation of technological knowledge. In the localized technological change approach, the introduction of innovation is the changing result of a series of circumstances and factors that affect the generation of technological knowledge. The incentive to innovate is translated into innovating only if a set of rather specific, complementary conditions about the generation of technological knowledge are satisfied. The firm can react creatively by introducing new technology and, therefore, can innovate only if there is a stock of easily accessible knowledge. This depends upon two conditions. First the internal learning conditions and the ability of each firm to mobilize and valorize the learning processes. The second key factor to be considered is whether and how the firm can access the sources of external knowledge. External knowledge is, in fact, an indispensable complementary input in the recombination process that leads to the generation of new technological knowledge. External knowledge plays a key role that becomes all the more relevant when the prevalent size of firms is small.

In the Arrovian approach, technological knowledge is mainly viewed as the result of spontaneous and automatic learning processes. Localized technological change impinges upon this approach and praises the role of the competence and tacit knowledge based upon learning processes. The Arrovian analysis of learning as the basic engine for the accumulation of technological knowledge (Arrow, 1962b), in fact, has been greatly qualified and sharpened by the insight of Anthony Atkinson and Joseph Stiglitz (1969) who introduced the strong hypothesis that technological change can take place only in a limited technical space, defined in terms of factor intensity. Technological change is localized because it has limited externalities and affects only a limited range of the techniques, that is, those contained by a given isoquant, which is identified by the actual context of learning, in the proximity of the equilibrium conditions under which the firms have been producing. In other words, technological change can only take place in the technical space where firms have been able to learn: localization here is strictly defined in terms of factor intensity and with respect to the techniques in place at each point in time.

Learning indeed is one of the basic sources of new technological knowledge. As such, it exerts a strong and clear effect in terms of defining the cognitive space into which each firm can expand its current technological base. As a consequence, the new technological knowledge generated by each firm is constrained within the proximity of its current activities. In other words, learning exerts a powerful localizing effect, which limits the spectrum of possible discoveries. At the same time, however, the generation of new knowledge can take a wide variety of possible directions, impinging upon both the specific form of learning that is actively implemented and the context in which it takes place (Antonelli, 1995, 1999, 2001).

The resource-based theory of the firm presents learning as the joint product of current activities and hence assimilates knowledge to learning. Edith Penrose (1959) identifies the firm, its organization and its routines, as the privileged actor in the learning process. The firm precedes the production function, as its primary activity consists of the generation of new technological knowledge. Each firm, as is well known, learns and builds up new capabilities and eventually discovers new possible applications for production factors and competences that are found within its own boundaries. According to the resource-based theory, in other words, innovative firms are successful when they try to make the most effective use of production factors that are not only locally abundant, but also internally – within its own boundaries – abundant (Foss, 1997, 1998).

The economics of localized technological knowledge makes it possible to implement the resource-based theory of the firm and hence bring a bottom-up approach to the economics of knowledge in two cardinal ways: (1) emphasizing the contribution made by intentional decision-making that stems from the creative reaction of the innovative firm; (2) qualifying the conditions for generation as being shaped by the localization of the learning process. Let us analyse them in turn.

Knowledge is no longer regarded as the automatic by-product of learning, but rather the result of an intentional process and explicit decision-making. The role of the Schumpeterian creative reaction, emphasized in the localized technological change approach, makes it possible to overcome this limitation (Schumpeter, 1947). The innovation process is activated when and if emerging mismatches between the expected and actual conditions of both product and factor markets and performances induce firms to change their routines. Only then is tacit knowledge accumulated by means of learning processes actually converted into technological knowledge and new technologies are finally introduced (Antonelli, 1995, 1999).

The appreciation of the role of intentional decision-making in the generation of new knowledge, and specifically the identification of the creative reaction that pushes firms to actually generate new knowledge, provides the first major point of departure from the notion of knowledge as the automatic and spontaneous outcome of learning. Firms are reluctant to change their routines, their production processes, their networks of suppliers and marketing activities as much as their goals and their understanding of the product and factor markets. Firms can overcome their intrinsic inertia and resistance to change only when there is a powerful failure mechanism at work. Firms are pushed into taking advantage of the tacit knowledge acquired through learning processes by the emerging mismatches between their own beliefs, based upon perceptions and related plans, and the actual conditions of the markets for products and production factors. Only when such a mismatch takes place and the quasi-irreversibility of the decisions implemented impedes simple adjustments, are firms pushed, by emerging losses and performances below expected levels, to react creatively and introduce innovations.

The transformation of a competence based upon learning processes into new, actual technological knowledge requires specific and dedicated effort, where learning is a necessary, but not sufficient, condition for the generation of new knowledge. External factors play a key role both in the intentional generation and the exploitation of technological and organizational knowledge. The combined effect of internal learning, external knowledge and the conditions for exploitation associated with the intensive use of idiosyncratic factors (as a result of introducing biased technological change by intentional decision-making) is the path-dependent and idiosyncratic character of the knowledge generated by the firm in its efforts to build up its distinctive competences. Here is the second major point of departure from the conventional notion of technological knowledge generation (Aghion and Tirole, 1994).

The generation of new knowledge is not an automatic and spontaneous product of internal learning processes. Intentional and selective strategies are necessary in order to generate new knowledge. Technological knowledge intentionally generated by firms has a strong idiosyncratic character that is influenced both by the characteristics of internal learning processes and by the characteristics of local factor and product markets.

Particular institutional conditions external to each firm favour the outcome of creative reaction and, therefore, encourage the rate of innovation. The efforts of firms to face the new product and factor market conditions can yield the introduction of actual productivity-enhancing innovations only if and when the access to external knowledge, an essential input into the generation of new knowledge, is possible and enables its acquisition at costs that are below equilibrium levels. Such conditions take place only in highly qualified circumstances. With such appropriate conditions, the creative reaction sets off a self-sustaining chain reaction. In such circumstances each single firm, as affected by innovation introduced by other firms, can react by introducing further innovation. The access to the local sources of technological knowledge provides a key input in the process of generating localized technological knowledge.

4. The role of external factors in the localized generation of technological knowledge

4.1 FROM TECHNOLOGICAL EXTERNALITIES TO PECUNIARY KNOWLEDGE EXTERNALITIES

The aim of this chapter is to explore the role played by external knowledge into the generation of new technological knowledge. The traditional analysis originating from the contributions of Nelson (1959) and Arrow (1962a) and implemented by the methodology elaborated by Griliches (1979, 1992) and Jaffe (1986), rests upon the notion of knowledge as a public good and, consequently, the notion of technological externalities applies. In this approach, knowledge spills over into the ambient and it is not necessary to have any inter-action between 'inventors' and 'imitators' or 'knowledge producers' and 'knowledge users'. Such knowledge externalities stem from a number of key characteristics of technological knowledge as an economic good, that is to say, non-divisibility, non-appropriability, non-rivalry in use and non-excludability. Such pervasive technological externalities in the generation and exploitation of technological knowledge make it difficult for the market to provide incentives and to organize the production and dissemination of knowledge. There is a vast literature exploring the implications in terms of market failure and articulating the need for public subsidies.

If knowledge is a public good or, as lately articulated in the new growth theory, a quasi-public good, the notion of 'technological externalities' can apply. Once discovered, in fact, technological knowledge can be accessed and used freely by all parties. Imitators can easily take advantage of knowledge generated by third parties: inventors can retain only a share of the stream of economic benefits that stem from its economic applications. At least a fraction of the technological knowledge generated by each firm affects the general efficiency of the production function of other firms.

The literature on knowledge spillovers has grown exponentially in recent years. Firms, clustering in geographic and knowledge space can take advantage of knowledge spillovers and grow much faster than isolated firms. This literature has developed the Marshallian understanding of externalities, where knowledge is a production factor spilling into the industrial districts with no costs for prospective users either to acquire or to use it. In this approach, external knowledge can be accessed with no interaction, transaction or communication costs.

The new growth theory has been developed further with the distinction being drawn between generic and specific technological knowledge. Generic technological knowledge is germane to a variety of uses, while specific technological knowledge is embodied in production processes and routines, and, as such, it has strong idiosyncratic features. Specific knowledge can be appropriated by 'inventors'. Generic knowledge instead retains the typical features of the Arrovian public good. The appropriability of specific knowledge provides sufficient incentives to invest in knowledge-generating activities. The assumption regarding the intrinsic complementarity between generic and specific knowledge is the basic engine of the process. Generic knowledge is generated by innovators engaged in introducing new specific knowledge embodied in new products and new processes. Specific knowledge is produced by taking advantage of generic knowledge that is available collectively. The spillover of generic knowledge helps new specific knowledge to be generated by third parties and yet does not reduce the incentives to generate new knowledge because of the strong appropriability of the specific applications. Each firm has unlimited access to the spillovers of generic knowledge and this can be used freely. The total factor productivity of firms is directly influenced by knowledge spillovers (Romer, 1986, 1990; Grossman and Helpman, 1994).

According to the new growth theory, unconditional and unconstrained access to generic technological knowledge leads to the spontaneous and ubiquitous increase of total factor productivity and hence to the automatic and steady growth of output. The evidence does not confirm these theoretical assumptions. The new growth theory is not able to account for the great differences across firms and regions, sectors and industries and, most importantly, historic times in the actual rates of introduction of new technologies (Aghion and Howitt, 1992, 1998; Jones, 2002).

These limitations of the new growth theory stem from two specific points. First, it does not explore the implications of the dual nature of knowledge as, at the same time, an output and an input; consequently, it is not able to appreciate the consequences of the non-exhaustibility and cumulability of knowledge because, once generated as an output, it enters the generation of new technological knowledge as an indispensable input. Second, it does not appreciate the costs associated with the utilization of knowledge, once generated, as an input in the generation of new knowledge (Cohen and Levinthal, 1989).

The new insight upon the intrinsic characteristics of the generation of knowledge elaborated by the notion of recombinant knowledge provides additional elements to criticize the new growth theory. According to Martin Weitzman, the generation of knowledge is characterized by the continual recombination of existing units. New technological knowledge, in other words, consists of the novel organization of elements of knowledge that have been already generated. This approach stresses the key role of technological knowledge as an input into the generation of new knowledge and prompts a more systematic exploration of the conditions and factors that affect the availability, accessibility, use and costs of existing knowledge (Weitzman, 1996, 1998).

The identification of the evident limitations of the new growth theory and the suggestions of the recombinant knowledge approach prompt exploration of an alternative analytical path, based upon the notion of pecuniary externalities. Pecuniary externalities provide a novel and fruitful tool to examine the relationship between the generation of technological knowledge, economic growth and total factor productivity growth. So far, it has found little application, as the literature has concentrated attention more systematically on the consequences of knowledge non-appropriability in terms of 'direct interdependence' non-mediated by the market mechanism. The application of the notion of pecuniary externalities to the economics of knowledge provides a coherent framework, which can take into account the emergence of innovation systems created by the regional and sectoral convergence of the localized strategies of knowledge generation and exploitation of many firms.

As is well known, the Marshallian literature has identified two quite different types of externalities: (1) technological externalities and (2) pecuniary externalities. Technological externalities consist of direct interdependence among producers. Pecuniary externalities consist of indirect interdependence. In the former case, the interdependence is not mediated by the market mechanisms. In the latter, instead, interdependence takes place via effects on the price system (Viner, 1931; Meade, 1952; Scitousky, 1954; Martin, 2007).

Technological externalities exist when unpaid production factors enter the production function. According to Scitovsky this is the case of technological external economies. They apply when

> The producer's output may be influenced by the action of persons more directly and in other ways than through their offer of services used and demand for products produced by the firm. This is the counterpart of the previous case, and its main instance is inventions that facilitate production and become available to producers without charge. (Scitovsky, 1954: 144)

Pecuniary externalities have been used very little in the economics of innovation while a large body of empirical and theoretical research has been based upon the notion of technological externalities. Pecuniary knowledge externalities, as distinct from technological externalities, play a key role in shaping the direction and the rate of technological change, and the dynamics of the convergent processes of knowledge generation and exploitation that lead to the emergence of geographical and technological systems of innovation.

Pecuniary externalities apply when the prices of production factors differ from equilibrium levels and reflect the effects of external forces. According to Scitovsky (1954), pecuniary external economies consist of 'interdependence among producers through the market mechanism' (p. 146).[1] There are positive pecuniary externalities when the market price of production factors happens to be lower than equilibrium levels due to the effects of market interactions among firms in the growth process.

Pecuniary externalities have long been a fruitful tool for understanding the relationship between structural change and growth. They have been used to understand the effects of interplay between industries, in the dynamics of the division of labour: increasing demand by downstream industries favours increasing levels of division of labour in upstream and lateral industries. This, in turn, leads to higher levels of specialization and the introduction of innovations that eventually engender lower prices, in intermediary markets, for capital goods and other intermediary inputs. In this case, pecuniary externalities stem from the effects of the dynamics of demand-led growth (Young, 1928; Kaldor, 1981). Alternatively, pecuniary externalities have been used to describe the triggering effects and vertical transmission mechanisms by means of which growth in upstream industries has an effect on downstream users. The poor supply of advanced intermediary inputs by upstream industries may cause development traps (Rosenstein Rodan, 1943).

More recently pecuniary externalities have been used to study intersectoral dynamics within filieres. Ciccone and Matsuyama (1996) show that the limited availability of specialized inputs may force the producers of downstream users to use, as distinct from generate technologies, production techniques which are too labour-intensive. Arora, Fosfuri and Gambardella (2001b) studied the mechanisms by which the growth of specialized upstream suppliers in developed countries improved access to technology and lowered investment costs for downstream users in developing countries in the chemical industry.

In these analyses however the users of technological knowledge, generated and made available through market transactions by upstream specialized suppliers, are passive. Consistent with standard microeconomics, agents are not able to react creatively to the stimulations provided by upstream activities; hence they cannot intentionally generate their technological knowledge, or change their technology.

So far, the notion of pecuniary externalities has found little application in understanding the generation of technological knowledge as distinct from its adoption, as well as in understanding the direction of technological change, as distinct from its rate.

Pecuniary knowledge externalities become relevant as soon as: (1) firms are credited with the creative capability to generate intentionally technological knowledge and to introduce technological changes that are consistent with their specific and contextual conditions and (2) the active role of knowledge users is recognized. In order to command new technological knowledge, generated by third parties, and take advantage of it, users need to perform specific activities that entail specific resources. This is true for the adopters and imitators of new products and processes when technological knowledge is embodied, for the customers of patents and licences when knowledge is disembodied, and for the receptors of knowledge spillovers. In all cases, users can access external knowledge only at a cost: such costs have an effect on a firm's technological choices. Hence the need for pecuniary knowledge externalities (David and Rosenbloom, 1990).

The appreciation of pecuniary externalities makes it possible to understand how the lower relative prices of (1) specific knowledge inputs, (2) other intermediary production factors and (3) knowledge as an output, affect the emerging and intentional direction of technological change. Hence pecuniary knowledge externalities apply to the analysis of: (1) the knowledge generation function when the cost of external knowledge as an input is considered, (2) the production functions of other goods when the costs of other intermediary inputs are considered and (3) the revenue functions when the price of knowledge as an output is considered. In all cases, such price levels are determined by the path-dependent characteristics of the localized regional, institutional, historical and industrial context (David, 2001, 2007).

The characteristics of the context into which firms are localized are especially important in terms of pecuniary knowledge externalities that shape the direction of technological change, both with respect to the costs of knowledge generation and the opportunities for knowledge exploitation. The notion of pecuniary knowledge externalities makes it possible to integrate into a single framework the analysis of the direction of technological change as shaped by the effects of the actual costs of the external knowledge inputs that are indispensable in the generation of new knowledge, and by the effects of the prices of other intermediary inputs that can be conveniently bundled with new knowledge so as to increase its appropriability (Antonelli, 2009).

In both cases, firms have a clear incentive to search for potential complementarities between internal and external factors and intentionally characterize their innovative strategies so as to implement the interface between internal and external factors, achieve dynamic complementarities and increase their productivity and profitability (Bresnahan, Gambardella and Saxenian, 2001).

4.2 THE LOCALIZED GENERATION OF TECHNOLOGICAL KNOWLEDGE: THE DISTRIBUTED MODEL

In the last decade, this novel analytical framework has been shaken by: (1) the discovery of knowledge governance costs, (2) the new appreciation of knowledge complementarity as distinct from knowledge cumulability and (3) the discovery of the key role of knowledge as both an input and output in an intentional process of knowledge generation. Let us analyse these aspects in more detail.

(1) Progressively, the evidence gathered in the empirical literature has shown that the acquisition of technological knowledge by both users and imitators is not free. Knowledge does not spontaneously spill into the ambient: its acquisition requires some dedicated resources. Imitation costs are relevant (Mansfield, Schwartz and Wagner, 1981) as well as absorption costs (Cohen and Levinthal, 1990; Griffith, Redding and Van Reenen, 2003). The characteristics of the system, into which knowledge flows, matter in terms of knowledge governance costs expressed as transaction, interaction and communication costs (Nelson, 1993; Martin, 1999).

This literature shows that technological externalities are not a satisfactory tool of analysis: they do not consider the efforts that are necessary for the actual acquisition of external knowledge. Dedicated interactions and specific resources are necessary in order to take advantage of the knowledge that spills over into the ambient. External knowledge has a cost: it cannot be treated as a cost free factor. Here the application of the notion of pecuniary externalities, as distinct from 'technological externalities' becomes relevant. It is clear, in fact, that the costs of using existing external knowledge exist, although they are often below its marginal productivity; because of the intrinsic non-exhaustibility and non-divisibility of knowledge their levels can be lower than the costs of early generation, at least in specific and positive geographic, historic, institutional and sectoral contexts (Bresnahan and Gambardella, 2004; Breschi and Malerba, 2005; Antonelli, 2007).

(2) Much attention has been paid to the analysis of knowledge indivisibility articulated in terms of cumulability, that is to say, diachronic indivisibility: new vintages of knowledge build upon the previous advances. Recent developments in the economics of knowledge have made it possible to understand the role of synchronic knowledge indivisibility better. The notion of knowledge complementarity has been elaborated in terms of the interdependence between different modules of contemporary knowledge generated by different agents and possibly in different fields. The legacy of Hayek

(1945) finds new support: technological knowledge is viewed as dispersed and fragmented into a variety of complementary and yet specific and idiosyncratic applications and contexts. In such a new framework, knowledge is viewed as a collective activity (Antonelli, 2001, 2007). A systemic approach to understanding the determinants of the rate and the direction of technological change is progressively implemented. In an approach in which there is knowledge complementarity, weak divisibility and interdependence among learning agents, firms and public research centres become central attributes of specific national innovation systems articulated in technological, industrial and regional subsystems characterized by interaction and communication networks, where the dissemination of and access to technological knowledge takes place (Freeman, 1991; Patel and Pavitt, 1994; Feldman, 1999).

(3) The new understanding of knowledge as both an output and input reinforces the empirical evidence on the role of the costs of and access to external knowledge. More precisely, technological knowledge is a costly input both for the production of other goods and the generation of new technological knowledge. The role of knowledge as an essential input, in turn, adds a new element to explain the intrinsic complementarity between external and internal sources of knowledge for the production of new knowledge (David, 1993; Arora, Fosfuri and Gambardella, 2001a).

The generation of new technological knowledge consists mainly of the recombination of existing knowledge. New technological knowledge is but the result of reorganizing the structure and relations between existing bits of knowledge. The access to existing knowledge becomes a key condition for assessing the actual chances of generation of new knowledge. A command of all the existing knowledge is clearly impossible for each agent: hence the key role of external knowledge (Weitzman, 1996, 1998).

These advances have important implications for our understanding of the effects of the local, as opposed to global, and specific, as opposed to general, contexts, in regional, industrial and institutional terms, on the costs and the characteristics of the technological knowledge being used and generated by each firm.

External knowledge does not freely spill over into the ambient. External knowledge can be accessed at a specific and identifiable cost that varies according to the different characteristics of the local context. Knowledge governance costs, articulated in transaction, networking and absorption costs, matter. Hence pecuniary knowledge externalities are a fertile tool of analysis that makes it possible to appreciate what determines and affects the different levels of costs of external knowledge as an essential input.

In some specific locations, heavy governance costs add to the purchasing costs of external knowledge. In others, knowledge governance costs are very low: the access to the local pools of knowledge is easy and the total costs of external knowledge, including purchasing and governance costs, are much lower than their marginal productivity. Such circumstances, however, do not hold everywhere and all the time, but only in highly idiosyncratic conditions.

External knowledge remains an essential input in the generation of new knowledge: no firm can invent alone. As a consequence, pecuniary knowledge externalities are likely to shape the direction of technological change. Firms will try to direct their research efforts according to the local endowments in terms of knowledge pools and their relative access costs. Pecuniary externalities stemming from access to dispersed fragments of knowledge, possessed by different agents, provide an opportunity for these agents to integrate fragmented knowledge synchronically and to use it as an essential input for the generation of new knowledge, at costs that in specific circumstances are below equilibrium conditions.

External knowledge, that is to say, knowledge possessed by other parties, has a crucial role. In the generation of knowledge, firms act as 'integrators' of internal skills and competence with external sources of knowledge. Knowledge external to the firm, at each point in time, is a necessary and relevant complement to knowledge internal to the firm, if new knowledge is to be generated. The conditions governing access to external knowledge are a key factor in assessing the chances of new knowledge being generated. The generation of new knowledge is the specific outcome of an intentional action and requires four distinct and specific activities: internal learning, formal R&D activities, the acquisition of external tacit knowledge and the acquisition of external codified knowledge. Each of these is indispensable. Firms that have no access to external knowledge, and cannot take advantage of essential complementary knowledge inputs, can generate very little (if any) new knowledge, even when internal learning combined with R&D activities provides major contributions. Also, the opposite is true. Firms that do not perform any

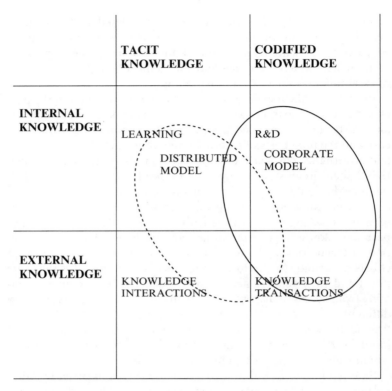

Figure 4.1   The generation of technological knowledge

knowledge generating activity cannot generate any new knowledge, even when they have access to rich pools of knowledge. No firm, in fact, can innovate in isolation (Antonelli, 2007). Figure 4.1 provides a synthetic account of the main points of our analysis.

These activities can be classified according to two dimensions. The rows identify the two extremes of the involved internal/external knowledge. No firm can command the overall knowledge available at each point in time: hence external knowledge is an essential input that complements the internal generation. The columns define the two extremes of tacit and codified knowledge. All codified knowledge requires an essential component of tacit knowledge in order to be used and integrated.

None of the four inputs is supplementary as all are essential complements. The recombinant generation of new technological knowledge consists in the active integration and recombination of the four distinct and yet strictly complementary sources of knowledge. The mix of components, however, can vary. In order to steer the recombinant generation of new knowledge, firms act as system integrators of internal sources of knowledge, such as intramuros R&D activities and learning processes, with external knowledge. According to the different weights of each component, alternative models can be identified.

The corporate model emphasizes the role of the internal generation of codified knowledge based upon R&D activities and formal transactions in the markets for knowledge (Chandler, 1962, 1977, 1990; Teece, 2000).

The Italian distributed model (see Chapter 8) emphasizes the polycentric character of the generation process of new technological knowledge (Ostrom, 2010). It is based upon the systematic recombination of existing knowledge (Weitzman, 1996, 1998). As such it is characterized by the relevance of such inputs and activities as the internal tacit knowledge, acquired by means of internal learning processes, and the external tacit knowledge, accessed by means of systematic knowledge interactions. In the distributed model formal R&D activities geared towards the generation of codified knowledge play a much lesser role than in the corporate model.

In the distributed model, external knowledge is an essential input into the generation of new knowledge. External knowledge can substitute internal sources of knowledge only to a limited extent: fully-fledged substitutability between internal and external knowledge cannot apply. Unconstrained complementarity, however, also appears inappropriate. Building on the large empirical evidence regarding the role of external knowledge in the Italian case study evidence, the hypothesis of a constrained multiplier relationship can be articulated. External and internal knowledge, both in their tacit and codified forms, are complementary inputs where each one is indispensable (Patrucco, 2009).

Because technological knowledge is intrinsically indivisible, the successful generation of new knowledge depends upon the access to external knowledge. External knowledge is necessary, but only potentially useful: systematic efforts have to be made in order to exploit such possibilities. To do this, firms rely on knowledge exploration strategies to identify the sources of knowledge and to assess whether and to what extent they can rely upon external or internal knowledge to produce new knowledge. Only when a firm is able to fully coordinate all the relevant learning and research activities conducted within its boundaries with the relevant sources of external knowledge, both tacit and codified, can new knowledge be successfully generated. Knowledge procurement is just as relevant as intramuros research activities in the generation of new knowledge. The purchase of patents and licences in knowledge markets by means of knowledge transactions, however, is not the only source of external knowledge. External knowledge can also be accessed by means of a variety of other tools, including the hiring of qualified personnel, who embody competences acquired by means of learning in other companies, and an array of interaction modes with public research centres, customers, suppliers and competitors.

4.3   EXTERNAL KNOWLEDGE AND GOVERNANCE: TRANSACTION, COMMUNICATION AND NETWORKING COSTS

The acquisition of and access to external knowledge are expensive both in terms of actual purchasing costs and in terms of knowledge governance costs. Knowledge governance costs include all knowledge transaction, communication and networking costs. Knowledge transaction costs are the costs associated with exploration activities in the markets for disembodied knowledge such as search, screening, processing and contracting. As is well known, the assessment of the actual quality of the knowledge can be difficult when the vendor bears the risks of opportunistic behaviour and dangerous disclosure (Williamson, 1996).

The acquisition of external knowledge requires qualified interactions with other agents: dedicated effort is necessary to create the institutional context in which external knowledge can be acquired. The capability of agents to access external technological knowledge depends on the fabric of institutional relations and shared codes of understanding, which help to reduce information asymmetries, limiting the scope for opportunistic behaviour and building a context into which reciprocity, built-up trust and generative relationships can be implemented (Cohen and Levinthal, 1990).

Knowledge communication is necessary when knowledge is dispersed and fragmented, retained by a myriad of heterogeneous agents and yet characterized by high levels of indivisibility with important potential benefits in terms of externalities stemming from its integration and recombination. However, knowledge communication is not automatic. It is the result of a lot of intentional activities designed to create a context in which the combination of variety and complementarity is facilitated.

Systematic networking is necessary to establish knowledge communication flows. The network structure of the system plays a key role in shaping the flows of knowledge communication and hence the availability of external knowledge. Specific, dedicated networking activities are necessary in order to manage the flows of knowledge that are not internal to each firm and yet cannot be reduced to arm's length transactions. Networking activities make knowledge interactions, as distinct from knowledge transactions, possible. Networking activities are a highly specific – indispensable – ingredient of the basic governance of knowledge (Freeman, 1991).

Firms often rely on networking interactions with other independent parties, to increase the proprietary control of their knowledge, to acquire external knowledge and to exploit it better. External knowledge can be acquired by taking advantage of the spillovers from academic activity and from localization in the proximity of other firms. Qualified user–producer interactions, both upstream, with suppliers, and downstream, with customers, are the source of key inputs into the production of new knowledge. Knowledge search and its utilization is implemented better within networks of interactions based upon constructed and repeated interactions, qualified by contractual relations. The array of networking tools is ever increasing and includes both formal and informal mechanisms. Joint ventures, dedicated research clubs, sponsored spin-offs, patent-thicketing, technological platforms, cross-licensing and in-house outsourcing are the main types of formal cooperative tools. Co-localization within technological districts and membership of epistemic communities are typical forms of networking procedures (Antonelli, 2007).

The basic assumption here is that the levels of knowledge governance costs have a key role in assessing the actual levels of the total costs for the prospective users of external knowledge (Arrow, 1969, 1974).

An understanding of the costs of external knowledge has important implications for the direction and the amount of technological knowledge being generated by the firm. When efficient markets for knowledge are available, the selection of knowledge activities that firms retain within their boundaries is much more effective. Usually the scrutiny of knowledge generating activities and their eventual valorization is, in fact, a demanding task. The exploration of external sources of knowledge and knowledge outsourcing becomes common practice. Firms may rely on external providers for specific bits of complementary knowledge. Knowledge outsourcing on the demand side matches the supply of specialized knowledge-intensive business service firms. Universities and other public research centres can complement their top-down research activities aimed at producing scientific knowledge with the provision of elements of technological knowledge to business firms.

The stronger the pecuniary knowledge externalities, the stronger the incentives for firms to choose to develop the characteristics of the technological knowledge that fit the characteristics of the context into which they are embedded. A variety of factors affect this process: the cognitive distance among agents, the complementarity in competence and research agenda, the levels of trust and the institutional setting. Geographic proximity plays a key role too (Boschma and Frenken, 2006).

Firms that have access to cheaper external knowledge, can generate a larger amount of knowledge with a given amount of resources available to fund research activities. The unit costs of knowledge, generated in a conducive environment, are clearly lower than the unit costs of knowledge generated in a 'hostile' context by a single firm 'forced' to rely almost exclusively on its own internal competence.

This analysis has many important implications for the role of the local context into which firms are embedded. It is clear, for instance, that when and where external knowledge is cheap, both because of low purchasing costs in the markets for codified knowledge, and low knowledge governance costs, firms will rely less on internal learning and research activities. Instead, when and where the access conditions to external knowledge are less easy, firms will rely more on internal research and learning activities. Such an analysis provides a clue to understanding the puzzling evidence of the low levels of formal research activities of firms localized in fertile and dynamic technological districts.

NOTE

1. As Scitovsky (1954) notes: 'This latter type of interdependence may be called pecuniary external economies to distinguish it from technological external economies of direct interdependence' (p. 146).

5. The role of external factors in the localized exploitation of technological knowledge: localized appropriability and directed technological innovation

The analysis of knowledge exploitation provides further elements of insight into the understanding of the introduction of technological innovations (March, 1991).

In the Schumpeterian approach, technological knowledge can be appropriated and exploited effectively through downstream integration both in the creation of new firms and by incumbents that can take advantage of existing barriers to entry and hence to imitation. This takes place when innovators are large corporations that enjoy the advantages of barriers to entry based upon increasing returns to scale (Schumpeter, 1942). Existing barriers to entry become barriers to imitation for new products. Lead times provide innovating incumbents with the opportunity to reap the advantages of economies of scale before potential competitors are able to imitate the innovation. The corporation is the institution that provides innovators with the opportunity and the incentives to appropriate and exploit technological knowledge (Chandler, 1962, 1977, 1990).

David Teece has much enriched the Chandlerian analysis of embodied appropriation. He suggests that firms can try to exploit their technological knowledge by bundling it with complementary assets that are under their exclusive control (Teece, 1986, 1998, 2000). According to this approach, firms try to search for complementary assets depending on the characteristics of their proprietary knowledge. The bundling of knowledge with other assets that are under a firm's exclusive command becomes an effective strategy to appropriate technological knowledge and hence to exploit it better.

This analysis of knowledge exploitation can be differently implemented with the notion of localized appropriability. Localized
appropriability is the possibility for inventors to better appropriate
the stream of benefits stemming from the introduction of innovations by means of the strategic use of selective inputs that are under
the exclusive command of the innovator. They are the result of the
downstream vertical integration of knowledge, purposely generated,
in products and production processes that are highly idiosyncratic
and, as such, make it possible to retain a long-lasting cost advantage.

Firms have a strong incentive to try to direct the generation of
technological change according to the characteristics of the idiosyncratic inputs that have been identified. In order to achieve localized
appropriability firms need to elaborate a clear technological strategy. This approach is the opposite of the one put forward by David
Teece. According to Teece, firms search for complementary assets,
once they have a piece of technological knowledge they want to
exploit. In our approach, instead, the identification of idiosyncratic
production factors becomes the focusing mechanism that directs the
generation of new technological knowledge and the introduction of
technological innovations. This approach is the result of quite a long
analytical process that should be carefully considered (Antonelli,
1995, 1999).

Recent advances in the economics of knowledge enable important
progress in understanding the key role of pecuniary externalities in
knowledge exploitation. The analysis of the characteristics of localized knowledge appropriability embodied in idiosyncratic production factors plays a key role in shaping a firm's intentional strategy
regarding the direction of technology. The firm is viewed as a learning agent, capable of creative reactions induced by market forces.
Building upon learning processes, each firm elaborates and intentionally implements both knowledge generation and exploitation
strategies. These strategies include the exploration of factor markets
and the identification of the idiosyncratic production factors whose
intensive use is convenient.

An important step forward can be made when the role of production factors, external to the firm, but idiosyncratic because they are
available only in a specific context, is appreciated. Localized appropriability becomes relevant. Localized appropriability results from
the embodiment of knowledge into downstream activities which are
characterized by the highly intensive use of production factors that

are external to the firm, and both idiosyncratic and locally abundant. The bundling of knowledge with other production factors, that are idiosyncratic and localized to a degree that makes it difficult for imitators and competitors to access them, means that localized appropriability is possible. The identification and valorization of the local and idiosyncratic resources, whose intensive use is convenient, becomes a clear and strong focusing device along which firms can align their research and learning activities.[1]

In short, when the generation of new knowledge is directed towards the introduction of new biased technologies that consist of using locally abundant production factors intensively so as to reduce production costs, the local social value of technological knowledge is larger. The private share of such a larger social value is larger when directed technological change, biased towards the intensive use of pecuniary externalities engendered by local idiosyncratic production factors, makes it possible to exploit the new technological knowledge better. This is due to barriers to entry and imitation which prevent the dissipation of the economic rents stemming from the introduction of new biased technologies, and hence increase de-facto knowledge appropriability.

The search for new, more effective, uses of locally abundant production factors is a powerful alignment mechanism for the research strategies of innovators and it is a strong incentive to the generation of directed technological knowledge. The biased production technology that uses the locally abundant and, hence, cheaper production factors most intensively is more efficient and profitable, because it engenders systematic cost asymmetries that are long lasting, when competitors do not have access to the same factor markets.

Pecuniary externalities matter in shaping the direction of knowledge generation because of their effects in terms of exploitation. The relative abundance of key idiosyncratic inputs, that other competitors cannot access in the same conditions, resulting in average market prices being lower, means that firms have the opportunity to increase the appropriability of their knowledge, providing that the firm is able to make intensive use of those key inputs. Pecuniary externalities are crucial in shaping the strategies for the valorization of the distinctive competences and the economic success of innovative firms. An analysis of the conditions for localized knowledge appropriation and exploitation enables firms to identify idiosyncratic production factors. The introduction of directed technological change biased towards their intensive usage provides firms with the opportunity for a better exploitation of technological knowledge.

An understanding of the intentional, contextual and resource-consuming activities necessary to actually generate new technological knowledge leads us to dig deeper into the analysis of the factors affecting the direction or characteristics of the new knowledge generated by firms. The conditions for knowledge appropriation and exploitation exert a powerful feedback upon the generation of new technological knowledge.

Following this line of thought, it now seems increasingly clear that not only is the generation of knowledge the result of intentional activities that build upon internal learning processes, but it is constrained by an array of external and localized complementary conditions. Knowledge exploitation, as well, is heavily constrained and shaped by the specific way it is used. The localized conditions determining how knowledge is used, radically affect its appropriability: hence, the notion of localized appropriability has important consequences (March, 1991; Antonelli, 2003).

Learning firms need to strategically select the direction of their innovation activities. Although learning localizes the cognitive base to a limited spectrum of rays emanating from the original focal point of activity, there are still many possible directions along which the generation of new technological knowledge can be aligned. A variety of possible discoveries can be the outcome of the intentional valorization of learning processes and the consequent accumulation of tacit knowledge. New technological knowledge impinges upon the basic ground provided by: learning by making the current products, learning by using the current technologies and capital goods and learning by interacting with the actual variety of suppliers, competitors and customers. The tacit knowledge and the competences acquired can be implemented and valued in a variety of possible directions.

The choice from an actual array of possible discoveries becomes a crucial issue. The intentional choice of the direction of the possible discoveries marks the second strong departure from the deterministic notion of the firm as an agent moving along a predefined trajectory based upon past learning. As a matter of fact, at each point in time the firm is faced by a variety of possible directions towards which its creative activities can be directed. Each possibility needs to be assessed and the relative profitability needs to be valued both from the viewpoint of the costs of introduction and the revenue stemming from its use.

This approach clearly contrasts the notion of technological trajectory suggested by Nelson and Winter (1982), according to which the dynamics of a process is fully determined at the onset, and applies the alternative framework of path dependence according to which the occurrence of small events along the process in non-ergodic dynamics do alter the rate and direction of the process (David, 1975, 2001, 2007).

An important step forward can be made here, if the factors that constrain or stimulate the selection of the direction of the sequential steps – acting as focusing mechanisms – are identified and analysed within a single framework. The characteristics of knowledge and idiosyncratic production factors help to identify the role of such focusing mechanisms. The conditions for valuing and exploiting new technological knowledge become relevant focusing devices in the identification of the correct strategies for the generation of new knowledge.

With a given technology and assuming standard substitution among inputs, producers have a clear incentive to increase the intensity of the utilization of inputs characterized by pecuniary externality. Hence, the intensity of such factors will be higher in some specific locations than in others. In a dynamic context where technology is endogenous, innovators have a strong incentive to direct the introduction of new technologies so as to increase the intensity of production factors that are available at prices below their marginal productivity. Consequently, in a dynamic context, the utilization intensity of the factors that happen to be characterized by pecuniary externalities will be much higher than in a static context. Technological change works as a meta-substitution process.

Pecuniary externalities become a factor of specialization and, in a dynamic context, where technological change is endogenous, they play a major role in shaping the direction of technological change. Pecuniary knowledge externalities provide a novel and fruitful tool for understanding the relationship between the generation of technological knowledge and its exploitation. So far, it has attracted little attention, as the literature has explored more systematically the consequences of knowledge non-appropriability in terms of 'direct interdependence' non-mediated by the market mechanism.

As a matter of fact, the notion of pecuniary knowledge externalities provides the foundations on which can be built a new understanding of localized appropriability and hence a new view of the incentives to generate new technological knowledge.

The identification of the sources of pecuniary externalities embedded in local endowments of idiosyncratic production factors, in fact, provides the opportunity to substantially increase both the absolute effects of the technological change that a firm can generate and its appropriability. The intentional direction of technological change towards the systematic exploitation of pecuniary externalities – stemming from the local endowments of idiosyncratic production factors – makes it possible to increase the gains in terms of efficiency for a given level of resources invested in the generation of new technological knowledge, in terms of productivity and appropriability of new technologies.

The new understanding of the role of localized knowledge appropriability leads us to a new and better understanding of the idiosyncratic character of local resources and how this affects production and competition. In fact, it provides a new basket of analytical opportunities with which to understand the key role of the specific and localized conditions that affect a firm's actual chances to exploit the technological knowledge it can generate.

The productivity of new technological knowledge, when applied to the actual production process, and the appropriability of the economic value stemming from its use, are much influenced by the relative price of the production factors being used. The identification of production factors that are idiosyncratic becomes a crucial issue. Production factors are idiosyncratic when firms can exert a specific control on them, which assures low and exclusive acquisition costs. Firms which are able to identify idiosyncratic production factors can direct the introduction of new technologies so as to increase their use in the production process, use them intensively and thus extract much higher rents from their knowledge-generation activities for a much longer period of time.

The identification and valorization of idiosyncratic resources becomes a clear and strong focusing device along which firms can align their research activities. The generation of new technological knowledge can be directed towards the exploitation of such idiosyncratic production factors, so as to reduce production costs and create barriers to entry and to imitation. Such barriers to entry and imitation based upon the intensive use of idiosyncratic production factors prevent the economic rents stemming from their introduction from being dissipated and hence increase appropriability. The appreciation of the role of localized knowledge appropriability and hence of biased technological change towards the intensive use of idiosyncratic production factors becomes a powerful tool for understanding the criteria by which a firm selects the direction of the generation of new technological knowledge. A full-fledged economics of the distinctive innovative competence of the firm, one including the context in which the firm is based, can be elaborated impinging upon these elements.

NOTE

1. Following a well-established line of analysis of technological change at the macroeconomic level, it is well known that the intensive use of more abundant, and hence cheaper, production factors leads to a larger increase in productivity (Kennedy, 1964; Samuelson, 1965; Ruttan, 1997; Acemoglou, 2002). Despite this, little attempt has been made, so far, to integrate such an approach – centred upon the analysis of the aggregate direction of technological change – with an analysis of what conditions knowledge-generation strategies at the firm and regional level. When the endowments of both tangible and intangible inputs differ, the direction of technological change towards the exploitation of local pecuniary externalities based upon the intensive use of locally abundant factors has a strong effect on the performance both at the level of the economic system and at the level of the firm (Antonelli, 2007).

6. The emergence and decline of innovation systems

The analysis developed so far makes clear that externalities are endogenous. It should be evident by now that externalities are external to each individual firm, but by no means are they external to the system of firms under analysis. Externalities are internal to the system and change as a consequence of the actions and interactions of the firms.

As is well known, Alfred Marshall elaborated the notion of externalities to account for increasing returns at the firm level. The notion of externalities enabled Alfred Marshall to justify increasing returns as the product of conditions external to each firm, rather than internal. In his original analysis, however, the factors that accounted for increasing returns were external to each firm, but internal to the system into which firms were embedded. They do not fall from heaven and they are not given and static. Quite the opposite, they are the result of a recursive process of emergence that takes place when the conduct and the performances of the firms and their interactions affect the structural characters of the system and these, in turn, affect the context of action of each individual firm.

Externalities and, specifically, knowledge externalities are a specific and yet dynamic and changing attribute of the system that is produced by the interaction of the individual agents that belong to the system. The levels of knowledge externalities are, in fact, influenced by the density of firms and by the structure of their relations. The effects can be both positive and negative and pecuniary externalities enable to grasp them both. The quantification and measure of both positive and negative effects – on costs and prices of knowledge, respectively, as an input and an output – of the density and proximity of firms, allows for the identification of the satisfactory size for clusters.

The recursive and systemic dynamics of technological change can now be explored in more detail. The actual capability of firms to react creatively to out-of-equilibrium conditions, generating new technological knowledge and changing their own technologies, depends upon the proper combination of internal knowledge and competence, and the localized availability of knowledge externalities and interactions. At each point in time, in fact, the reaction of firms is qualified and constrained by their location and the consequent conditions of access to external knowledge. When external knowledge cannot be accessed properly, the reaction of firms is adaptive and consists of standard switching upon the existing maps of isoquants.

The creative reaction of firms, however, consists both in their strategic mobility in multidimensional space and in their innovative capability. Firms can change their location, enter and exit product and factor markets, create new links and communication channels, change their position in vertical inter-industrial linkages and in regional districts, and hence firms can change their knowledge base, their complementarities, with respect to other firms. Firms can introduce institutional innovations that help the emergence of new markets and new forms of organization of the system at large (Lane, 2009).

Their reaction can become creative as opposed to adaptive and engender the actual introduction of successful, productivity-enhancing innovations, when and if the interactions and feedbacks shaped by the structure of the system provide the access to external knowledge and external learning conditions. The intensity and the effects of interactions are shaped by the structure of the system and, specifically, by the network topology of agents distributed in the multidimensional space, at each point in time. The distribution of agents in the multidimensional space is itself the endogenous result of their past locational strategies. Clearly, knowledge externalities are internal to the system: they depend upon the specific combination of activities and channels of communication in place among agents. Knowledge externalities depend upon the structure of the system. The organization and composition of the structure of the system into which firms are localized exerts a key role in shaping the dynamics both at the aggregate and the individual level.

An understanding of the constraints and opportunities provided by pecuniary externalities, stemming from horizontal knowledge indivisibility and localized appropriability, makes it possible to elaborate, in a single framework, an analysis of the incentives that contextual and localized factors exert in shaping the direction and the characteristics of the new knowledge generated by firms, and to stylize the path-dependent dynamics of the convergent processes that lead to the emergence of regional and sectoral systems of innovation.

First, the new appreciation of knowledge indivisibility has led to an understanding of the role of external knowledge. In turn, a better assessment of the cost of external knowledge has stressed the role of governance costs in the provision of external knowledge as an input into the production of new technological knowledge. Second, the new analysis of localized knowledge appropriability, based upon the conditions of usage and application to downstream production processes, has shed new light upon the incentives to bias technological change towards the intensive use of idiosyncratic production factors. For the use of external knowledge as an input, pecuniary knowledge externalities, as distinct from technological knowledge externalities, emerge as a key factor. For the factor bias of new technologies, pecuniary externalities, stemming from the lower costs of crucial inputs, other than external knowledge, are important. The combined appreciation of these two elements becomes a powerful tool for understanding the dynamics of knowledge convergence engendered by knowledge externalities.

In this framework, the combined effect of the availability of external knowledge and of locally abundant idiosyncratic inputs explains, at one and the same time, the emergence of path-dependent local and sectoral systems of innovations, the features of regional specialization and the directionality of technological change.

The availability of external knowledge, in fact, pushes firms to increase the complementarity of their knowledge base so as to take advantage of emerging pecuniary knowledge externalities. At the same time, the opportunities provided by the local idiosyncratic endowments and the local structure of factor costs – as shaped by indirect interdependence within vertical filieres – push firms towards the introduction of locally converging technological changes directed towards the intensive use of idiosyncratic factors that pecuniary externalities make cheaper and which, in turn, tend to increase knowledge exploitation.

An understanding of the specific directionality of technological change, beyond simple factor intensity, is important. Technological knowledge cannot be regarded as an undifferentiated homogeneous body, but rather as a bundle of highly idiosyncratic and circumscribed items possessed by individual agents, localized by their own circumscribed competences, more or less interconnected by a web of communication channels. At each point in time, innovation systems are the nodes of such networks of communication channels. They are the result of the intentional search and implementation of knowledge complementarities among agents originally dispersed in knowledge space or clustered in other nodes. Learning agents able to generate new knowledge, try to exploit knowledge pecuniary externalities and move within the knowledge space, hence they direct technological knowledge towards well-specified characteristics that are shaped collectively. The collective convergent directionality of new technological knowledge contributes to the emergence of structured collective pools of knowledge. As such, innovation systems, characterized by the structure of communication channels and knowledge complementarities, exhibit dynamic features (Durlauf, 2005; Frenken, 2006; Guiso and Schivardi, 2007).

An understanding of the effects of pecuniary knowledge externalities in shaping the direction of technological change makes it possible to explain, at one and the same time, the convergence of the technological paths of firms towards local pools of complementary knowledge and the emergence of structured systems of innovation based upon the local availability of distinctive sources of both tangible and intangible inputs (Durlauf and Johnson, 1992; Matsuyama, 1995).

In this light, local and sectoral systems of innovation are no longer the exogenous result of fortuitous, institutional blending (Boschma, 2005; Malerba, 2005). They can be seen as nodes of communication channels that are the result of an endogenous emerging process that shares the complex dynamics of the creation of the Internet network (Pastor-Satorras and Vespignani, 2004; Antonelli, 2007).

A firm that is located in a conducive knowledge environment, and is able to identify and access the local pools of knowledge at low costs, is induced to take advantage of this and hence to root the generation of its new knowledge in the characteristics of its environment. The amount of knowledge generated by each firm is larger when it is able to align its research strategies in such a way as to take advantage of locally abundant knowledge. Consistently, in downstream applications, firms can rely upon a larger increase in efficiency with the same amount of budget funding the generation of new knowledge. The amount of external knowledge that is used in the knowledge-generation process has a direct bearing not only upon the amount of knowledge being generated, and hence on the shift efficiency engendered in the production process, but also on its characteristics. Firms that rely more upon external knowledge are more likely to produce complementary knowledge.

Let us now consider the effects of the direction of technological knowledge in terms of knowledge exploitation. When factors are not equally abundant in each local factor market, it is clear that the unit costs of the goods manufactured using locally abundant factors intensively are lower than the costs of the goods manufactured with inputs that are available to every firm at the same price. On the top of this, we see that the efficiency of the two production processes differs because of the larger amount of knowledge that has been generated by the firms that have a better access to external knowledge and are better able to take advantage of it with the introduction of a bias in the direction of their knowledge. The workings of the two mechanisms is consistent and, clearly, the average costs of the goods that are manufactured using idiosyncratic technology are lower than the average costs of the goods that are manufactured using generic technology.

Finally, we must consider the price at which the goods that have been manufactured with the new technologies can be sold. The products manufactured with a more idiosyncratic technology, using locally abundant factors more intensively, that is not available under the same conditions to competitors, enjoy systematic cost asymmetries with respect to imitators and hence can take advantage of substantial barriers to entry and to mobility. In product markets characterized by monopolistic competition, incumbents protected by barriers to entry and to mobility, can fix high prices for their products, far higher than those of competitors.

The technological path of each firm will reflect the characteristics of both its own internal quasi-irreversibilities and learning processes, and the local context. The initial conditions play a key role in defining the context of action. The external context, however, at each point in time, powerfully affects the dynamics. The direction of the process is constrained by the initial conditions, but it can change at each point in time. The past dependence limits, at each point in time, the span of possible directions. Path dependence consists of the continual redefinition of a limited span of possible directions.

The convergence of the research strategies of each firm can gain momentum as result of strong incentives orienting research projects towards local pools of common knowledge. Positive feedbacks are likely to reinforce the process, as the efforts to increase the complementarity of the research activities of firms enrich the local pools of knowledge, with the result that the chances to access external knowledge increase. At the same time the increasing awareness of the opportunities for better knowledge exploitation, provided by the intensive use of idiosyncratic and locally abundant production factors, increases the intentional convergence of the knowledge generation strategies towards a common direction, shaped by the collective identification of the local idiosyncratic inputs. At the population level, the effects of individual convergence are reinforced by selection mechanisms. The success of the localized knowledge-exploitation strategies acts as a powerful focusing mechanism that, by means of selection processes, favours the survival and growth of firms that have selected a convergent path of knowledge generation and exploitation.

Systems of innovation emerge. They develop in technological districts and clusters when the generation of new technological knowledge is reinforced by the emerging structure of complementarities, implemented by communication channels, provided by the intentional research strategies of firms discovering new sources of complementarities and moving in the knowledge space. In special circumstances, the emergence of innovation systems – driven by highly performing network structures that have emerged through the collective dynamics of a myriad of agents in search of potential complementarities – may lead to Schumpeterian gales of innovations.

As Figure 6.1 shows, each firm is rooted in a well defined location in a Lancastrian knowledge space represented for the sake of simplicity by two characteristics: A and B. The graph depicts the potential knowledge complementarities, where each firm is able to move in such a knowledge space and generate new knowledge taking advantage of increased proximity and reinforced communication channels with other firms clustering in nodes (the shaded regions). As a result, new systems of innovation based upon nodes of coherent knowledge complementarity emerge (and others decay) while the direction of technological knowledge is shaped by the emergent collective convergence of each firm's research strategy (David, Foray and Dalle, 1995).

Pecuniary externalities, however, are neither exogenous nor, by

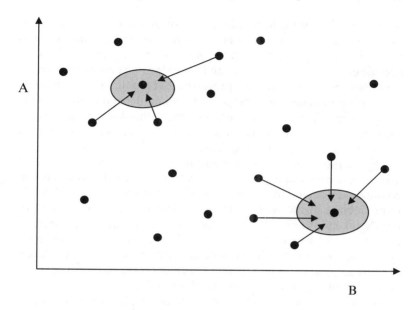

Figure 6.1   The emergence of innovation systems

definition, static. The convergent dynamics may exhibit both positive and negative effects. On one hand, the amount of external knowledge available within the district keeps increasing and its costs become lower and lower. On the other hand, however, knowledge govern-ance costs may increase, as the number of firms accessing the same knowledge pools increases, because of the effects of congestion in coordination. Density may have negative effects in terms of reduced knowledge appropriability: the case for excess clustering can take place when proximity favours the uncontrolled leakage of propri-etary knowledge. In the same way, the price of idiosyncratic inputs may increase with the increasing levels of their derived demand as shaped by the introduction of directional technological change.

The dynamics of the process reflects the interplay between the positive and negative changes of the levels of pecuniary externalities both in knowledge generation and knowledge exploitation. The con-vergence of the direction of technological change and the emergence of innovation systems in geographical and technological space takes place as long as the rising levels of knowledge governance costs and the rising prices of the idiosyncratic inputs do not exhaust pecuniary externalities. Innovation systems emerge depending on the relative weights of the positive and negative pecuniary externalities. In specific contexts, the interplay can lead to logistic processes of emergence with S-shaped dynamic processes that identify critical masses. Innovation systems can emerge and decline depending on specific factors, such as the characteristics of the technological knowledge, the types of competition in product and factor markets and the institutional context (Beaudry and Breschi, 2003).[1]

The characteristics of the system, in terms of knowledge governance mechanisms and hence the levels of knowledge transaction, communication and interaction costs, are crucial to assess the long-term viability of the system dynamics. The analysis, so far, has not jointly taken into account what the positive and negative effects of the number of agents, that are active in the same knowledge pool and share basic knowledge complementarities, have upon the levels of knowledge appropriability and hence upon the price of the products that embody new technological knowledge.

At each point in time the emergence of new innovation systems may be blocked by a number of countervailing forces. The process is far from being past dependent: it is shaped, at each point in time, by the ability of the actors to counter the dissipation of pecuniary externalities. Both at the firm and the regional level, these processes are likely to take place with a strong non-ergodic and sequential stratification (David, 1994). The path-dependent dynamics stem from the interplay of past dependence and intentional action. The internal stock of knowledge, acquired by each firm through learning, together with the organizational and architectural features of the interaction networks that frame the local pools of knowledge and of the economic structure, are the past-dependent components, as, at each point in time, they are the result of historic accumulation. The amount of knowledge being generated, the direction of technological change being introduced, the levels of knowledge governance costs and the price of locally idiosyncratic production factors are the result, at each point in time, of the intentional action of agents. Hence, they provide opportunities for intentional action to change the original path. At each point in time, the intentional action of the embedded agents adds a new layer to the original structure: the original shape exerts an effect that the new layers can modify, according to their thickness and density.

Also, an understanding of the key role of pecuniary knowledge externalities, available in the localized context where technological knowledge is being generated, makes it possible to appreciate the specific forms of knowledge complementarities among firms. Much empirical analysis has explored the relations between the variety of economic activities as a source of Jacobs externalities. It is necessary to take a step forward and qualify the kind of variety. Jacobs externalities can be considered as economies of scope at the regional level. A wide ranging literature on the theory of the firm has shown that some combinations of production processes characterized by technological complementarity do yield increasing returns (Milgrom and Roberts, 1995). Other combinations, such as in the case of uncorrelated diversification, can actually yield negative returns to variety. In a similar way, an analysis of pecuniary knowledge externalities and directed technological change suggests that 'positive' and 'negative' Jacobs externalities can be identified. In particular, positive Jacobs externalities emerge when the convergence of the competence and the technological knowledge being generated sets up actual horizontal complementarities.

At each point in time, the generation of new knowledge by each firm is influenced by the dynamics of internal learning, by the structure of local interactions that shape the access to the knowledge generated within the system, and by the structure of local endowments. Each firm, however, is able to interact with the system and to change it. This takes place at different levels: by introducing changes in the structural conditions and in the topology of communication channels of the systems; with the introduction of organizational innovations in knowledge governance mechanisms; and by changing the factor markets through innovations that affect the supply of the idiosyncratic production factors. The emergence of innovation systems is the result of continual feedbacks between the structure of the system and the innovative action of its agents.[2]

NOTES

1. Once more, analysis of the Internet shows striking similarities between the dynamics of communication systems and the emergence and decline of innovation systems. See D'Ignazio and Giovannetti (2006).

2. See Marshall (1890 [1920]):

> The development of the organism, whether social or physical, involves an increasing subdivision of functions between its separate parts on the one hand, and on the other a more intimate connection between them. Each part gets to be less and less self-sufficient, to depend for its wellbeing more and more on other parts, so that any disorder in any part of a highly-developed organism will affect other parts also. This increased subdivision of functions, or 'differentiation,' as it is called, manifests itself with regard to industry in such forms as the division of labor, and the development of specialized skill, knowledge and machinery; while 'integration,' that is, a growing intimacy and firmness of the connections between the separate parts of the industrial organism, shows itself in such forms as the increase of security of commercial credit, and of the means and habits of communication by sea and road, by railway and telegraph, by post and printing-press. (Book VIII, I, § 3 and 4)

7. A model of localized technological change cum pecuniary knowledge externalities

7.1 THE BASIC MODEL

We can now put together in a simple model all the elements that have been introduced so far.

Let us assume that a myopic firm or a group of myopic firms has made plans and set the basic conditions of their production process selecting the levels and combination of inputs according to the expected conditions of product and factor markets. These firms are characterized by substantial bounded rationality that impede long-term foresight. Their production factors are characterized by substantial irreversibility: all changes both in the mix and in the levels require dedicated resources and are expensive. Then, unexpected changes in product and factor markets engender a reaction. Their reaction can be either passive or creative, according to the conditions of access to external knowledge, an indispensable input into the generation of new technological knowledge.

More specifically, we argue that firms, stirred by unexpected events, constrained by the irreversibility of their production process, hence localized in terms of competence, production mix and levels of inputs, and by the historic path through which they have defined their conditions at each point in time, will be able to introduce technological innovations that actually increase the overall efficiency of their production process, only if the system into which they are localized provide them with access to pools of external knowledge at costs that are lower than equilibrium ones.

Let us assume that the production process is characterized by substantial irreversibility: the firm can change only a portion of the

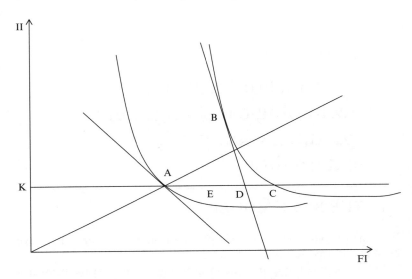

Figure 7.1   Localized technological change cum pecuniary
              knowledge externalities

inputs that happen to be flexible. In Figure 7.1 the vertical axis represents the irreversible inputs (II) that can be identified with capital, and the horizontal one represents the flexible inputs (FI) that can be identified with labour. Let us now assume that the firm has been able to choose the correct mix of production factors according to the conditions of product and factor markets. In Figure 7.1 point A identifies the equilibrium.

The firm is burdened by bounded rationality and it is not able to foresee all the possible states of the world: hence it is unable to elaborate correct expectations about the evolution of both product and factor markets in the long run. We now assume that unexpected events take place both in product and factor markets: wages as well as the demand for the products of the firm increase beyond expectations. The textbook firm, with no irreversibilities, would be able to move on the existing map of isoquants and change its technique to point B.

The myopic firm characterized by irreversibility of the production process, instead, can only move along the ray originating from K that indicates the given and irreversible endowment of fixed production factors. In order to adjust to the new and unexpected changes, the myopic firm will be able to move to point C at the intersection between the new desired isoquant along the ray K of the given endowment of fixed input.

The technical solution C belongs to the existing map of isoquants, but implies a substantial increase of production costs. The firm, in other words, is now pushed to produce far away from equilibrium conditions and will find itself on a point of the average cost curve that is well above the minimum. At this time, the generation of new technological knowledge becomes necessary and crucial. In order to change technique A and move to technique C the firm needs to command new technological knowledge: its competence is, in fact, localized and limited in a small portion of the space of techniques rooted around point A. If the generation of new technological knowledge is successful, the firm will be able to introduce localized technological changes and move along the ray K and possibly reach point D. At point D, the firm will be again in equilibrium.

All technological changes that enable the firm to move from point C and point D, however, will not increase the actual efficiency of the firm with respect to the equilibrium point B. Both B and D belong to the same new isocost. The firm able to reach point D will be able to reduce the decrease in efficiency of the production process engendered by the constraint of the irreversibility of its production factors. However, only if the generation of technological knowledge is so effective as to enable the firm to introduce localized technological changes along the ray K that go beyond point D, will the firm actually be able to increase its total factor productivity. The conditions of the generation of technological knowledge clearly play a crucial role.

7.2 THE KNOWLEDGE GENERATION FUNCTION

Following Nelson (1982) and Weitzman (1996, 1998), we can specify a knowledge generation function. External knowledge is the qualifying input, together with internal knowledge obtained by means of R&D activities and the valorization of learning processes. External knowledge is a non-disposable input, for nobody can command all the knowledge available at any point in time. Internal and external knowledge are complementary inputs that have to be combined in order to produce new technological knowledge.

In our case, the generation function T and the cost equation C of technological knowledge can be written as follows:

$$T = (IK^a \ EK^b) \text{ with } a + b = 1 \qquad (7.1)$$

$$C = pIK + uEK \qquad (7.2)$$

where T represents new technological knowledge generated with constant returns to scale by means of internal knowledge (IK) and external knowledge (EK); a and b are their respective output elasticities. Here, p and u represent their respective unit costs. The unit cost of internal knowledge consists of the market price of the resources that are necessary to perform R&D activities. The costs of external knowledge are the resources that are necessary to screen, understand, purchase and acquire knowledge possessed by other agents in the system, including non-trivial efforts in terms of knowledge communication, including reception and absorption activities, as well as knowledge networking. Such technological knowledge does not spill freely in the air. Dedicated activities are necessary in order to identify and acquire it. Moreover, additional resources are necessary in order to find a new use for it. The acquisition of external knowledge is not free: in fact, pecuniary externalities replace technological externalities.

There are conducive contexts characterized by high-quality knowledge-governance mechanisms, which means that because of knowledge non-exhaustibility, the costs of using existing technological knowledge are far below the costs of generating it. Pecuniary knowledge externalities result in the costs of external knowledge (u) being lower than the costs of internal sources of new knowledge (p) and also being below equilibrium levels (u^*). It should be noted that the latter would hold if and when knowledge were a standard economic good.

Pecuniary knowledge externalities are found in economic systems where the costs of external knowledge are below equilibrium levels. Pecuniary knowledge externalities are found if, when and where knowledge-utilization costs differ sharply from its generation, and when knowledge-governance at the system level is effective and the knowledge-governance mechanisms are highly efficient. It is important to stress again how important knowledge-governance costs are. When knowledge-governance costs are high, the actual costs of external knowledge are close to 'equilibrium' levels. Hence, there are

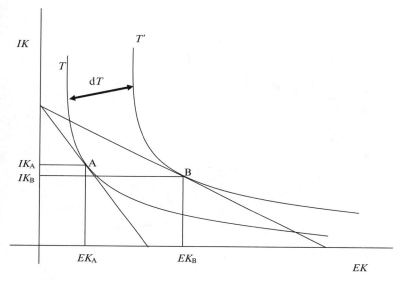

Figure 7.2   The Nelson–Weitzman knowledge generation function

no pecuniary knowledge externalities. When knowledge-governance costs are high the dynamics for new growth are hampered.

Pecuniary knowledge externalities are available only in specific circumstances and locations and are the result of the path-dependent evolution of the institutional and economic context. Specifically, they are the result of the specific organization of the modes of interaction and transactions within regional and industrial systems that have emerged through the polycentric governance of complex economic systems (Ostrom, 2010).

When pecuniary knowledge externalities apply, the maximizing firm will find the equilibrium at point B and produce a larger quantity of knowledge (*T'*), as shown in Figure 7.2. The equilibrium technique will consist in using external knowledge more than internal knowledge. In a system characterized by positive pecuniary knowledge externalities, a firm will produce more technological knowledge than in a system where external knowledge has higher costs.

With positive pecuniary knowledge externalities in the upstream generation of technological knowledge, the costs of technological knowledge generated by the firm are below equilibrium level: $s < s^*$ (see below).

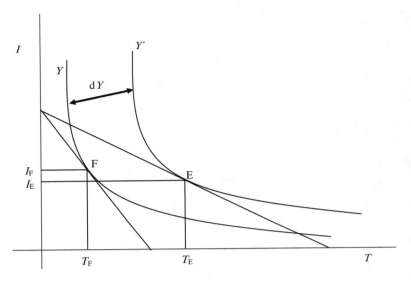

Figure 7.3   The Griliches production function

This has important implications regarding a firm's output. As shown in Figure 7.3, positive upstream effects of external knowledge, available at costs that are below equilibrium levels, will result in the firm being able to generate technological knowledge at lower costs and hence to produce a larger quantity of Y. The firm will, in fact, select the equilibrium point E, instead of F, where a firm that has no access to pecuniary knowledge externalities would go. The equilibrium at E implies a smaller demand for the bundle of tangible inputs (I), a more intensive use of the technology (T) and a larger output Y'. As a matter of fact, the amount of excess output dY generated by the firm that can take advantage of positive pecuniary knowledge externalities can be considered the residual, that is to say, the excess output that cannot be explained in equilibrium conditions.

7.3   THE GRILICHES PRODUCTION FUNCTION

Let us formalize this crucial point. According to Griliches (1979), technological knowledge directly enters a standard Cobb–Douglas production function with constant returns to scale. Hence:

$$Y = (I^f \, T^g) \text{ where } f + g = 1 \qquad (7.3)$$

$$C = cI + sT \qquad (7.4)$$

where for the sake of simplicity I is a bundle of tangible inputs, c is their costs, T is technological knowledge and s its cost, f and g are the output elasticities of the two production factors. Standard maximization leads to the identification of the equilibrium quantities of production factors.

We know that total factor productivity A is measured by the ratio between the real levels of output RY, and the theoretical ones generated by the equilibrium level use of production factors:

$$A = RY \, / \, I^* \, T^* \qquad (7.5)$$

where I^* and T^* are the equilibrium quantities of production factors and A measures total factor productivity.

Now it is clear that if and when:

(1) the costs of external knowledge in the upstream knowledge generation function are lower than in equilibrium ($u < u^*$);
(2) the output in terms of technological knowledge is larger than in equilibrium conditions, that is, the actual levels of T (RT) are larger than the equilibrium levels (T^*) ($RT > T^*$);
(3) the costs for technological knowledge that enters the Cobb–Douglas production function for all the other goods are also lower ($s < s^*$);

then firms produce more than expected and hence experience an 'unexplained' increase in the actual levels of output, that are larger than the expected ones ($RY > Y^*$).

These elementary passages enable us to state the basic proposition that total factor productivity levels and their increase depend upon the discrepancy between the equilibrium costs of external knowledge and the actual ones. Hence, we can put forward the basic proposition that total factor productivity levels stem from pecuniary knowledge externalities:

$$A = f(u/u^*) \qquad (7.6)$$

Total factor productivity growth can be explained as being due to positive pecuniary knowledge externalities, because knowledge is a production factor both for the production of goods and for the generation of further knowledge. Further, it is characterized by non-exhaustibility and its production function is shaped by the complementarity between external and internal sources of knowledge (see Antonelli, 2011b).

The working of pecuniary knowledge externalities is compatible with equilibrium conditions at the firm level while at the aggregate level, the system is far from equilibrium. As long as there are pecuniary knowledge externalities, the typical system dynamics, stemming from the positive feedback generated by knowledge non-exhaustibility and knowledge complementarity, implemented by good knowledge governance mechanisms, are at work at the system level.

7.4   THE DYNAMIC INTERPLAY BETWEEN POSITIVE AND NEGATIVE PECUNIARY EXTERNALITIES

The tradition of analysis proposed by Griliches (1979, 1992) has understood the positive effects of the non-appropriability of knowledge in terms of the uncontrolled spillover of knowledge from 'inventors' to third parties.

Applying the notion of pecuniary externalities to the economics of knowledge makes it possible to appreciate and identify not only the positive effects of knowledge spillovers within clusters but also the negative effects in terms of reduced knowledge appropriability. Clustering clearly affects knowledge appropriability.

Traditional analysis based upon the contributions of Arrow (1962a) has focused attention on the negative effects of the non-appropriability of knowledge in terms of missing incentives for the generation of new knowledge. Pecuniary knowledge externalities do not always exist and they are not exclusively positive. Agglomeration in geographical and technological space, within technological clusters and technological systems, respectively, has negative effects that are seldom identified. The density of firms accessing the same knowledge pools may have negative consequences in terms of reduced appropriability of technological knowledge. The clustering of firms in the same region favours the uncontrolled mobility of qualified workers and hence the leakage of sensitive information and competence. The likelihood of informal contacts among workers of different companies is increased and favoured by repeated interactions and the complementarity and interdependence of research activities. Once more, firms are exposed to the uncontrolled loss of proprietary knowledge.

As Kenneth Arrow (1962a) has pointed out, knowledge is indeed characterized by non-rivalry in use. While two or more parties cannot share the simultaneous usage of the same tangible good, repeated usage of knowledge by many parties at the same time is possible. Each user does not deprive or limit the conditions of usage of other parties.

Knowledge, however, is characterized by substantial rivalry in exchange. Firms can extract substantial monopolistic rents from the exclusive action of original and unprecedented technological knowledge. The innovative firm can charge monopolistic prices for products that embody new technological knowledge as long as it is able to retain its exclusive action.

Non-rivalry in use and non-rivalry in exchange coincide only when perfect competition applies. But perfect competition applies only when all firms have access to all technological knowledge available with no restriction. When the access to knowledge is restricted, perfect competition no longer applies. Knowledge holders have a clear incentive to delay the dissemination and leakage of knowledge to third parties.

In Schumpeterian competition, non-rivalry in use and non-rivalry in exchange differ widely. As is well known, in fact, the exclusive command of proprietary technological knowledge impedes imitation and hence lengthens the duration of monopolistic rents.

A full account of the negative effects of clustering requires the analysis of the reduction in the levels of mark-up engendered by an increase in the number of clustering firms. An increase in the number of firms co-localized, in fact, engenders a decline in the levels of the market price of the goods manufactured with directed technological changes, which intentionally use locally abundant and idiosyncratic inputs intensively. It is clear, in fact, that the larger the number of co-localized firms that rely upon strategies of localized appropriability that impinge upon the same pools of idiosyncratic inputs, the closer prices will be to marginal costs. Access to the same pools of

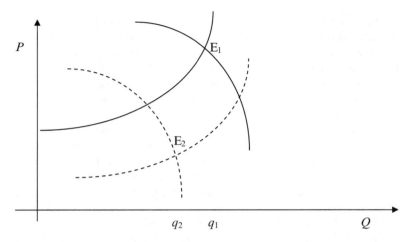

Figure 7.4   Positive and negative pecuniary knowledge externalities

knowledge reduces the costs of external knowledge as an input into the generation of new knowledge, but reduces its appropriability, too.

The understanding of the dual role of knowledge as an output and an input makes it possible to use the notion of derived demand. The non-appropriability of knowledge, as sketched by the dotted supply and demand schedules in Figure 7.4, has effects on both demand and supply. The effects on the derived demand side are negative. This is because the prices for knowledge are lower than they would be with a pure private good characterized by full appropriability and exhaustibility, and they push the position of the demand curve downward (see the shift of the derived demand curve from the solid to the dotted line in Figure 7.4). The effects on the supply side, however, are positive as they push down the supply curve as well. The costs of the production of new knowledge are, in fact, lower – with respect to pure private goods – when the access to external knowledge that spills over from original inventors is possible at a cost that is lower than in the case of a pure private good. Hence, the actual amount of knowledge generated in the system may be much closer to equilibrium levels. The price of knowledge may be lower. The actual extent to which such positive and negative effects apply and their relative weight depend very much upon the localized conditions of action of agents.[1]

When such effects are taken into account the notion of net pecuniary knowledge externalities can be introduced. Net pecuniary knowledge externalities are the result of the joint assessment of both negative and positive effects. The latter reduce the costs of external knowledge and, consequently, because of the increase in total factor productivity, the costs of goods. The former reduce the price at which knowledge, as a good (or as an input that incorporates the new knowledge), can be sold. The levels of net pecuniary externalities depend upon the combined effects of positive and negative pecuniary knowledge externalities. It is easy to derive the formal conditions to identify the optimum size of the local pools of knowledge.

The negative effects of pecuniary knowledge externalities stem from the reduction in the appropriability of technological knowledge, hence in the reduction of knowledge rents and eventually of revenue (RV). The price of the goods that embody the proprietary technological knowledge declines as a consequence of the reduction in appropriability towards perfect competition conditions, away from monopolistic levels. The stretch of time along which the generator of an innovation can exert an exclusive and hence full command of the stream of economic benefits of its introduction is trimmed by the number of firms that can use the same technology.

The larger the number of firms that share the same access conditions to the same pools of technological knowledge the lower the chances of stretching appropriability through time are. We know that the value of output depends on the quantity and its price P:

$$Y = PQ \qquad (7.7)$$

We assume that the competitive market price of these goods (P) is a fraction of the monopolistic prices (P^*) at which firms are able to innovate in isolation with perfect appropriability of their technological knowledge. More specifically, we can assume that the price (P) at which the good that embodies new knowledge is sold, is a function of the levels of monopolistic prices (P^*) divided by the number N of firms that can access and share the same pools of technological knowledge pools reducing its appropriability:

$$P = z \, (P^* \, / \, N) \qquad (7.8)$$

where $z' < 0$, $z'' > 0$. We assume, in fact, that the larger the number of firms, the lower the prices for the goods that embody the localized technological knowledge.

Hence, we can see that the negative effects of pecuniary externalities, consisting in the reduction of knowledge rents and hence in the fall of revenue (RV), are a function of the number (N) of the firms that share the same pools of technological knowledge (see Figure 7.5, top panel).

At the same time, we know from Equations (7.1)–(7.6) that the total factor productivity of production processes that benefit from the access to the local pools of knowledge is a function of the size of the pools. Hence, we know that the positive effects of pecuniary knowledge externalities consist in the reduction of average production costs (AC) made possible by the increase in total factor productivity that is engendered by the access to technological knowledge in the local pools at costs that are below equilibrium levels. AC of the same output (Y) are influenced by the costs of external knowledge which, in turn, are affected by the same number of firms N:

$$AC = v(C^* / N) \qquad (7.9)$$

where we can assume that $v' < 0$, $v'' < 0$.

If the positive effects of the density of firms, in a given innovation system, in terms of pecuniary knowledge externalities are larger than their negative effects in terms of reduced knowledge appropriability, a local system can emerge and consolidate. Net positive pecuniary externalities (NE) are found when the positive effects, in terms of pecuniary knowledge externalities, are larger than the negative effects, in terms of reduced appropriability and hence traduced levels of knowledge rents:

$$NE = (\Delta AC - \Delta RV) \qquad (7.10)$$

The distributions of the positive net pecuniary externalities are typically quadratic and always positive: they start at 0 levels (for z'' > v''), grow up to a maximum and then decline to zero. Hence, we can better specify Equation (7.10) as follows:

$$NE = m \left(N(t) - (N^2(t)) \right) \qquad (7.11)$$

The entry of new firms will be attracted by the positive net externalities (NE). When $NE > 0$, new firms will try to enter the system. The increase of the number (dN) of firms that enter and interact within

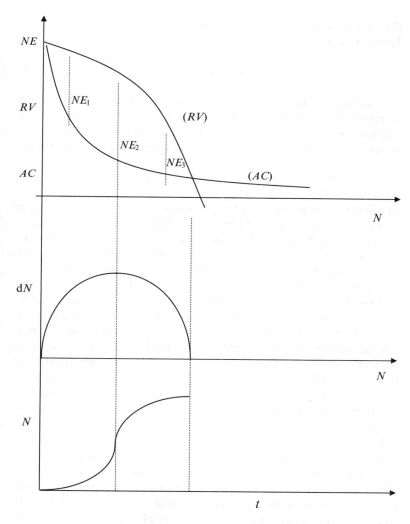

Note: *NE*: Net positive knowledge externality; *RV*: Effects of knowledge externalities on revenue; *AC*: Effects of knowledge externalities on costs.

Figure 7.5   *The dynamics of the pecuniary knowledge externalities trade-off and the s-shaped diffusion process of innovation systems*

the system depends upon levels (*m*) of positive net externalities. Hence we can write:

$$dN = m \,(NE) \qquad (7.12)$$

If we assume that the entry (d*N*) of new firms is a function of the levels of net externalities, and we know that the distribution of *NE* is quadratic in *N*, we can conclude that the dynamics of firms entry, as dependent upon the number *N* of firms, takes a quadratic shape:

$$dN(t) = o \,(N(t) - (N^2(t))) \qquad (7.13)$$

In such circumstances the entry process of new agents in the system may follow a hump-shaped process (see Figure 7.5, middle panel).

Net pecuniary knowledge externalities provide the incentive to enter knowledge pools. Entry will take place as long as they are positive. The flow of entry will take a quadratic shape and accelerated flows of entry are likely to take place in the proximity of the optimum size of the cluster. Beyond that level, firms will enter at a reduced rate. Entry will stop as soon as the negative effects of reduced knowledge appropriability are larger than the positive effects, in terms of reduced costs of external knowledge. The specific form of interplay between the positive effects on the costs of external knowledge and the negative effects on knowledge appropriability can acquire a quadratic form. In such circumstances the dynamics of the process will follow an S-shaped path (see Figure 7.5, bottom panel).

Pecuniary knowledge externalities enable us to grasp the negative effects of the agglomeration of firms and their access to the same localized pools of knowledge. At the same time, the appreciation of the effects of externalities upon the price of the goods that are manufactured with the support of localized technological knowledge enables us to account for their strong effects upon the direction of technological change. Firms, in fact, will try to make the most intensive use of the production factors that are locally abundant, as their use can become a major barrier to entry and to imitation for firms that cannot access the same production factors under the same conditions.

Pecuniary knowledge externalities, in fact, qualify the exploitation of technological knowledge. Firms that become aware of the specific characteristics of the local supply of technological knowledge at costs that are lower than equilibrium levels, try to increase the intensity of use of these production factors that other firms – localized in other districts and in other innovations systems – cannot imitate easily.

The identification of the idiosyncratic aspects of the local pools of technological knowledge becomes a powerful factor affecting the direction of technological change.

Figure 7.6 highlights graphically the effects of the introduction of technological changes directed towards the intensive use of locally abundant production factors, including competence, in respect to the effects of neutral technological changes that are not biased in favour of locally abundant factors. Knowledge rents in the former case are clearly much larger and last much longer. Hence $(RV)_2$ is larger than $(RV)_1$. In the former case, the number of firms that can take advantage of net positive externalities is much larger and the absolute size of positive net externalities is also much larger. The latter case applies to systems of innovations where firms are not able to direct technological change towards an intensive use of locally abundant resources: they are smaller and the size of net positive externalities is also smaller; they do not last as long, in terms of entry of new firms.

The introduction of biased technological change directed towards the intensive use of locally abundant factors enables firms to take collective advantage of the command of the local resources and hence to use this form of quasi-exclusive control as a source of barriers to entry and to imitations towards firms that are not co-localized and hence cannot share the same access conditions to the same pools of localized technological knowledge.

The negative effects of reduced appropriability that take place with biased technology – when firms are able to direct technological change towards an intensive use of locally abundant production factors – are much smaller than the negative effects that stem from the decline in the prices for the manufactured goods that incorporate the technological knowledge generated with the help of pecuniary knowledge externalities that do not incorporate any bias. In the 'neutral' case, local firms are pushed to cut prices on the internal markets. In the case of the introduction of directed technological changes, instead, the local system of innovations act as a collective monopolist that has a strong and shared incentive to participate in a

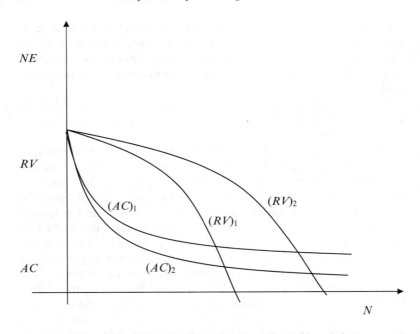

Note: *NE*: Net positive knowledge externality; *RV*: Effects of knowledge externalities on revenue; *AC*: Effects of knowledge externalities on costs.

Figure 7.6   Net pecuniary knowledge externalities with directed technological change

strategy of appropriation of the benefits stemming from the shared localized pools of technological knowledge, with respect to external competitors.

On the other hand, firms able to direct their technological change towards production processes that make intensive use of locally abundant and hence cheap inputs, available in local factor markets at prices that are below equilibrium prices, will experience higher rates of growth of total factor productivity and larger benefits in terms of the reduction of average costs (see the curve $(AC)_2$ in Figure 7.6).

As a result, agglomeration is no longer an unconstrained strategy. The size of the local knowledge pools can be too small or too large. There is also, depending on specific conditions, an 'optimum' size of the local pools of knowledge. The governance of the local pools of knowledge plays a key role. The organization of the local systems, in fact, has important effects: next to the sheer size, in terms of density and number of firms, the quality of the connections and the context of knowledge interactions and transactions all affect the actual costs of external knowledge. They are also endogenous, as they are the product of the interactions and strategic action of firms that try to increase their command of external technological knowledge. The analysis of the dynamic complexity of the condition of access to external technological knowledge becomes crucial to understand the change through time of innovation systems.

7.5 CONCLUSIONS

Summing up, in the localized technological change approach, innovation activity is interpreted as the result of a particular form of *creative reaction* triggered by unexpected changes in product and factor markets and made possible by pecuniary knowledge externalities. More specifically, the introduction of innovation is the result of a series of circumstances and rather special complementary factors. When the external context is conducive and supports the attempts of firms to try to react by means of the generation of new technological knowledge and the eventual introduction of technological innovation, a self-sustaining chain reaction is set off. Innovation is, therefore, the result of conditions of disequilibrium which, in their turn, determine an imbalance. Each single firm is affected by innovation introduced by other firms and it reacts by introducing further innovation. The conditions for the generation of technological knowledge play a key role in this context.

The generation of technological knowledge is a collective, highly imperfect and heterogeneous activity. First of all, it is not only an output, but also an input, an essential intermediary factor of production that is relevant both in the generation of new technological knowledge and in the generation of other goods. The dynamic efficiency of each firm, and of the system at large, depends upon the factors affecting the generation and dissemination of knowledge.

The identification of the dual characteristics of technological knowledge as both an output and an input in the production of other goods and in the production of further knowledge, together with an understanding of the intrinsic complementarity between external and internal sources of knowledge (both non-disposable inputs in the generation of new knowledge), make it possible to apply the notion of pecuniary externalities in a novel context.

Pecuniary knowledge externalities are a powerful analytical tool that applies to the analysis of external knowledge as a necessary and yet costly production factor in the generation of new knowledge. The use of the notion of 'technological' externalities is consistent with the view that external knowledge falls from heaven like manna and spills freely in the atmosphere.

The distinction between pecuniary and technological externalities in the economics of knowledge and innovation is fruitful. Making such a distinction suggests that an understanding of the characteristics of knowledge and geographical space into which firms are rooted plays a key role in the implementation of successful strategies for the localized generation and exploitation of knowledge. Pecuniary externalities help to explain the role of external factors in shaping both the rate and the direction of technological change. Distinguishing between pecuniary externalities and technological externalities in the economics of knowledge suggests that an understanding of the full range of characteristics of the space into which firms are rooted – including the structure of knowledge governance mechanisms, the local factor markets and the vertical structure of inter-industrial relations – plays a key role in the implementation of successful strategies for localized knowledge generation and exploitation.

When, instead of focusing only on the diachronic building of knowledge, the role of the synchronic integration of knowledge, dispersed among a variety of agents, is considered, pecuniary knowledge externalities stemming from the localized complementarity of agents emerge as a crucial factor in shaping the generation of new knowledge.

Because of intrinsic knowledge indivisibility, both in terms of knowledge cumulability and complementarity and its twin character of being both an input and an output, the acquisition of technological knowledge external to each firm is a necessary and indispensable activity in the generation of new knowledge. Hence, firms are pushed to select the generation of new knowledge so as to make the best use of external knowledge that is available within the local knowledge networks. Firms have a strong incentive to generate a localized technological knowledge that favours the introduction of an intentionally biased direction of technological change in downstream applications. The intensive use of locally and possibly internal production factors, that are highly idiosyncratic and hence cheaper for a limited number of users, favours both the productivity of new biased technologies and their profitability, because it reduces the risks of imitation by rivals, who do not have access to the same factor markets. Such inputs are made idiosyncratic to the innovating firm by the selection of locational factors and their intentional creation. In so doing, firms implement and benefit from localized appropriability. Localized appropriability adds to the appropriability provided by the intellectual property right regime.

Strong positive external effects, in terms of: (1) reduced knowledge generation costs, stemming from knowledge complementarity; (2) reduced production costs, engendered by the ensuing technological innovations that make an intensive use of locally abundant factors; and (3) increased knowledge localized appropriability based upon the use of idiosyncratic – either locally available or internally created – production factors, all provide a clear incentive to direct the generation of new knowledge according to the local knowledge networks and endowments. This strategy can exert positive effects not only on the growth of firms but also upon regions and industries able to implement the local pools of collective knowledge by means of effective knowledge governance mechanisms.

The dynamics of the process can last as long as institutional and organizational changes are introduced so as to counteract the decline in the levels of pecuniary externalities stemming from increasing knowledge governance costs and decreasing relative abundance of idiosyncratic inputs. The continual recreation of pecuniary knowledge externalities is crucial for the process to keep momentum.

The localized context of action emerges as a fundamental aspect of the innovation process, one that makes it possible to understand that a variety of paths to innovation can exist and be successful. An understanding of the key role of the localized context where technological knowledge is being generated and exploited, opens up new prospects of empirical enquiry regarding the variety of types of knowledge that different groups of firms, active in different contexts, have an incentive to generate.

Depending on the local endowments, articulated in material inputs, skills and mechanisms of knowledge governance, firms have clear incentives to identify and implement a specific typology of technological knowledge and the resulting technological innovations. In a heterogeneous system, where local endowments differ, firms do not compete on the same knowledge frontier but, instead, they have a strong incentive to identify the kind of technological knowledge that is most appropriate to their own specific conditions and traditions. Such specific conditions are not only internal to each firm, as the resource-based theory of the firm argues, but also external. Consequently, a variety of localized paths to technological change are likely to emerge and consolidate. Firms based in countries and regions with a stronger scientific infrastructure have an advantage in the introduction of science-based technologies. This is not necessarily the case for firms based in countries where the endowment of human capital is lower or different. The distinction between skills acquired on-the-job and skills based upon formal education, for instance, has important ramifications. The specific characteristics of the industrial structure also play a major role here. Firms based in countries and regions specialized in capital goods have a structure of incentives to align their knowledge generating activities that differ from the one of firms based in countries specialized in final goods. In the globalizing learning economy, regions have a strong incentive to pursue dedicated and specialized knowledge strategies based upon their own endowments in terms of both knowledge generation and knowledge exploitation mechanisms (Scott and Storper, 2007).

Pecuniary knowledge externalities are a crucial tool to understand the complex dynamics of network creation that underlies the path-dependent emergence of local and sectoral innovation systems as well as the dynamics of innovation cascades. As such, pecuniary knowledge externalities are an important tool for implementing an articulated economics of complexity.

Our argument, according to which firms prompted by increasing demand, may introduce technological innovations that can increase total factor productivity only if and when external knowledge is available at costs that are below equilibrium, identifies the key conditions in the cost equation for the generation of technological knowledge and in the profit equation for its exploitation – without affecting the output elasticity of inputs and the specification of both the knowledge and the output production functions. In so doing, we reverse the new growth theory and elaborate a frame that can account for the variety of specific contextual conditions that may or may not lead to the actual introduction of productivity-enhancing technological innovations.

Pecuniary knowledge externalities are not always present or universally positive. Agglomeration within geographic and technological clusters can turn out to be negative, in terms of reduced appropriability of proprietary knowledge. Agglomeration within clusters yield positive effects only when the effects of pecuniary knowledge externalities upon the costs of external knowledge are stronger than the effects of pecuniary knowledge externalities upon the prices of the goods that embody the new technological knowledge. A clear case of excess agglomeration has been identified in terms of reduced knowledge appropriability. Uncontrolled leakage and reduced exclusivity of proprietary knowledge can impede the long-term sustainability of such a process of self-propelling growth.

The quality of knowledge governance mechanisms, including the assessment of intellectual property right regimes, is crucial for the actual viability of public policies based upon knowledge externalities. The implications of the analysis conducted so far for analysing the Italian evidence are quite important.

The next section of this book can be considered an enquiry into the conditions that determined in the Italian case, in the 1950s–90s, the availability of external knowledge at costs that were below equilibrium levels and an empirical investigation of the consequences, in terms of total factor productivity and output growth and introduction of directed technological change biased in favour of capital-intensive process innovations.

NOTE

1. At the firm level it is clear that firms have a strong incentive to implement, on one hand, exploitation strategies in order to reduce the negative effects of non-appropriability and hence minimize the uncontrolled leakage of their proprietary knowledge, while, on the other hand, they are induced to adopt exploration strategies, in order to maximize the benefits of knowledge spilling in the atmosphere. It is clear that both the exploitation and exploration of knowledge require dedicated activities and relevant resources.

PART II
The Italian evidence

8. Technological change in a distributed innovation system

The model of localized technological change cum pecuniary knowledge externalities elaborated in Part I provides a coherent analytical framework that implements and empowers the notion of creative reaction and localized technological change – constrained by the irreversibility of production factors that limit standard adjustment process based upon substitution processes – with the notion of pecuniary knowledge externalities.

The main theme and the basic hypothesis of this book claims that an increase in wages and demand pulls can stir learning firms to actually introduce technological innovations only if, when and where the access conditions to external knowledge enable them to generate new technological knowledge at costs that are lower than equilibrium ones. This model should enable us to grasp the specific characteristics of the process of technological, structural and organizational change, experienced by the Italian economic system in the second part of the twentieth century.

The rate of technological change experienced by the Italian economy was the result of the mix between the stimulations provided by the demand pull and the amount of pecuniary knowledge externalities, made available by the localized pools of technological knowledge within vertical filieres and industrial districts framed into a distributed process of knowledge generation and exploitation. The direction of localized technological change has also been influenced by the specific conditions of the localized availability of the pools of knowledge. It is clear, in fact, that firms that could rely upon vertical user–producer relations between upstream producers and downstream users of capital goods had a strong incentive to increase the capital intensity of their production process and to introduce more process than product innovations.

The application of the basic tools of complex system analysis to social sciences and the economics of innovation are particularly helpful for appreciating the emergence and the characteristics of the Italian distributed model of knowledge generation, dissemination and exploitation. This frame recognizes that innovation takes place in organized contexts, characterized by qualified interactions among heterogeneous and creative agents that are able to act intentionally to face unexpected events. The outcome of their interactions is determined by the structured contexts into which they are embedded. At the same time, however, their actions and interactions may have the twin effect of generating new technological knowledge and introducing technological innovations so as to affect the performances of the system. They also affect the organization, the structure of the system, the knowledge governance mechanisms with an indirect effect that has consequences in time. The action of agents has both a direct and indirect bearing upon the aggregate outcomes of the dynamics. In this approach, neither the interactions nor the organized structures into which they take place are exogenous, as they are determined internally by the dynamics of the system. The individual and intentional action of creative agents is central in the dynamics of the system, yet no individual agent can claim responsibility or even a long-term view on the eventual results of his or her action (Arthur, Durlauf and Lane, 1997; Lane, 2009; Antonelli, 2011a).

The Italian evidence, as analysed by an increasing number of detailed case studies, supports the view that the polycentric architecture of the connections and ensuing knowledge interactions among agents in geographical, technological and industrial space was most important to generate the levels of pecuniary knowledge externalities able to actually convert the stimulus of increases of wages and demand pull into technological innovations. The architecture of inter-industrial flows of goods and services within industrial filieres, and their implications in terms of qualified knowledge interactions among users and producers, and networking activities within industrial districts, played a central role in determining the effective amount of knowledge being generated, and in making possible the actual introduction of technological and organizational innovations.

This evidence confirms that the distributed model of generation of technological knowledge that emerged in the Italian economic system in the second part of the twentieth century could take advantage of learning processes both internal and external to firms so as to magnify the actual amount of technological knowledge being generated. The relationship between traditional indicators of the effort to generate new knowledge, such as the expenditures in R&D activities, and the effective amount of technological change being introduced needs to be qualified and implemented with the assessment of the typology of the architecture of connection and interaction in place. A 'good' architectural and behavioural organization of interactions and connections within the system enables the generation of technological knowledge and the consequent introduction of much technological change even with low levels of expenditure in R&D activities.

Two dimensions of the architectural and behavioural organization of the structure of connections and interactions appear most relevant in the Italian case: the horizontal intra-industrial flows of interactions among agents within technological districts and the vertical inter-industrial ones within filieres. The analysis of the emergence of technological districts makes it possible to grasp the complementarity among firms that belong to the same industry and share the access and the implementation of common pools of localized knowledge. The analysis of the flows of pecuniary externalities among industries within vertical filieres makes it possible to understand the dynamics of a self-sustained innovation process based upon innovation cascades. Bidirectional feedbacks have been at work. Downstream users provided a strong demand pull effect – based upon high rates of investment and hence derived demand for upstream products – and active user–producer interactions. Upstream producers contributed with the introduction of new vintages of capital goods incorporating technological advances that fed total factor productivity growth (TFP), and hence continual reduction of production costs and increasing of market share for downstream users.

Geographical and relational proximity in regional and knowledge space between users and producers gives downstream firms privileged access to the product innovations introduced by upstream manufacturers, that could be used timely and effectively as new production factors. The supply of new idiosyncratic inputs by upstream producers pushes downstream users to direct their technological change towards an intensive use of them, also in order to increase knowledge appropriability. The increased derived demand for these idiosyncratic products activates demand pull effects upon the rate and direction of technological change in upstream industries. These dynamics have been explored by many case studies.

The ground-breaking analysis on the emergence and successful growth of the new district of ceramic tiles in Sassuolo by Romano Prodi (1966) showed how the introduction of a major process innovation in furnace technology and the downstream growth of a consumer goods industry were twice intertwined. Prodi carefully showed to what extent the enrichment of the furnace technology manufactured by upstream mechanical engineering companies was the result of the feedback provided by downstream users, with quite an original anticipation of the user–producer approach eventually implemented by Eric Von Hippel (Von Hippel, 1988, 2005). At the same time, Prodi showed how the fast growth of the sales of tiles, especially in international markets, was the origin of the strong growth of investments embodying the new vintages of process innovations and how it stirred the ingenuity of upstream machinery producers that had to cope with the fast growth of their derived demand. In such a framework, the limitations of the 'automatic' Kaldorian generation of new technologies, eventually embodied by investments, was overcome. In Prodi's analysis, in fact, the demand pull process was coupled with qualified and fertile user–producer interactions that could support the actual generation of new advanced technological knowledge.

Some years later, Russo (1985) explored the same case of Sassuolo analysing in detail how the introduction of technological innovations in the upstream mechanical engineering industry – specializing in the production of furnaces – activated a flow of user–producer vertical interactions with the downstream users, that fed further introduction of innovations upstream. At the same time the division of labour in downstream activities increased with the emergence of new layers of specialization in complementary activities. The cooperation of firms in each layer became stronger and stronger to face the impetus of the changing conditions in both factor and product markets. Firms specialized horizontally in specific and yet complementary niches, both in terms of product and geographic markets. The interplay between division of labour and technological change acquired all the characteristics of a self-sustained process: the new technologies offered new opportunities for the specialization of firms in new layers of the production process, as much as the division of labour and the increasing length of the filiere offered new opportunities for the generation of new technological knowledge and its effective exploitation by means of the introduction of further waves of technological changes.

More recently, Russo (2000) has provided an original empirical investigation of the key role of external knowledge in the generation of technological knowledge in the case of the ceramic tile industry of the Sassuolo district. Russo systematically explored the origins of 'kervit', a major process innovation. The use of the notion of generative relationships, put forward by Lane and Maxfield (1997), implemented by the application of ethnographic methodology, enabled Russo to trace the emergence of learning processes within a local productive system and to explore the role of dynamic complementarities in fostering the innovation dynamics. This innovation is, in fact, the result at the same time of a complex web of interactions among users and producers, and of the interaction between learning processes within firms and among firms. Specifically, Russo shows how the introduction of the kervit innovation was the final result of a learning process activated by user–producer interactions with upstream producers led by the inventor – at the time, an employee of a company and the eventual creator of a new firm that deposited and exploited the resulting patent. The crucial role of the relationship between the generation of technological knowledge within a company and the creation of new firms for its exploitation has been eventually confirmed by a variety of other empirical studies that show how the introduction of technological innovations is the result of learning processes that lead to the creation of new knowledge-intensive firms, often with the support and the financial participation of the owners of the originating company.

Fiorenza Belussi has provided fascinating evidence on the key role of proximity and interaction within industrial districts and vertical filieres in the fashion industry. Here the generation of new knowledge is tightly related to the interactions between a great variety of specialized providers that converge to the final introduction of soft innovations based upon design and fashion. These innovations affect a huge array of downstream industries specializing in consumer goods, ranging from shoes, garments, furniture, leather, wood products to plastic. The fast rates of introduction of soft innovations in these industries are key to their continual penetration of international markets in rich niches, characterized by low levels of price elasticity and very high levels of revenue elasticity. These innovation processes cannot be grasped without the understanding of the close knit interactions between technological innovations and changes in design and fashion, on one hand, and upon the relations among firms along the vertical filieres relating each layer both upstream and downstream, on the other hand (Belussi and Pilotti, 2002; Aage and Belussi, 2008).

Many analyses of the filieres that relate garment, textiles and the chemical and mechanical engineering industries, stress the positive interplay between the dynamics of division of labour, the creation of new intermediary markets, and the rates of generation of technological knowledge and introduction of technological innovations. The creation of new intermediary markets and the increased specialization of downstream firms in well-defined production layers provided opportunities for the bottom-up introduction of new dedicated technologies, as much as the introduction of technological innovations in the upstream chemical and mechanical industries provided an opportunity to identify new downstream market niches (Antonelli and Marchionatti, 1998).

An important step towards a dynamic extension of the analysis is made when the origins of the local supply of idiosyncratic factors are investigated. The introduction of technological innovation in upstream industries is a major source of the local supply of such idiosyncratic factors. Firms active in downstream industries and clustering in the same geographic space can take advantage of the introduction of innovations in upstream industries. Proximity, both in knowledge and geographical space, favours the early adoption of new production factors and facilitates user–producer interactions. Co-localized firms can make better use of upstream innovations than remote firms. Co-localized firms have a privileged access to the new technologies both as adopters and adapters.

The supply by upstream innovators of new products, that can become production factors in downstream industries, provides the opportunity for downstream users, who are co-localized and/or have privileged access to these innovations, to strategically take advantage of their localized availability, and stimulates them to generate new technological knowledge and eventually introduce new technologies that use them intensively.

The case study of Pier Paolo Patrucco on the Emilian district of the plastic industry provides illuminating evidence of the role of the systemic interactions within a district and along the filiere between the upstream producers of machinery and chemical components and the downstream users specializing in plastic products. This case study documents how the emergence of technology systems is the result of interdependent dynamics in the generation and diffusion of complementary bits of localized technological knowledge. Technological communication, both horizontal among competitors and vertical among suppliers and customers – including both final consumers and upstream providers of capital and intermediary goods – is the crucial element assessing the collective conditions under which technological knowledge is accumulated and diffused. The case study of the emergence of the Emilian technological system in the plastics sector shows that the interplay between industrial dynamics and policy interventions of local institutions to support R&D efforts and technological interrelatedness, are the determinants of the systematic production, accumulation and distribution of localized technological knowledge (Patrucco, 2005).

The innovation capabilities of firms within each layer are conditional to the flows of technological knowledge that take place within each layer and between layers, embodied in the advanced inputs supplied by the upstream providers and vice versa. The supply of pecuniary knowledge externalities by upstream innovators provides the opportunity for the creation of new activities in downstream applications. Innovative users, in turn, push upstream producers to introduce further innovations.

The book by Belussi, Gottardi and Rullani (2003) provides a superb collection of case study evidence capturing one central aspect of the emergence of the distributed model of knowledge generation: the complementarity between transactions in tangible goods and knowledge interactions. Such complementarity becomes evident when transactions are repeated and take place within a long-term contract. Repeated transactions in the intermediary markets for capital goods provided the opportunity to implement knowledge interactions that were fruitful both for the customers and the vendors of tangible goods. Such qualified user–producer interactions were the result of the implementation of coherent technological filieres that acted as effective communication channels for the bilateral exchange of tacit knowledge, made possible by the emergence of intermediary markets with low transaction costs. These intermediary markets were increasingly articulated and sophisticated, along chains of specialized suppliers, through processes of vertical disintegration, the birth of new specialized firms and increased division of labour. Italian small firms, as a result, were able to achieve higher rates of growth, as they were able to make a systematic use

of external knowledge, that is knowledge generated by other firms –
including the corporate part of the economy – the technology generated in other countries, and, to a large extent, the pool of collective
knowledge implemented within industrial districts and technological
filieres.

In his analysis of the Italian industrial districts, Lane (2002)
presents this peculiar form of market system as the emerging property of an organized complexity based upon structured transactions
enriched by interactions. Agents interact in the market place by
means of structured transactions. Such transactions are far from the
typical impersonal exchange depicted in textbook microeconomics. These transactions take place within the context of long-term,
incomplete contracts and, as such, are recurrent, personalized and
based upon reciprocal trust and confidence. They are characterized
by intense user–producer interactions where both parties cooperate
in valorizing the shared learning processes. Long-term, incomplete
contracts emerge from recurrent interactions and shared interest so
as to provide the context into which transactions are enriched by
forms of tacit cooperation.

The notion of transaction-based interactions is important as it
identifies a key aspect of market interactions falling between the
extreme cases of 'perfect transactions' and 'perfect interactions'.
The former miss the appreciation of the rich context into which real
transactions in real market places take place, and may apply to quite
a limited spectrum of actual exchanges concerning only perfectly
homogeneous and highly standardized commodities. The latter fail
to appreciate the economic aspects of social interactions and risk
portraying collective innovation processes as the by-products of
spontaneous exchanges of gifts by cooperative agents with no rent-
seeking perspectives. The notion of transaction-based interactions
captures the wide spectrum of circumstances that characterize real
market exchanges and enables us to appreciate the convergence of
the rent-seeking behaviour of intentional agents, trying to maximize
their individual benefits through participation in the social exchange
centred upon an innovation. The Italian case study evidence provides substantial support for the notion of an original distributed
process of knowledge generation, dissemination and exploitation as
a collective process, shaped by coalitions of interactive and intentional agents engaged in enriched transactions within a structured
context, based upon relevant pecuniary knowledge externalities.

The analysis of the direction of technological change within industrial districts confirms the effects of pecuniary externalities upon the direction of technological change, and makes it possible to better understand the feedback dynamics of the process that leads to cascades of innovations. The selection by downstream users of new directional technologies – making intensive use of innovative production factors provided by upstream industries under favourable conditions – increase their derived demand for upstream suppliers. Hence, the possibility of increasing the division of labour in upstream industries is further enhanced and consequently the specialization and the incentives and opportunities to introduce innovations are also enhanced. Such a process will engender new pecuniary externalities with the continual interaction between upstream and downstream innovation activities.

Innovation cascades emerge as soon as the supply of idiosyncratic production factors is no longer regarded as exogenous or static, but rather the endogenous result of the interaction among innovative firms active in different layers of the filieres and value chains. Innovation cascades are the result of the efforts of innovative users taking advantage of the new technologies being introduced by innovative suppliers. The changing conditions of downstream markets will, in turn, engender further feedback for upstream suppliers. Innovation cascades are the result of the complementarity of downstream and upstream innovation processes.

The framework elaborated so far provides the basic elements for understanding not only the persistent growth of many 'traditional' sectors organized in industrial districts, but also the growth dynamics of many new knowledge districts, where there are knowledge-intensive business suppliers based upon skilled manpower. The interplay between pecuniary externalities in knowledge generation and knowledge exploitation provides the context in which small firms, with low levels of formalized R&D activities, were able to introduce fast rates of innovation based upon horizontal complementarity between their own knowledge base and the systematic direction of the new technologies towards the use of locally abundant production factors supplied by upstream innovators.

The growth of the Italian industry in the second part of the twentieth century, with special reference to the industries of general machinery, machine tools, food, garments, textiles, furniture, jewellery, leather, tiles and other consumer goods, shows how reciprocal access to the local pools of the competence and expertise of designers, marketing experts and stylists provides the opportunity to increase a firm's capability of generating technological knowledge. The growth of upstream niche sectors specializing in the supply of high quality and dedicated inputs ranging from machinery to intermediary inputs, designed to support downstream production, provided the second boost to the dynamics. The local supply of capital and intermediary inputs gave downstream users the opportunity to increase the exploitation of the new knowledge being generated, as well as the opportunity to take advantage of intensive user–producer interactions. The creation, through innovation cascades, of vertical filieres articulated in an increasing number of layers of specialized activities has been the ultimate result of the dynamics of converging technological change. The paradox of low levels of R&D activities and considerable increases in total factor productivity levels seems to be solved: as a matter of fact, such an organization of industrial and technological activity is far more knowledge intensive than aggregate statistics can measure.

An understanding of the polycentric mechanism of knowledge generation that is at the heart of the sustained introduction of technological knowledge in the Italian case, makes it possible to grasp the relevance of process innovations and the capital-intensive direction of the technological changes introduced. Technological change in the Italian case – in the traditional industries since the 1950s, in the whole industrial system later on (see Chapter 11) – has been mainly directed towards capital-intensive technologies and process innovations, instead of product innovations, because of the origins of technological knowledge. The key role of user–producer relations, in fact, favoured the generation, exploitation and incorporation of technological knowledge generated along the vertical filieres that relate upstream producers of capital and intermediate goods to downstream producers of final goods.

The study by Parisi, Schiantarelli and Sembenelli (2006) presents comparative evidence on the determinants of the introduction of process and product innovations at the firm level. Their results show that firms with high levels of investment in fixed capital have much higher chances of introducing process innovations embodied in new capital goods. Firms able to perform R&D activities had much stronger chances of introducing a new product. Our analysis of the effects of the specific characters of the generation of technological knowledge in the Italian case, makes it possible to appreciate the results of this study. The weakness of R&D activities and the key role of investments are, in fact, fully consistent with the evidence about the prevalence of process innovations biased in favour of capital-intensive technologies that characterize the Italian experience.

The dynamics of sectoral relationships has been a crucial factor in the process of technological and structural change that characterized the growth of the Italian economy after World War II. In fact, it seems reasonable to argue that Italian industry developed a special innovation system, pulled by the strong growth of the international demand and based upon intensive user–producer interactions within a context of unfolding intermediary markets. Such an innovation system enhanced the positive feedbacks between higher levels of division of labour, diffuse generation of new technological knowledge – sustained by the systematic valorization of learning process internal both to firms and local innovation systems – and fast rates of introduction of new technologies.

This context sustained the creative reaction pulled by the strong increase in the international demand of firms specializing in durable and non-durable consumer goods industries and facilitated the growth of strong sectors specialized in the manufacture of capital and intermediary goods. This, in turn, led to the introduction of further technological innovation which was mostly incorporated in machinery and intermediary inputs, and gave life to a system of virtuous interaction between process innovations introduced by user firms and product innovations introduced by upstream producers. These virtuous interactive processes were possible because of the strong qualified relations between user and producer industries.

These relations were built up in the Italian economy during the period 1950–90, and were encouraged and strengthened by the typical spatial and organizational structure of the productive process, characterized by numerous industrial districts and by many key manufacturing local labour systems centred around some regionally rooted medium-sized industrial firms. Yet our approach differs from the line of interpretation elaborated by Brusco (1982), Fuà (1983) and Becattini (1989). The latter stresses the key role of the changing conditions of labour markets and of industrial relations. In this approach, industrial districts are primarily the result of a process of increased specialization and division of labour as a device to reduce the minimum efficient size of firms and increase the opportunities to achieve a better command of labour relations and a substantial reduction of unit wages. The sharp difference in the wage levels between large and small firms cannot be questioned. Our interpretative frame, however, stresses the intimate relations between the innovation process and the increased specialization and division of labour within industrial filieres, and highlights specifically the cumulative relations between the enhanced levels of division of labour, the creation of intermediary markets, the process of localized and polycentric generation of technological knowledge and the eventual introduction of technological innovations, made possible by user–producer interactions within districts but along the vertical filieres.

In this way, a two-fold process of structural change and of localized technological change developed: the structuring of vertical and diagonal industrial filieres (value-added chains), together with the shaping of mechanisms of interaction, accumulation, transmission and exploitation of mostly tacit technological knowledge, strengthening the polycentric character of the distributed innovation system.

The empirical evidence provides a consistent body of research that acknowledges the key role in the generation of new technological knowledge of tight user–producer interactions between the upstream manufacturers of capital goods (in the mechanical engineering sector), intermediate goods (also in the chemical industries), and the downstream producers of consumer goods. This evidence stresses the relevance of the unfolding variety of intermediary markets that have characterized the developments of the vertical relations among users and producers. Firms activate the convergence of their knowledge generation activities in an effort to take advantage of the local pools of collective knowledge, and direct the exploitation of the new knowledge being generated towards the intensive use of locally abundant and yet idiosyncratic production factors. In turn, the supply of such locally abundant factors is a result of the rapid rate at which innovations are introduced by firms in upstream industries that rely upon pecuniary knowledge externalities based upon enforced knowledge complementarities. The process leads to the eventual emergence of an articulated structure of layers of vertical and horizontal complementarities among highly specialized service firms with high levels of vertical flows of exchanges within intermediary markets (that is, between layers), and horizontal knowledge interactions within each layer (Patrucco, 2003, 2009).

The Italian case can be considered a model of a distributed

innovation system alternative to the corporate model. In the corporate model, the generation of technological knowledge is mainly based on large firms that have identified a specific knowledge generation activity mainly based upon R&D to generate codified knowledge. In the corporate model, learning activities play a lesser role. External knowledge is important, but it is mainly acquired by means of specific knowledge transactions formalized as long-term contracts with universities and other public and private research centres. Transactions enable the acquisition of codified knowledge embedded in patents and blueprints.

In the distributed model, learning activities and external knowledge are the primary source of a blend of technological knowledge that has a much stronger tacit content. The generation of such technological knowledge relies on a variety of learning processes such as learning-by-doing, learning-by-using and learning-by-interacting. Learning processes allow the accumulation of competence based primarily on tacit knowledge. Seniority and long-term relations (between skilled workers and managers within family-owned firms) qualify industrial relations and provide the context for the valorization and appreciation of the tacit knowledge accumulated by means of learning processes. External tacit knowledge is a key source of technological knowledge: it is acquired mainly by means of qualified interactions, rather than formal transactions. Knowledge interactions take place with both customers, competitors and vendors of capital and intermediary inputs. Proximity within industrial districts and clusters also favours knowledge interactions because of intense inter-firm mobility of skilled personnel. Vertical mobility among firms that co-operate within the same filiere plays a key role as it provides the context into which user–producer interactions take place, and enables the generation of tacit knowledge.

The Italian model of distributed innovation is consistent with the national innovation system (NIS) approach that has been developed in a long process of theoretical elaboration in the area of economics of innovation.[1] The analysis of the emergence of the Italian innovation system also enables us to appreciate the limitations of the standard NIS approach. In the latter, in fact, very little attention is paid to analysing the process that leads to the creation of a virtuous system of interdependent feedbacks and interactions that are at the core of the systemic approach and to its possible degeneration.

From this viewpoint, the Italian evidence suggests that attention should be paid to the system dynamics approach elaborated in the new context of the economics of complexity (Anderson, Arrow and Pines, 1988). The emergence of the Italian Innovation System can be viewed as the result of the regional spreading of intensive user–producer interactions that has been taking place since the early 1950s, originating from the industrialized core regions of the northwest. In that part of the country, the mechanical engineering industry progressively became the main manufacturing activity, while new industries specializing in light consumer goods such as textiles and clothing, furniture and leather products, spread progressively in the northeast, centre and southeast of the country. The fast growth of the latter industries provided an increasing derived demand for capital goods and advanced intermediary inputs manufactured mainly (initially) in the northwestern industrialized triangle. The interactions produced mutual benefits with positive effects in terms of the growth of a dedicated competence in providing the final goods industries with updated and innovative capital and intermediary inputs that sustained the rapid penetration of Italian exports in the international markets. The analysis of the historical process highlights the endogenous character of the emergence of the national innovation system. The key element here, in fact, is dynamic coordination between two distinct processes: the specialization of the old industrialized regions in the provision of capital and intermediary goods and the specialization in consumption goods of the new industrializing periphery. This dynamic coordination should be regarded as the fragile product of a system of interactions that gained strength and structure. From this viewpoint, it was much more the result of a path-dependent process exposed to localized positive feedbacks – so as to become path creating – rather than a past-dependent process (where the hysteretic elements were set from the outset). As a matter of fact, the Italian Innovation System seems to be the result of a growing complementarity between the core of large companies, dating back from the early twentieth century and regionally concentrated in the northwestern part of the country, and new industrializing regions that found the opportunity for growth in specialization in light consumption industries, with the opening of European and international markets after World War II. The ability of the northern industries to identify an emerging captive market in the derived demand of the new emerging industries in the new industrializing periphery and to become the dedicated suppliers of capital and intermediate goods, is the result of a historic process. User–producer interactions provided large benefits to both parties: the industrializing periphery discovered the advantages, in terms of fast TFP growth, of the supply of process innovations embodied in the dedicated capital goods provided by the advanced northern industries; the mechanical engineering industries of the north could benefit from the interactions with the product innovations introduced by the firms based in the new industrial districts and clusters.

The main hypothesis is that innovation, that is to say, the capacity to generate and to promptly adopt innovations, and therefore increase the overall efficiency of the economic system and, consequently, TFP, depends not only on the innovative efforts of single agents but also, and perhaps above all, on the interdependence of the various innovative processes, and ultimately on the architecture of the system in which the agents operate. Therefore, the outcome of the special combination of elements which make up the system depends on the typology of the dynamic relations which tie the actors together and on the capacity of the system to evolve in such a way as to develop the most functional architecture for its growth.

The functioning of the Italian innovative system is based on the combination of three specific and strictly interdependent processes:

(1) the pressure of the demand for innovative capital equipment and intermediary inputs exerted by traditional and durable consumer goods manufacturing industries on the upstream industries. The 'made in Italy' and some other key national industries (textiles, clothing and leather, furniture, building materials and ceramics, food, white goods, automotives and so forth) pulled their suppliers' growth and innovative capacity both through the typical Smith-Young-Kaldor dynamics (where an increase in the size of the market is at the origin of an increase in division of labour, specialization, learning, investment and development of new technologies), and through collective and shared learning-by-doing and -using, made possible by strong virtuous localized relationships between users and producers of capital goods and key intermediary inputs;

(2) upstream sectors' total factor productivity growth, which trickled down on user industries as technological externalities, and which nourished their TFP dynamics as pecuniary (knowledge) externalities, also due to users' direct involvement (creative

adoption) in the development of incremental innovations, crucially based on external, shared knowledge;

(3)   the directionality of technological change biased (especially by traditional sectors) towards the introduction of capital-intensive process innovations, as a result of knowledge exploitation strategies aimed at taking advantage of idiosyncratic resources – such as the localized pools of knowledge, centred upon capital and intermediary goods production, and stemming from the key role of user–producer relations in the generation of technological knowledge – and the enlarged supply of capital at low costs.

NOTE

1.   See Nelson (1993), Fagerberg (1987), Freeman (1997) and Antonelli (1999, 2008a, b). This approach highlights the systemic character of innovative processes, the importance of interdependence among the actors, the importance of the structural context in terms of geography, institutions and sectors. The large amount of empirical research carried out in this area has made it possible to confirm the relevance of the theoretical model, not only through the identification of various operational levels – so as to distinguish between national, regional and local systems – but also to highlight a variety of innovative systems which have proved to be successful (see Edquist, 1997; Cantwell and Iammarino, 2003; Malerba, 2005). Two fundamental points are confirmed. First, a domestic innovation system is the result of a set of regional, industrial and institutional subsystems. Secondly, various domestic innovation systems can give different innovative results because of the specific conformation of the various subsystems as well as of their relationship structure. In the national innovation systems approach, the structural architecture of the system, in terms of the topology of the network of connections and channels of knowledge externalities, plays a central role in interpreting the innovative capacity of single actors.

9. The measures of innovative activity in Italy

9.1 INTRODUCTION

Italian economic growth in the second half of the twentieth century provides large and systematic evidence of fast rates of total factor productivity growth, and yet low levels of effort in the generation of technological knowledge, as measured by traditional indicators such as expenditure on R&D activity or patents. A mainly quantitative approach, which includes some interpretive tools explicitly based on the economics of innovation, is adopted here. The analysis concentrates on industry, because of the particular relevance it assumed during the examined historical period, the contribution it made to overall productivity growth, the innovation processes developed and the role played in national and international technology flows.

The role of innovation is crucial when interpreting the Italian economic growth experience in the four decades after World War II. Total factor productivity increased significantly for Italian industry, in comparative terms, until 1990 notwithstanding the severe international productivity slow down that has prevailed since the early 1970s. The empirical analysis shows how total factor productivity experienced a fast increase, not only in modern industries, but also in traditional sectors. The rejuvenation of the traditional industries clustered within industrial districts appears to be one of the key characteristics of the process. In this context, the emergence of key sectors specializing in the supply of dedicated capital and intermediary goods was, at the same time, an input and an output of the process leading to the creation of industrial and technological filieres where systematic user–producer interactions implemented internal learning processes.

Our analysis aims to draw attention to the relevance and uniqueness of technological change which characterized the industrial system in Italy. Therefore, we identify and evaluate the significant elements of empirical evidence which show how, contrary to current opinion, the Italian economic system had a notable capacity to innovate, producing relevant technological change both with regard to its rate and direction. By focusing attention together on total factor productivity, on indicators of R&D activity, patenting at home and abroad, and on the purchase on international markets of unincorporated technological knowledge – keeping in mind the empirical evidence of the previous chapter – it is possible to provide an interpretation of the Italian puzzle consisting of very low levels of statistically recorded classical innovation activity and yet high levels of total factor productivity growth. The basic argument is that the emergence and functioning of an original innovation system centred on internal learning and user–producer interactions in industrial filieres and manufacturing clusters have increased the dynamic efficiency of the low levels of R&D activities and engendered fast rates of introduction of innovations. In fact, the innovative ability of Italian firms was based much more on processes of creative reaction based upon the systematic development of localized learning and intensive user–producer interactions than on the traditional mechanism of formal research as revealed by statistics regarding R&D and patents.

This chapter offers a descriptive analysis of the evolution of the (visible) production of technological knowledge in Italy in the second half of the twentieth century, crosschecking three kinds of indicators: (1) the expenditures on R&D, (2) transactions in the technological balance of payments and (3) patents granted to Italian residents by the United States Patent and Trademark Office. We then perform TFP calculations for the Italian economy, to highlight the wide heterogeneity both in diachronic terms and synchronic terms, across sectors – industrial branches in particular – and regions, and to identify through a *shift-share analysis* the relevant locus of technological innovation/efficiency gains and the evolution of sectors' and regions' contributions to the overall productivity dynamic. From an analytical point of view the decision to integrate these four indicators is quite significant, reflecting the long debate on the limits of each single indicator, and aiming to maximize their specific strong points and overcome their specific weaknesses.

9.2 RESEARCH AND DEVELOPMENT

The statistical data on R&D expenditures cover activities mostly carried out by big companies and public institutions, and so favour formalized research activity. They confirm that in Italy both the public sector and above all the private sector invested few resources in research activities.

The data (see Figures 9.1 and 9.2) show that the overall volume of R&D expenditure increased both in absolute terms and relative to gross domestic product (GDP), starting in 1963 from a modest figure (0.6 per cent of GDP compared to an average 1.9 per cent for the six main Organization for Economic Co-operation and Development (OECD) countries). However the gap between the other main industrialized countries remained considerable and the R&D/GDP ratio remained anchored at rather low levels, incompatible with Italy's economic position on the international scene (1.3 per cent against 2.4 per cent in 1990).[1] In this evolution, the relatively modest weight of R&D expenditure of Italian enterprises has a crucial part (see Figure 9.3).[2]

The *regional* pattern of public and private R&D activity (see Figures 9.4–9.6) shows a strong concentration (75 per cent of national R&D in 1978–95) in only three regions: Piemonte (26 per cent), Lombardia (35 per cent) and Lazio (14 per cent).[3] The northern and central regions cover 93 per cent of the Italian total over the whole 1978–95 period, leaving the eight southern regions (with more than 35 per cent of the Italian population) an increasing but tiny share. Over the period, only the above-mentioned three regions and Liguria invested more than 1 per cent of their regional gross product in R&D. Second tier good performers were Emilia Romagna (whose share increased the most) in the northeast and Toscana in the centre.

The analysis of the pattern of R&D expenditure by *economic sector* shows a strong and rather stable concentration (see Figure 9.7). Manufacturing industry was the most important contributor to Italian R&D, both in absolute and value-added terms. R&D expenditures in the manufacturing sector were concentrated in few branches: in the early 1990s transportation equipment accounted for 30 per cent (and within that group, the aeronautical industry alone accounted for 12 per cent), then electrical and electronic machines with more than 25 per cent, followed by chemicals with a little less

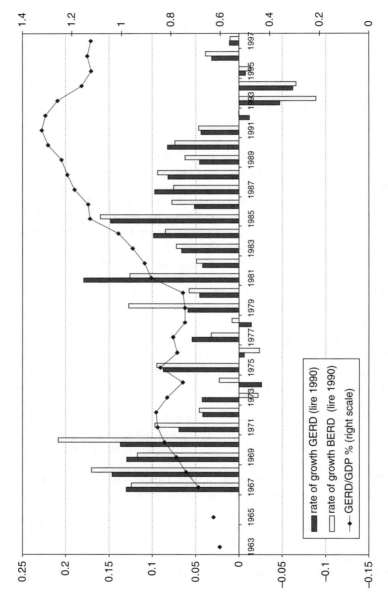

Figure 9.1   Domestic expenditure on R&D in Italy

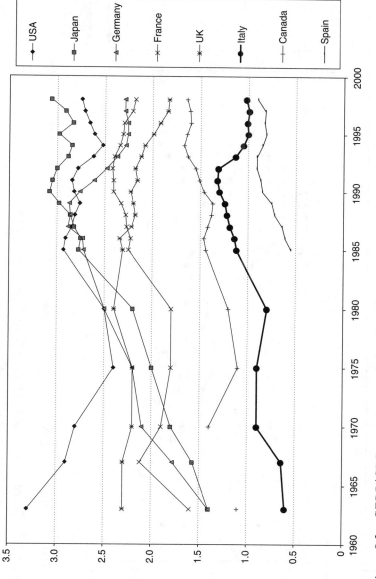

Figure 9.2   GERD/GDP percentage ratio in selected countries

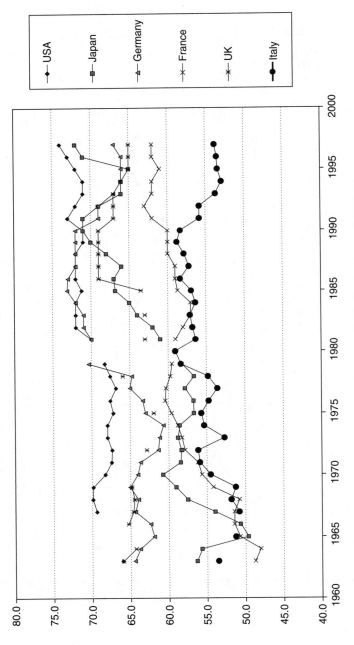

Figure 9.3   Business enterprise sector expenditure on R&D (percentage of GERD)

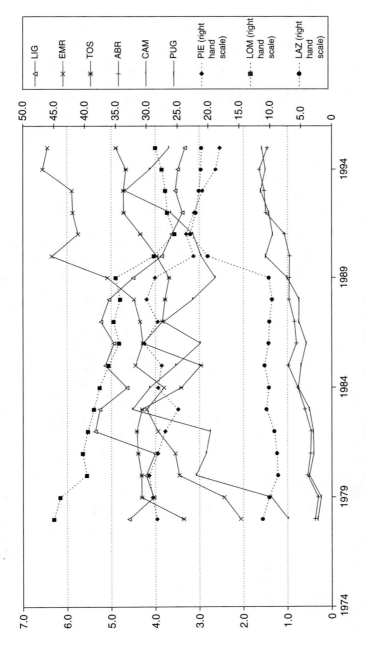

Figure 9.4 Italian regions R&D (percentage of total for Italy)

97

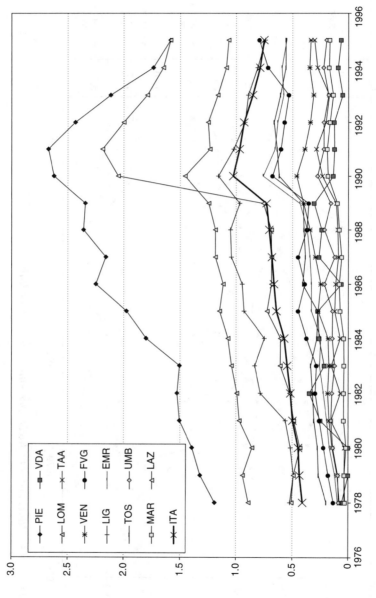

Figure 9.5   Regional R&D/Gross Product (%): northern and central Italy

Figure 9.6   Italian regions

(pharmaceutical firms alone accounted for almost 15 per cent of total expenditure).[4] The evolution of the pattern of R&D expenditure by sector reveals some interesting trends: the 1960s and 1970s were characterized by the growth of R&D in sectors at the technological frontier (in the fields of electronics, chemicals, nuclear power); since the 1980s there has been a relative fall in research activity in high-tech industries and an intensification in intermediate technological industries (automotive industry, machine tools, electrical machines and appliances). In the long run, the mechanical industry, in particular, made up ground.[5]

Comparing the six most industrialized OECD countries, the pattern of R&D expenditure in Italy by sector was different in the early 1960s, while two decades later it was even more so. At the beginning, the following stand out: the low weight of transportation in total R&D expenditure (then this difference with the other main countries narrows as result of the Italian automotive R&D

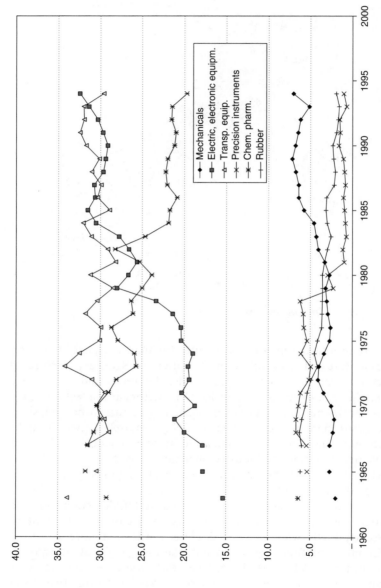

Figure 9.7 Share of manufacturing industry expenditure on R&D (%) in selected manufacturing sectors in Italy

growth and of the falling weight of military aerospace research abroad, which was never high in Italy); and the significant role of the rubber and plastic materials industry (then declining to a low contribution in international comparison). In the 1980s, the Italian case was different because of the lower than average weight of the electronics industry and the higher weight of chemicals.[6] The gap in absolute terms is quite relevant in almost all of the sectors for the whole period, considering that in transportation equipment (excluding aerospace), one of Italy's leading sectors, investment in R&D in 1981–85 was, on average, equal to 40 per cent of what it was in the other main OECD countries and that this percentage falls to 30 per cent for chemicals and less than 20 per cent for the electric/electronic equipments sector; and R&D statistics for more recent years confirm these findings.[7] At the same time, in the second half of the 1980s not only was the absolute size of R&D expenditure smaller than that of Italy's competitors but the ratio of R&D to turnover was smaller too. The relative disadvantage of Italy's major chemical companies (including pharmaceutical) was evident, while it was less marked in the car and the rubber industries. The ratio between investment in R&D and turnover for the leading firms in the branches of machine tools and robotics was instead in line with foreign competitors.[8]

In short, such data certainly confirm that R&D activity was, for the whole period, a marginal and even 'eccentric' phenomenon in the overall system. The extreme character of these figures, suggest that, in Italy, R&D expenditures cover only a very limited part of the production of technological knowledge useful for industrial innovation. Such expenditures reflect a kind of behaviour and operational criteria typical of large firms active in sectors with a strong scientific base, with laboratories with scientific staff, rare in the Italian industrial landscape. Most of Italian industry is characterized by a completely different kind of firm, often small and in traditional sectors. The particular dimensional structure of the Italian industrial system is, in fact, one of the main reasons for the low level of R&D activity; the original specialization model, biased towards traditional sectors, being a second major determinant of the low involvement of domestic firms in R&D activity.[9]

9.3   PATENTING ACTIVITY

The statistics regarding patents granted by USPTO can be considered a useful measure of the flow of science-based innovations which the (few) Italian large corporations developed. The overall share of patents granted in the United States to Italian residents in the 1950–2000 period was rather modest. The comparisons between Italian patents and other foreign patents issued in the United States show (see Figures 9.8–9.11):[10] the limited number and share of Italian patents in the initial period; the growth of the Italian share during the 'economic miracle years' up to the historical maximum of 4.1 per cent in 1963, and a (limited) catch-up with respect to the main industrialized countries, with the significant exception of Germany; and the decline of Italy's patent share during the subsequent three decades. Since the mid-1960s up to the early 1990s, however, the gap with respect to the other industrialized countries, excluding Japan (the big winner of this phase), narrowed. During the 1990s, the dynamic of Italy's patent activity in the United States diverged from the overall trend of her competitors (notably South Korea's performance). Certainly, Italy did not experience, not even during its economic boom period, any 'take off' in foreign patent activ-

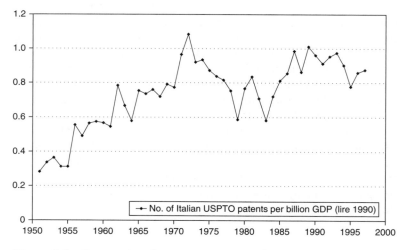

Figure 9.8   International patent activity: Italy 1

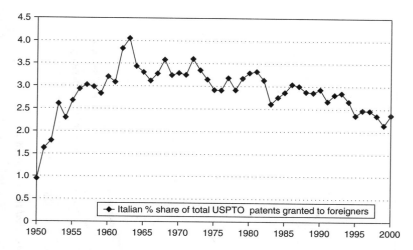

Figure 9.9   International patent activity: Italy 2

ity similar to those of Germany and Japan (in the 1950s and the mid-1960s, respectively).[11]

The regional pattern of patenting activity, as emerges from data for Italian patents at the European Patent Office in the 1980–90 period, shows a lower concentration than R&D (see Table 9.1).[12] Behind the two northwest big players (Piemonte, 16 per cent, and Lombardia, 39 per cent of European Patents granted to Italians on average in the benchmark years 1980, 1985, 1990), other regions show good relative performances (notably Emilia Romagna, Veneto, Lazio and Toscana; Marche improves significantly). Here, the technological catch-up of northeast and centre regions emerges more clearly; again the Mezzogiorno is far behind, with a mere 3 per cent of Italian EU-patents in 1990.

The data regarding the patents distribution by *sector* (SIC classification) reveal an interesting pattern: the single most important Italian contributor during the whole period 1950–2000 was machinery and mechanical equipment (30 per cent), followed by chemical products (22 per cent), and electric and electronic machinery (15 per cent).[13]

A comparison of the Italian pattern of distribution of patents by sector in respect to other countries highlights quite a different hierarchy of the main contributing sectors: while initially, the non-electric

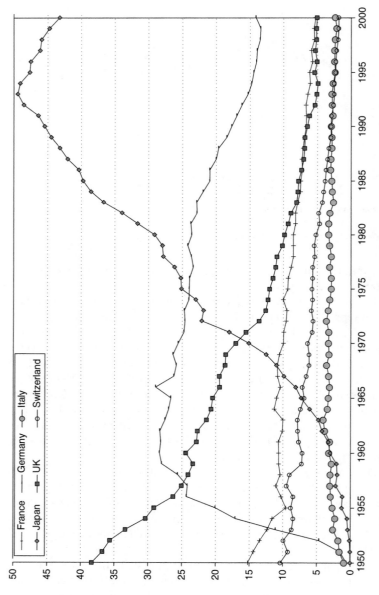

Figure 9.10   Selected countries percentage share of USPTO patents granted to foreigners 1

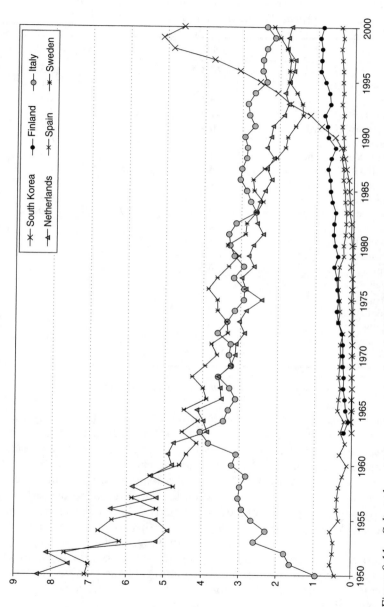

Figure 9.11 Selected countries percentage share of USPTO patents granted to foreigners 2

Table 9.1 *Italian regions share (%) of patents granted by the European Patent Office to Italian residents*

	1980	1985	1990
Piemonte	14.5	17.9	15.3
Valle d'Aosta	0.0	0.0	0.1
Liguria	3.4	2.2	2.2
Lombardia	41.4	37.1	37.2
Trentino-Alto Adige	0.3	0.7	1.1
Veneto	7.1	10.1	10.1
Friuli-Venezia Giulia	4.0	3.5	4.4
Emilia-Romagna	13.7	10.8	11.6
Toscana	4.0	5.7	6.1
Umbria	1.8	0.8	0.7
Marche	0.8	0.7	2.0
Lazio	4.5	7.2	6.2
Campania	1.3	0.7	0.6
Abruzzi	0.8	0.5	0.7
Molise	0.3	0.0	0.0
Puglia	0.5	0.7	0.3
Basilicata	0.0	0.1	0.0
Calabria	0.3	0.1	0.1
Sicilia	0.8	0.9	1.0
Sardegna	0.5	0.2	0.4
Total	100.0	100.0	100.0

Source: Our calculations on Crenos Data Bank on European Patents.

machines sector was the first contributor to patenting activity for Italy, as for other countries; in the 1990s, the electric and electronic equipment sector became the leading contributor for the others, but remained only third in Italy, behind the chemical products sector (third in other countries).[14] The share of patents in the electric and electronic equipment field remained lower for Italy over the whole period, mirroring the high share of the first position non-electric machinery. In respect to European main trading partners, there is a certain similarity to Germany (as the three main sectors ranking, machinery, chemicals, electric and electronic equipment, was the same), but for Italy, contrary to the German case, the contributions of the precision instruments and transportation equipment sectors were much lower.

We calculated a specialization index (revealed technological

Table 9.2 Index of revealed technological advantage: Italy (USPTO patents)

USPTO PRODUCT FIELD	1950–63	1964–73	1974–88	1989–2000	1950–2000
Food and kindred products	1.13	0.65	0.88	1.09	0.96
Textile mill products	1.69	1.03	0.72	1.03	0.96
Chemicals and allied products	1.03	1.43	1.33	1.57	1.43
Petroleum and natural gas extraction and refining	0.33	0.79	0.34	0.89	0.60
Rubber and miscellaneous plastics products	2.56	1.35	1.07	1.19	1.20
Stone, clay, glass and concrete products	0.87	0.79	0.78	0.79	0.80
Primary metals	0.69	0.76	0.77	0.62	0.72
Fabricated metal products	1.22	0.80	0.91	1.10	1.00
Machinery, except electrical	1.10	1.07	1.22	1.28	1.22
Electrical and electronic machinery, equipment and supplies	0.60	0.77	0.74	0.63	0.67
Transportation equipment	1.32	0.82	0.81	0.76	0.83
Professional and scientific instruments	0.90	0.63	0.62	0.61	0.63
All other SICs	1.23	1.11	1.19	1.29	1.22

Source: Our calculations on USPTO (2001), Cantwell (2002).

advantage index) in order to identify the relative strengths and weaknesses of Italian technological innovative performance, obtaining some light and some dark areas (see Table 9.2):[15]

- specialization in the machinery sector progressed significantly in the long run;
- the process of technological specialization in the chemical industry proceeded vigorously up to the mid-1960s, reaching, after some troubles, appreciable levels;
- in the sphere of electric and electronic machines there was a (timid) process of relative specialization only in the first 25-year period, then de-specialization prevailed, with the index well below one.

Overall, during the long post-World War II phase, the mechanical industry faced the problem of technology and made a more than average effort to equip itself with levels of technological skills and innovative capacity to sustain its successful presence on national and international markets. Industrial machinery, in particular, developed a well-structured technological base, establishing itself as an area of relative national technological strength.

Instead, Italy's patenting profile remained seriously inadequate in the fields of electronics and precision instruments. The failed attempt of Italian firms to make their mark in advanced electronics was apparently a serious problem for the evolution of the technological strategies of Italian industry.[16]

9.4   ACQUISITION OF FOREIGN NON-INCORPORATED TECHNOLOGY

Italian payments of the Technological Balance of Payments (TBP), that is, the purchase by Italian firms of non-incorporated technological knowledge developed abroad, appears to be significant, when compared to the modest sums invested in R&D. The volume of resources invested by Italian firms in purchasing non-incorporated technology is another important indicator of the resources devoted to the accumulation of technological knowledge directly aimed at the introduction of innovations, another crucial input of Italian innovative activity.

In the 50 years after World War II, Italian technological trade experienced sustained growth (see Figure 9.12).[17] Italy's effort to purchase technology abroad stands out among OECD countries up to the late 1970s (see Figure 9.13); also the TBP coverage ratio (receipts over payments) improved (see Figure 9.14).

The sectoral distribution shows the concentration of purchases in the field of electronics (29 per cent in the 1972–88 period) and of sales in the field of mechanics (13 per cent) and chemicals (25 per cent); at the end of the period the traditional sectors gained ground, too, as sellers of technology. These results confirm that electronics was the Achilles' heel of Italian technology, while mechanics in its many forms represents its strength, and the chemical industry represented the challenge once won, but mostly neglected.[18]

The marked difference in the way non-incorporated technology

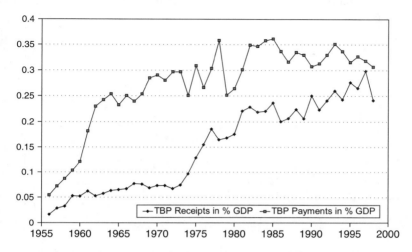

Figure 9.12   Technological balance of payments in Italy

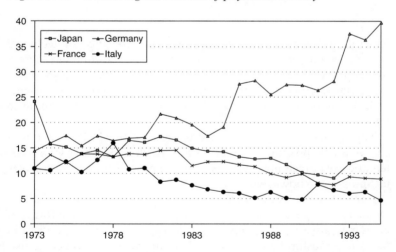

Figure 9.13   Selected countries percentage share of total TBP payments of the eight main OECD countries

was purchased (patents and licences, 75 per cent of total expenses in 1972–88) and transferred (technical assistance and designs, 48 per cent of receipts) reflect, together with the weakness of domestic research activity and industry's peculiar specialization, the original

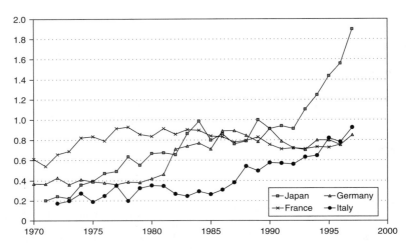

*Figure 9.14   Technological balance of payments coverage ratio in
            selected OECD countries*

(emergent) Italian innovation system: the relevance of technical
assistance and *know-how* as a form of transfer of technology signals
the country's strength in intermediate technologies (especially,
industrial machinery), in rejuvenated traditional technologies (made
in Italy), and the importance of specific and localized learning in
industrial innovation processes.[19]

The technical and geographical patterns of the TBP show Italy's
characteristic position as an economy which makes heavy and systematic use of recombination as the main process for generating new
technological knowledge.

Italy bought (codified) technology from the more industrialized
countries (63 per cent of total payments in 1972–88) in the forms of
greater relative value (patents and licences) and sold (specific and
tacit) relationship-based technological knowledge (technical assistance, know-how and designs) to less developed countries (45 per cent
of receipts).

Finally, the high values of the ratio TBP payments/R&D for the
Italian economy (more than 35 per cent until mid-1980s), on one
hand point to a hard-won tendency to balance domestic and foreign
sources of technological knowledge and, on the other hand, suggest
that the Italian process of 'technological emancipation' and the

formation of solid autonomous innovative capacity was incomplete. At the same time, it suggests that technological payments should be considered an integral and crucial part of the national innovative effort, a complementary factor to R&D, an important input of Italian industry localized innovation processes. In the period under consideration, Italian firms made, in fact, a considerable effort of creative adoption: they acquired codified/scientific foreign technological knowledge and used it in processes of technology recombination, which allowed adoption, adaptation and valorization of the specific knowledge resulting from localized learning (see in Chapter 10, the machinery industry case).

9.5 LOCALIZED TECHNOLOGICAL CHANGE AND TOTAL FACTOR PRODUCTIVITY

R&D expenditure, patents and TBP expenses, as a matter of fact, measure different levels of elaboration of resources invested into that special economic process defined as the generation of codified knowledge and the eventual introduction of technological innovation, but certainly do not sufficiently cover the much wider range of innovative activities typical of Italian firms. Combining the three indicators with the analysis of the evolution of total factor productivity at a disaggregate level can help to build a wider and better-grounded interpretive framework.

Only by integrating the three statistical series with the study of the evolution of total factor productivity can the analysis be considered valuable. Innovative activity is certainly fuelled by R&D expenditure, by successive patents which enable (admittedly, with variable coefficients of transformation) innovations to be developed and by trade in non-incorporated technology, but a much wider range of economic actions is covered so as to include the choice which governs the use of intermediate inputs and investment decisions. Innovation is the result of a variety of activities. Learning processes of various kinds play a major role in the accumulation of the competence that is necessary to generate new technological knowledge and eventually to introduce innovations. The access to external knowledge is a crucial factor in the generation of new technological knowledge. The adoption of new capital and intermediary goods incorporating technological innovations is an essential component of the innovation process. In the end, it is particularly helpful to consider the notion of creative adoption, which stresses the blurring of the distinction between innovation and adoption, and highlights the increasing awareness of the amount of creative efforts that are necessary to adopt an innovation and to adapt it to the specific characteristics of the production process, and the product and factor markets of each firm (Kleinknecht, van Montfort and Brouwer, 2002).

R&D indicators are able to grasp only a fraction of such activities; while much R&D is funded and performed to generate novelties that are not able to increase the efficiency of the production process; also, R&D statistics, being an input indicator, are not able to account for the different levels of efficiency in the generation of new technological knowledge. As is well known, only a fraction of the technological innovations being introduced is represented by patent statistics. Neither R&D nor patent statistics account for innovations in organization, input mix and markets. In the search for additional indicators, innovation counts suffer the subjective character of the claims upon which they are based.

Total factor productivity instead can explain the full bundle of the economic effects of the introduction and diffusion of an innovation. Hence, total factor productivity indicators are likely to provide an accurate measure of the actual amount and extent of the innovations being introduced.[20] This claim finds strong support in the results of the systematic application, to a variety of empirical cases including countries, regions, industries and firms, of the so-called Crepon–Duguet–Mairesse (CDM) methodology that provides reliable evidence about the consistent and converging representations of the intensity of innovation as measured respectively by patents, R&D activities and total factor productivity (Crepon, Duguet and Mairesse, 1998; Parisi, Schiantarelli and Sembenelli, 2006). From this point of view, a true and significant indicator of the actual amount of technological knowledge being generated and technological change being introduced in a distributed innovation system cannot be drawn up solely within the ambit of the activities typically defined in scientific and technological terms, as indicators of specific inputs in the generation of technological knowledge such as R&D expenditures, or indicators of some outputs such as patents, but only in wider economic terms. Only the growth of efficiency in productive processes, in all their complexity, can be considered to be a

Table 9.3   *Labour productivity levels (GDP per employee, USA = 100)*

	Italy	France	Germany	Japan	UK	Netherlands	USA
1950	**30**	37	34	16	54	49	100
1973	**54**	65	34	50	59	72	100
1987	**70**	82	75	71	68	74	100
% change							
1950–73	**80.8**	75.5	83.4	222.6	10.1	44.8	
1973–87	**27.8**	25.6	20.7	41.1	14.2	2.9	
1950–87	**131.2**	120.4	121.4	355.0	25.7	48.9	

Source: Our calculations on data by Broadberry (1996).

Table 9.4   *Labour productivity levels (GDP per employee, USA = 100): manufacturing industry*

	Italy	France	Germany	Japan	UK	Netherlands	USA
1950	**26**	32	37	8	38	33	100
1973	**45**	53	55	44	47	62	100
1987	**63**	65	59	81	56	72	100
% change							
1950–73	**72.7**	66.0	51.6	481.0	22.3	84.9	
1973–87	**40.4**	22.5	7.2	82.8	21.5	16.9	
1950–87	**142.5**	103.4	62.5	962.4	48.6	116.1	

Source: Our calculations on data by Broadberry (1996).

reliable and complete indicator of the intensity of innovative activity in progress in any given field. Combining the three indicators with the analysis of the evolution of total factor productivity at a disaggregate level can help to build a wider and more detailed interpretive framework that goes beyond the descriptive limits of the single measures and avoids summing up their weaknesses.

In comparative terms, Italian industry's capacity to increase its aggregate efficiency was remarkable and persisted for four decades (see Tables 9.3–9.5).

Our calculations of total factor productivity for the main economic sectors show that Italian growth was based, to a considerable

Table 9.5   Economic growth and TFP (average annual growth rates)

	Italy*	France	Germany	Japan*	UK°	USA
1951–73						
Real Product	5.2	5.6	6.3	9.8	3.7	3.7
Total Factor Productivity	3.4	3.1	3.5	4.1	1.9	1.2
TFP contribution to real product growth	64.3	56.1	55.1	41.4	51.4	31.5
1960–90						
Real Product	4.1	3.5	3.2	6.8	2.5	3.1
Total Factor Productivity	2.0	1.5	1.6	2.0	1.3	0.4
TFP contribution to real product growth	47.9	41.4	49.4	28.8	51.9	13.2

Notes: * first figure of 1952 ° first figure of 1955.

Source: Our calculations on data by Christensen, Cummings and Jorgenson (1980); Dougherty (1991).

extent, on efficiency gains and strengthening of innovation dynamics in the manufacturing industry. TFP growth was higher in manufacturing than for the whole economy and slowed down only slightly after 1973 (see Table 9.6).[21]

The Italian regions' industrial TFP performance is quite heterogeneous through time and territorial areas (see Table 9.7). The centre (Marche, in particular) and the northeast (Veneto, in particular) industries' strong efficiency gains of the 1960s – after a decade of significant internal catch-up against the northwest industrial triangle – and the lead of northeastern regions in the 1970s (Emilia Romagna, in particular), which brought the new industrialized regions close to the TFP levels of the northwestern first movers (Piemonte and Lombardia) must be mentioned. Also notable is the recovery of the north–western regions in the 1980s, which re-established a (challenged) hierarchy, maintaining the industrial 'triangle' by far the main contributor to national TFP levels, well above its value added (VA) share (see Table 9.8); the ephemeral industrial Mezzogiorno's

Table 9.6 Total Factor Productivity in Italy (average annual
growth rates): main sectors

	Agric.	Energy	**Manu-fact. Ind.**	Constr.	Industry	Services sal. * §	Private sector * §	Private sector without agric. * §
1955–73	2.5	4.1	**4.7**	0.8	3.4			
1955–63	2.6	4.9	**4.4**	0.9	3.5			
1964–73	2.5	3.5	**4.9**	0.7	3.3	4.2	4.0	3.7
1974–88	2.7	−3.1	**3.3**	−0.3	1.8	0.2	1.5	1.2
1955–88	2.6	0.8	**4.1**	0.3	2.7	2.1	2.7	2.3

Notes: * data available since 1961. § Without real estate renting and other services.

Source: Our calculations on data by Antonelli and Barbiellini Amidei (2007).

Table 9.7   Total Factor Productivity in Italian macroregions
(average annual growth rates): industry

	Northwest	Northeast	Centre	South	Southeast	Southwest	Italy
1963–69	2.5	3.8	3.1	5.2	6.3	4.9	3.5
1970–79	1.4	2.7	1.4	0.9	1.4	0.7	1.6
1980–89	2.2	1.0	0.9	1.5	1.6	1.5	1.6
1990–94	0.8	1.7	0.8	0.0	0.4	−0.2	0.8
1963–94	1.7	2.3	1.5	1.8	2.3	1.7	1.9

Source: Our calculations on data by Antonelli and Barbiellini Amidei (2007); Paci and Saba (1998); Paci and Pusceddu (2000); Svimez (1996).

catch-up, which fades away after a good 1960s performance, leaving the southern industry's contribution to national TFP levels well below its VA share.

The analysis within the manufacturing industry returns a wide heterogeneity of TFP dynamics both in diachronic and synchronic (across sectors) terms, and highlights significant changes in the hierarchy of the sectors as contributors to overall productivity dynamics (see Table 9.9). To identify 'the locus of technical progress' we performed a *shift-share analysis* on aggregation of sectors: the

*Table 9.8   Macroregional contribution (%) to Italian TFP levels
(Y/Y*): industry*

	TFP level – ind	Northwest (%)	VA share (avg.)	Northeast (%)	VA share (avg.)	Centre (%)	VA share (avg.)	South (%)	VA share (avg.)
1963–69	5.0	53.0	44.8	20.4	19.1	18.0	16.9	8.6	19.2
1970–79	7.4	45.9	41.4	23.1	21.5	18.6	17.4	12.5	19.7
1980–89	7.3	44.6	39.7	24.5	23.6	18.6	17.8	12.3	18.9
1990–94	9.2	45.6	39.5	24.2	24.4	18.2	17.7	12.0	18.3
1963–94	7.1	46.8	41.3	23.1	22.1	18.4	17.5	11.7	19.1

Source: Our calculations on data by Antonelli and Barbiellini Amidei (2007); Paci and Saba (1998); Paci and Pusceddu (2000); Svimez (1996).

'modern' sectors, relative to the Italian production system of the 1950s and 1960s (chemicals, mechanicals, transportation equipment and rubber), the 'traditional' sectors (food, textiles and clothing, wood and furniture) and the 'intermediate'/capital-intensive sectors (ferrous and non-ferrous metals, non metalliferous minerals, paper). Here, sectoral analysis helps to break down the productivity growth of manufacturing industry into the contribution of different branches' TFP dynamics and the composition effects which resulted from changes in industrial specialization (see Tables 9.10 and 9.11, Figure 9.15).[22]

The calculations reveal that the modern sectors, during the whole period 1955–88, had above average rates of TFP growth, and made the highest contribution to manufacturing TFP, bigger than their VA share (47 per cent against 42 per cent). Moreover, in 1974–88, when manufacturing TFP growth was slowing down, the contribution of the modern sectors increased significantly, proportionately more than their growing share of VA, so much so as to explain more than half of the total TFP growth (57 per cent against 47 per cent of the share of VA). Considering the results of the single branches, the mechanical industry stands out: in particular, in 1974–88 it becomes the most important single contributor to manufacturing TFP growth. The significant chemical industry's TFP contribution was instead eased out by the early (mid-1960s) interruption of the sector expansion.

The traditional sectors in 1955–73 turned out to be capable of increasing efficiency significantly, and resulted key contributors to

Table 9.9 TFP growth in Italy (average annual growth rates): manufacturing industry

	Modern sectors*	Traditional sectors**	Interme-diate sectors***	Manufact. industry	Ferr. & non min.	Non met. min.	Chem. pharm.	Mech.	Transp. equip.	Food bev. tob.	Text. app. foot.	Wood furn.	Paper	Rubber
1955–73	**5.0**	**5.0**	**3.5**	**4.7**	1.5	4.9	7.1	4.6	5.9	3.3	6.3	4.7	4.7	4.3
1955–63	**4.7**	**4.8**	**3.8**	**4.4**	3.5	3.3	10.4	3.9	8.4	2.0	6.9	3.5	4.3	–0.6
1964–73	**5.2**	**5.2**	**3.2**	**4.9**	–0.1	6.1	4.4	5.2	3.8	4.4	5.9	5.7	5.0	8.1
1974–88	**4.2**	**2.9**	**2.4**	**3.3**	1.9	1.9	10.8	3.8	1.4	2.6	2.8	4.1	4.0	3.7
1955–88	**4.6**	**4.1**	**3.0**	**4.1**	1.7	3.5	8.8	4.2	3.8	3.0	4.7	4.4	4.4	4.0

Notes: * chemical, mechanical, transp. equipment, rubber ** food, textile, wood *** ferrous min., non metal. min., paper.

Source: Our calculations on data by Antonelli and Barbiellini Amidei (2007).

Table 9.10   *Sectoral contribution (%) to TFP growth (average annual growth rates): manufacturing industry*

	TFP growth manuf.	Modern sectors* (%)	VA share (avg.)	Traditional sectors ** (%)	VA share (avg.)	Intermediate sectors *** (%)	VA share (avg.)
1955–73	4.7	40.9	38.1	41.5	37.8	17.6	24.1
1974–88	3.3	57.4	47.2	28.7	33.8	13.9	19.0
1955–88	4.1	46.9	42.2	36.6	36.0	16.4	21.8

Notes: * chemical, mechanical, transp. equipment, rubber ** food, textile, wood *** ferrous min., non metal. min., paper.

Source: Our calculations on data by Antonelli and Barbiellini Amidei (2007).

manufacturing TFP growth (more than their VA share, 41.5 per cent against 37.8 per cent). In the subsequent phase, after a drastic retrenching of their VA share (while keeping an important position in the Italian economy), they still account for almost 30 per cent of TFP growth. Throughout the 1955–88 period, instead, the intermediate/capital-intensive sectors contributed to manufacturing TFP growth proportionally less than their share of VA (16 per cent against 22 per cent). This was particularly hurt by the ferrous metals industry's performance.

The productivity slowdown was widespread, hitting almost all the industrial branches. Nevertheless, a significant compensating *effect* came from the *shift* of VA towards higher TFP growth/level modern sectors. At the same time, the areas where productive and innovative 'opportunities' were not fully achieved were mainly in the modern sectors, which were much less developed in Italy's productive system than in those of her main foreign competitors. The chemicals sector stands out, as it had been unable to complete its expansion, but also the transportation equipment industry was an 'underperformer', being essentially represented in the Italian industrial landscape almost solely by the branches of the automotive and motorcycle industry. The new high-tech industries (information technology, aerospace, fine chemicals and pharmaceuticals), after the progress made during the first fifteen years after World War II, remained in an embryonic state, were wiped off, or were confined to a productive niche, often new plants turned into isolated bushes. It is, therefore,

Table 9.11 TFP growth change shift-share analysis *(% sectors contribution; average annual growth rates): man-ufacturing industry*

	TFP growth manuf.		All manu-fact. sectors	Modern sectors* (%)	% points of avg. annual growth	VA share (avg.)	Tradit-ional sectors** (%)	% points of avg. annual growth	VA share (avg.)	Inter-mediate sectors*** (%)	% points of avg. annual growth	VA share (avg.)
1955–63	4.4	SECTORAL EFFECT	60.2	15.5	0.1	36.2	60.6	0.2	39.4	–16.0	–0.1	24.4
1964–73	4.9	SHIFT EFFECT	39.8	72.7	0.3	39.6	–27.2	–0.1	36.6	–5.7	0.0	23.8
Δ	0.4	*TOTAL*	*100.0*	*88.2*	*0.3*		*33.4*	*0.1*		*–21.6*	*–0.1*	
1955–73	4.7	SECTORAL EFFECT	112.7	37.9	–0.6	38.1	57.4	–0.8	37.8	17.4	–0.3	24.1
1974–88	3.3	SHIFT EFFECT	–12.7	–32.6	0.5	47.2	13.5	–0.2	33.8	6.4	–0.1	19.0
Δ	–1.4	*TOTAL*	*100.0*	*5.3*	*–0.1*		*70.8*	*–1.0*		*23.8*	*–0.4*	

Notes: * chemical, mechanical, transp. equipment, rubber ** food, textile, wood *** ferrous min., non metal. min., paper.

Source: Our calculations on data by Antonelli and Barbiellini Amidei (2007).

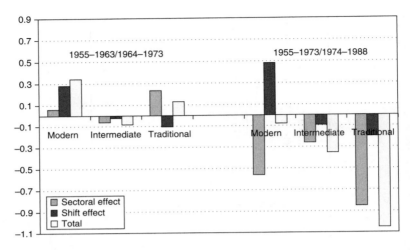

Figure 9.15   *TFP growth shift-share analysis, change between*
periods: manufacturing industry (sectors contribution;
points of average annual growth)

necessary to emphasize not only the positive effects of structural/
sectoral change and the success of the modernization of traditional
sectors but also the heavy opportunity costs involved, due to the
insufficient (in respect to main industrialized competitors) structural
evolution of the Italian industrial system towards new science-based
sectors, technologically more dynamic.[23]

To sum up, empirical evidence on TFP dynamics makes it possible to claim that technological change was not modest, regular or
neutral, but instead was intense, rapid, quite heterogeneous and, as
we will see in the next chapters, strongly *biased*. These results offer
new elements for reflection both at a macroeconomic level, when
applied to the study of long-run growth, and at an economic history
level, as Italy's catch-up is often depicted without a significant role
for technological innovation.

NOTES

1.   Also limiting the comparison to R&D civil programmes, a smaller but signifi-
     cant gap persisted.

2. In the 1960s, the corporate system acted as the driving force of R&D growth. The role of state enterprises was particularly interesting, in that it was a real tool of public research policy and played a central role in a failed (timid) attempt to develop a corporate centred national innovation system. In Italy, state action to support research carried out by (private) firms only began at the end of the 1960s (Law 1076 of 1968, Fondo IMI-Ricerca Applicata). See Antonelli, 1989; Giannetti and Pastorelli, 2007.

3. See Antonelli and Barbiellini Amidei (2007) for a description of the dataset on R&D expenditures at the national and sectoral level (see also Istat, 1978–85). Data on regional R&D were sourced from Crenos Databases Regio-IT 1960–96 (see Paci and Saba, 1998).

4. See Antonelli and Barbiellini Amidei (2007).

5. Machinery and mechanical equipment rose from 3 per cent in 1963–73 to 4 per cent in 1974–88 to 7 per cent of manufacturing R&D expenditures in 1989–97; the R&D/VA ratio for mechanical equipment overtook the one for manufacturing in the early 1980s.

6. The countries considered are Canada, France, Germany, Japan, Italy, the United Kingdom and the United States (see Bisogno, 1988).

7. See Istat (1995); OECD (2000).

8. See Onida and Malerba (1990); Parolini (1991).

9. Not surprisingly, up to 1985, the number of firms involved in Istat's annual census on R&D activity did not number 1000 units. R&D reached levels similar to those found in most advanced competitor countries only in a limited number of enterprises and industrial sectors. Recent European Community Innovation Surveys on innovation show more similarity in the share of Italian 'innovative' firms recorded by size with those of the European partners.

10. The comparison is within USPTO 'foreign' patents. United States residents' patents are excluded, in order to avoid evident effects of asymmetry in favour of domestic patenting activity for US firms. See Antonelli and Barbiellini Amidei (2007) for a description of the dataset on Italian patenting activity.

11. It is interesting to note that the data regarding patent applications submitted to the Italian Patent Office also signal difficulties emerging in the late 1960s. During the whole period under examination an increasing (but limited) share of Italian patents was issued by USPTO; the percentage of Italian external registrations reached significant levels during the 1980s, with the creation of the European Patent Office and the 'European patent'.

12. European patents data are the only available for Italian regions' patenting activity over this period. Data on Italian regions' patents were sourced from Crenos Data Bank on European Patents 1980–90 (see Paci, Sassi and Usai, 1997).

13. The three main sectors were followed, at some distance, by precision instruments (8 per cent), metal products (6 per cent), transportation equipments (4.5 per cent), rubber and plastic products (4 per cent); the traditional industries' shares were rather low (less than 1 per cent).

14. The comparison is again within USPTO 'foreign' patents. Data not displayed, see Antonelli and Barbiellini Amidei (2007).

15. The index is the ratio of the relative patents share (to other foreign patents) of the single Italian industries and of the Italian national share.

16. See Malerba (1988); Malerba, Torrisi and Bussolati (1996).

17. See Antonelli and Barbiellini Amidei (2007) for a description of the Italian TBP database.

18. Data not displayed, see Antonelli and Barbiellini Amidei (2007). An additional positive element for the machinery industry was the growing importance of sales of services with a high knowledge content (KIBS) to foreign firms. Such

forms of technology transfers (particularly towards developing and recently industrialized countries) remain, for the most part, outside TBP, an exception being the eventual supplies of non-connected technical assistance. The phenomenon emerged as being particularly important for Italy at the end of the 1970s (in 1979 a revenue of more than 260 billion lire against an income in TBP for the branch of machinery of 24 billion lire); the figures reflect sales by engineering and consultancy firms other than manufacturing firms (Scarda and Sirilli, 1982).

19.   The weakness of Italian industry in exporting codified non-incorporated knowledge is evident, and ancillary to the limited multinational growth of Italian firms. The weakness of international transfers of technology was even reflected in the relatively small amount of resources devoted by Italian firms to direct investment abroad, notwithstanding the huge internationalization effort reflected in export flows.

20.   When the consequences of introducing technological and organizational innovation have to be considered, economic theory offers a tool which is, at the same time, extremely simple but rather controversial: that is to say, the calculation of the residual and, therefore, total factor productivity. This procedure makes it possible to focus attention on the increases in output that cannot be directly traced to increases in the factors of production. However, the assumptions on which this methodology is based are rather restrictive and rely on the assumption of equilibrium and perfect competition in both the product and factor markets. For a methodological and historical outline of total factor productivity indexes and growth accounting since the seminal calculations of Abramovitz (1956) and Solow (1957), see Antonelli and Barbiellini Amidei (2007).

21.   The statistical material used to carry out the elaboration of the growth of total factor productivity for Italy is particularly questionable and heterogeneous. Continual changes in the criteria for the collection of national accounts means that continuous and homogeneous official historical series for the period from 1951 to the present day do not exist and so the variables and disaggregate data useful for our analysis are difficult to gather. Historic series built up by experts in national accounts are now available. Various statistical sources were reformulated during this research and now it is possible to study the evolution of total factor productivity in terms of value added for the whole of Italian industry and, in particular, for 10 sectors from 1951. More detailed studies, which make it possible to measure production functions in turnover and, therefore, to consider intermediate inputs, would be very useful so that increases in efficiency, which come from the introduction of new production processes, can be measured. The elaboration of production functions based on value added, on the other hand, provides results which can offer indications to evaluate overall increases in the efficiency of the productive processes, so mitigating factors which tend to distort the residual upwards. The calculations of the standard TFP-Solow residual for 10 industrial branches over the 1951–88 period presented here are based on a dataset built with data collected from various sources, notably: Golinelli (1998) for VA and labour units, and Annunziato, Manfroni and Rosa (1992) for capital; but also Rossi, Sorgato and Toniolo (1993) and Istat (1951–98). See Antonelli and Barbiellini Amidei (2007) for a description. The TFP calculations for the Italian regions' industry over the 1961–94 period (in which the data are available) are based on data sourced from Paci and Saba (1998) for VA and labour; Paci and Pusceddu (2000) for capital; and Svimez (1996) for wages.

22.   In our calculations, we used weights based on VA valued both at constant and current prices. Different weights do not modify the overall picture of the results.

In the tables presented here, the reference is to a share of VA at constant 1990 prices. For the calculation method, see Wolff (1985).

23. See Rossi (2003). Considering labour productivity levels in international comparisons, up to the early 1980s, the greatest progress was concentrated in traditional industries (largely in the area of made in Italy, the branches of textiles and clothing, leather and footwear, wood products and furniture, as well as ceramics), whose competitive advantages were the most difficult to defend against the new industrializing countries (see Dollar and Wolff, 1988; Broadberry, 1993). On the other hand, the hypothesis that since the 1960s, 'the relatively new sectors in terms of rate of technological change were also the most dynamic in terms of rate of growth of world exports' was not confirmed for years to come (Onida, 1978). For all the 1970s and beyond, higher rates of growth were registered in those sectors that were not the most technologically advanced, such as metal products, some basic branches of chemicals, plastic materials, rubber and capital goods, those 'specialized suppliers' sectors where Italy's exports gained ground.

10. Structural change and the building of systemic interdependence: the emergence of a distributed innovation system

The process of structural change that accompanied technological change, had a crucial influence on Italian economic and innovative performance in the post-World War II era.[1] The abundance of under-used labour in agriculture and the opportunities of employing it in more productive growing and emerging manufacturing industries made an important specific contribution to TFP growth, more and for longer than in the rest of Europe.[2] Yet, the crucial process in the Italian structural change was the growth and development of a strong machinery industry.

At the beginning of the 1950s, Italy stood out because of the high percentage of workers employed in agriculture.[3] Furthermore, Italy had an elastic supply of labour and the relations prevailing in the labour market favoured the establishment of a long virtuous phase (destined to have a traumatic end in the late 1960s), in which wages grew more slowly than labour productivity, facilitating high profits which encouraged investment (see Figures 10.1–10.3).

In the 1950s, Italy had the opportunity to 'exploit' the technological gap accumulated during the long Fascist dictatorship by taking part in Europe's unequalled process of catching up on the United States.[4] The process was, to a great extent, linked to the ability to adopt mass-production methods.[5] On the basis of this opportunity, the growth of internal demand (higher per capita income, spreading of modern consumption patterns) was an important factor leading to intense technological diffusion in manufacturing, especially with investments increasing production capacity.[6] Demand pull resulted in a significant lowering of average age and a technological modernization of

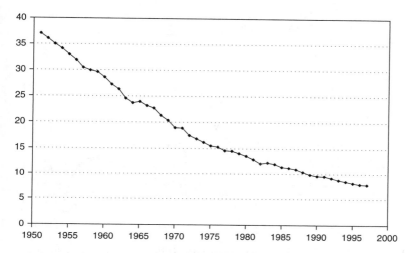

Figure 10.1   *Share of labour units in agricultural sector (%) on total Italian economy*

capital.[7] The Italian post-war *golden age* was a phase of very strong investment. Through this renewal of capital and the technology incorporated in it, industry, in fact, benefited from the spread of technical knowledge from more advanced countries and used the opportunity and stimulus to innovate production processes and products, adopting and increasingly adapting imported technologies.

In the subsequent phase, since the 1970s, if the average age of the stock of industrial capital in machinery and equipment rose, the process of *capital deepening* continued on intensely (see Figure 10.4).[8] In this phase, a typical process of induced biased technological change prevailed (see Chapter 11).

If investment in new machinery has generally represented one of the main channels for the introduction of new technologies for the most part of the industrialized countries in the twentieth century, this was especially true in the Italian case in the second half of the century.[9] Adopting new investment goods turned out to be the main source of innovation for firms of all kinds, sizes, and sectors up to the 1990s.[10] In the 1970s and 1980s, investment goods as a source of innovation appear to have been of the highest importance for the 'traditional' consumer goods industries (made

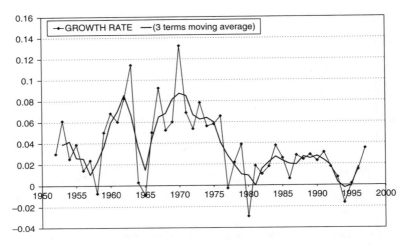

Figure 10.2   Real wage for labour unit: Italian manufacturing industry

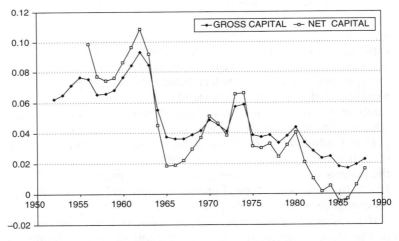

Figure 10.3   Real capital growth: Italian manufacturing industry

in Italy) and their intermediate inputs producers (textiles, chemicals, and so forth).

Structural change in Italy was accompanied on a much lesser scale by increased investment in human capital (classified according to the levels of education) with respect to physical capital. In the 1950s,

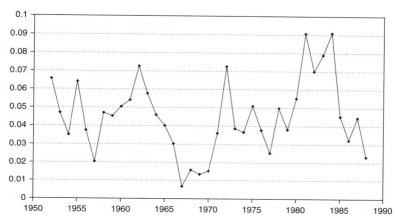

Figure 10.4   Real gross capital (machinery) per employee, growth rate – Italian manufacturing industry

the Italian workforce had low levels of human capital acquired by means of formal training and education, not only with respect to the United States, but also to many European countries and Japan.[11] Italy had a good supply of engineers (well qualified) and a skilled workforce.[12] The average level of education rose during the 50 years after World War II, but the most significant progress, especially in terms of university education, took place from the late 1960s.[13] The increased investment in the technical secondary education and in particular in the technicians educated and trained in the 'Istituti Tecnici Industriali' (technical-industrial high schools; see Figures 10.5 and 10.6)[14] was important for the development of the national absorptive capacity, that is, the capability to adapt the technologies being adopted (often from abroad).

Structural change also expressed the fulfilled opportunity to develop a domestic machinery industry, crucial in the emerging Italian innovation system. The ability to adopt external foreign knowledge depended initially on imports of foreign machinery: the data collected show that until the mid-1960s, a significant part of investment passed through the purchase of capital goods produced abroad (see Figures 10.7, 10.8).[15] In the two decades after World War II, however, a process of quantitative and qualitative growth of the rising Italian machinery industry was set in motion. Imported machinery provided an important impulse and was an important

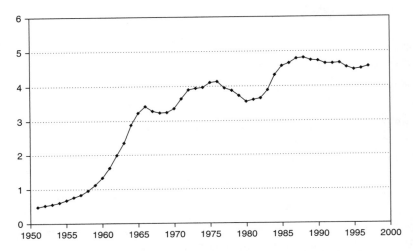

*Figure 10.5   Enrolled in technical industrial secondary schools on
industry's employees(%): Italy*

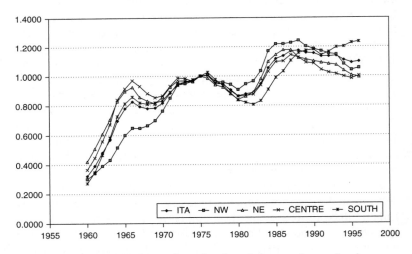

*Figure 10.6   Enrolled in technical industrial secondary schools on
industry's employees: Italian macro regions (index
1975 = 100)*

Figure 10.7   Equipment imports and exports: Italy

Figure 10.8   Equipment production and investment activity: Italy

input in the process of imitation, creative adoption and technological innovation for investing Italian industries as well as for domestic producers of capital goods. Increasingly, investing industrial
firms targeted domestically produced machinery. It was with the

economic *boom* of the early 1960s that internal demand for capital goods exerted decisive pressure on domestic industry: the strong and prolonged growth of investment, while initially finding the domestic productive structure unprepared and inadequate, set off significant upgrading, innovation and development of the sector. As can be seen from the data, domestic production of capital goods exceeded internal absorption from the mid-1960s.[16]

Within domestic production of capital goods, machine tools were already on a good track, textile machinery and wood and furniture machinery had grown since the 1950s, and from the 1960s the domestic production of machinery for the leather industry, machinery for the paper, printing, packaging and packing industries, machinery for the ceramics industry and for plastic materials also gained weight. Since 1965, the balance of specific commercial trade in capital goods has been positive (a similar profile emerges, on a bigger scale, for machine tools). Exports grew strongly in the long run and Italy gained a new significant and long lasting competitive advantage in this sector.[17]

Structural change and industrialization, as processes of increasing division of labour and specialization, led to the progressive development of upstream sectors and to the formation of articulated national manufacturing filieres. The emergence of a domestic machinery industry competitive in developing specialized machinery, tailored on the needs of the users, was crucial. Through creative adoption, increasingly reshaping new foreign technologies so as to increase their technological congruence with respect to the needs and characteristics of the industrial domestic users, the development of the Italian capital goods industry resulted, in fact, in a decisive boost to the diffusion of technological innovation and to productivity growth in important domestic manufacturing sectors. The growing supply resulted in a reduction in the price of capital goods (while the cost of labour was increasing and its ready availability decreasing), feeding capital deepening.

Starting in the 1960s, domestic demand for investment goods increasingly concerned more specialized and technologically sophisticated machinery, stimulating and feeding innovations by the national suppliers, shaped through interaction processes with the industrial users. The impulse of the demand of the growing Italian consumer durables industries (white goods, cars, motorcycles, typewriters, etc.), was important, stimulating more formalized innovative activity, through the purchase of licences abroad and the formation of joint research centres.[18] In this period, Italian industry, and the mechanical sector, in particular, benefited from the development of the technical secondary education in the 'Istituti Tecnici Industriali'. This educated human capital (endowed with good structured technical skills with some epistemic base) fruitfully matched the industry's internal development of skilled labour, and was pivotal to developing and successfully exploiting technological innovations along vertical manufacturing filieres. In the 1970s, the Italian machine tool industry entered a new and important phase of growth, with the development of the production of automated numerically controlled machines.[19] In a few years, as a result of the access to new technology and of incremental localized innovations, the spectrum of manufacturing processes where the use of numerically controlled machine tools was efficient increased. In particular, numerically control machines became attractive for small and differentiated production batches, helping the search for productive flexibility.[20] These technological and productive developments of the machine tool sector favoured the spread of decentralization and articulation of manufacturing industry's productive processes across Italian regions. During the 1980s, Italian producers were increasingly competitive in adapting and applying the new technologies to their typically specialized and customized machinery for traditional industries, thanks to the relationships linking producers, users and suppliers of components.[21] Also, in the 1970s and 1980s, the reliance of mechanical industry on foreign licences decreased and sales of know-how and technical assistance increased. At the end of the period analysed, the machinery sector accounted for a significant share of Italian industry's R&D, of sales of non-incorporated technology abroad and of Italy's international patenting activity (as seen in Chapter 9).

In so doing, the domestic machinery industry and related pecuniary externalities made a decisive contribution to the competitive strategy of Italian final goods producers.[22] The innovations incorporated in machinery contributed significantly to increase productivity, to improve quality and to widen the variety of products in the downstream manufacturing sectors. In particular, the innovative capacity of the Italian machinery industry made a significant contribution to the competitiveness of the country's traditional manufacturing sectors. The production of investment goods in Italy reached levels of technological excellence at an international level, above all, in the upstream sectors of traditional products in Italian industry. Textile machinery which is upstream to the textile and clothing industries, packaging machinery which is upstream to the food industry, specific machinery for the ceramics and wood industries, but also special machinery and robots which are upstream to the transport equipment, white goods and fine mechanics industries, offer unequivocal empirical evidence of the technological capability of the Italian capital goods industry and of the crucial role it played in the competitive growth of various Italian manufacturing industries.[23] As a result, the machinery sector played a central role in Italian industry TFP dynamics, as a growing advanced branch of Italy's productive system, as a supplier of goods, vector of technological change, and as a lever for technological and organizational innovation in users industries. In fact, the emergence of a competitive machinery industry can be considered the most effective, tangible and long-lasting single result of a bottom-up process of development that led to the accumulation of a widespread, collective and localized heritage of original technological knowledge, based upon processes of learning by doing, learning by using and learning by interacting. The emerging Italian distributed innovation system found in the machinery industry its original keystone.

We now have the building blocks to briefly examine the evolutionary process which led to the emergence of the Italian innovation system.

During the 1950s–60s phase:

- the expansion of the manufacturing base was greatly fuelled by a ready supply of labour at a low unit cost;
- the factor endowment was characterized by a relative abundance of semi-skilled workers, with low levels of education but with high levels of professional skills based on learning processes in quasi-craft production;
- the timely and profitable adoption by Italian industry of new technology incorporated into capital goods and diffused rapidly through high levels of investment;
- the import of innovative capital goods (foreign incorporated technology) initially prevailed; the crucial domestic machinery industry gradually emerges and develops (locally incorporated technology);
- product innovation prevailed, based on the imitation and

adaptation of foreign technology, also through the acquisition on international markets of non-incorporated innovative technology, in the form of patents and licences;
- the industrial base widened mainly due to the creation of new firms in the traditional sectors, spreading from the northwest triangle in the northeastern and central regions. Also, new durable goods industries enriched the national industrial base;
- The organization of the production of knowledge in Italy took place along two lines. On one hand, the group of large firms that had emerged at the beginning of the twentieth century, many under the control of the State, adopted a modified version of the 'American' model (based upon the pivotal role of the large corporation). The latter was in Italy articulated around the key role of direct public subsidies to State owned enterprises (SOEs) and 'influential' private firms to invest in new plants, preferably in southern Italy.[24] Italian corporations in this period were increasingly active in funding the generation of new knowledge and played an important role in the performance of R&D. Alongside the imitation and adaptation of the 'American' model, however, a second process took place, one where small firms played a crucial role: the accumulation and valorization of tacit knowledge based both on internal learning and the collective creation and usage of external pools of knowledge.

In the 1970s–80s phase:

- the ready supply of labour progressively dried up to such an extent that there were growing tensions in the labour market;
- at a macroeconomic level, the strong growth of unit wages (and of energy costs), the increased competitive pressure (in both domestic and international markets) induced technological innovation and pushed for the introduction of new capital-intensive and labour-saving technologies to reduce costs and increase efficiency; capital deepening progressed largely and pervasively;
- the northeastern and central regions industrial development continued and consolidated, together with northwest prevalence, while the southwest industrial catch-up dried up. 'Modern' sectors, relative to the Italian productive system of

the time, gained weight in the manufacturing industry (which was gaining ground in the national economy);

- an important component of the development of the mechanical and the chemical industry was the result of a process of 'ascent of the filieres', of building vertically integrated manufacturing chains. The strong derived demand of downstream sectors, mainly from traditional consumer goods industries (but also from producers of 'new' durable goods), pulled and stimulated innovation by upstream suppliers of capital and intermediate goods. The growth of innovative capacity in upstream sectors was also the result of intense processes of qualified and close interaction between users and suppliers of capital and inter-mediate goods. The suppliers' increased innovative capacity, in turn, favoured the downstream industries, both offering them customized capital and intermediate goods, which incor-porated significant technological innovation, spilling down pecuniary knowledge externalities. In the whole industrial system (upstream and downstream), a crucial role was played by strongly localized learning processes, both in spatial and technical terms. In this way, a virtuous system was set off in which product innovation in upstream industries stimulated, and was fed by, process innovations of downstream industries. The Italian industry, while experiencing a down-scaling of its growth path with many failures in heavy (capital/energy inten-sive) industries and in high tech industries, was able to create and exploit new technological opportunities based on a close vertical interdependence between adopting traditional sectors and modern innovating sectors: an authentic endogenous technological knowledge generating mechanism was actually activated. Throughout Italian manufacturing the soft innova-tion in design, marketing and brands gained relevance.

This process of virtuous and cumulative interaction was one of the most positive elements of the Italian growth model after World War II. With the slowdown of the innovative dynamism of the big corporations and the crisis of the SOEs, the small and medium enterprises- (SME) centred part of the Italian industry was able to implement an original model for the organization of the generation, dissemination and usage of technological knowledge. When the industrial sector had accumulated a sufficient degree of technological skills and had significantly articulated and structured the vertical linkages across its sectors, an original innovation system emerged capable of developing and capitalizing on its specific idiosyncratic characteristics and production factors. The growth of total factor productivity in downstream sectors appears to be the direct consequence of the growth of total productivity in upstream sectors, which, in turn, was pulled by the demand in downstream sectors and by knowledge externalities derived from the interaction with and within downstream industries. A systematic action of creative adoption was developed in the industrial system. It was based on *re-engineering* foreign technology, and was increasingly characterized by a strong domestic, idiosyncratic and localized component, which developed local skills and drew inspiration from virtuous processes of interaction between users and producers. It also exploited the development of *on-the-job* learning processes, especially in directing technological change in favour of the creative use of the locally abundant resources: semi-skilled labour in the first phase; specialized and dedicated (adapted to their specific needs) capital and intermediate goods together with technical skilled labour, in the second phase. Such technological options seem to lose part of their dynamic capacity from the 1990s.

NOTES

1. Structural change is traditionally defined by long-run changes in the relative share of the main economic sectors.
2. As shown by shift-share analysis of sectoral changes and their consequences on labour productivity and TFP dynamics (see Antonelli and Barbiellini Amidei, 2007). When the main industrial economies are compared, the structural effects in Italy were relatively more important and significant until the end of the 1970s (van Ark, 1996). See van Ark and Crafts (1996).
3. See O'Brien and Prados De La Escosura (1992). All countries experienced a strong decline in agriculture employment share, particularly in the first 20 years after World War II. However, Italy started with a much higher share (45 per cent of the total in 1951 compared to about 25 per cent in the main continental European countries).
4. See Zamagni (1990), Verspagen (1996), Barca (1997), Chandler, Amatori and Hikino (1999), Ciocca and Toniolo (1999). The Marshall Plan, in fact, provided supplies of American machinery and loans at reduced rates for the purchase of new equipment, while financing a wide range of initiatives favouring productivity. During the 1950s, many of the most important industrial plants were built up or modernized with American machinery (see Zeitlin and Herrigel, 1999; Antonelli and Barbiellini Amidei, 2007).

5. See Maddison (1996), Rossi and Toniolo (1996). In the 1950s, even in Europe, the automation of mass production machines became a central line of development for machine tool technology.

6. See Sylos Labini (1972).

7. Considering only the mechanical sector, the share of plant not more than five years old in Italy passed from 24 per cent in 1958, to 33 per cent in 1961 and to about 41 per cent in 1964. When machine tools are considered, at the end of the 1960s about 54 per cent of the stock of equipment was less than ten years old (see *Produzioni e Mercati. Le machine utensili*, in 'Bancaria' 1971), while in the mid 1970s, this share had risen to 59 per cent and almost 20 per cent of the stock of machine tools was less than five years old (see Antonelli and Garofalo, 1978). The average age of plant in the manufacturing industry was, in estimates at the time, less than in many other industrialized countries (see Cacace and Gardin, 1968). See also Wolff (1991).

8. With a different pattern: from a strong synergic growth of capital and labour, manufacturing passed after the early 1970s to capital growing at a lower rate and labour units employed less and less until a net decrease in the 1980s. Large firms, in particular, reacted with a combined strategy of increasing capital intensity, investing in automation and decentralizing production. In some industries (particularly heavy industries), there was significant investment aimed at enlarging productive capacity with State help. See Nardozzi (1974); Barca and Magnani (1989).

9. Classical economics, from the time of Smith, and Marx have centred the analysis of economic growth on the theme of the production of machinery because of its role in the processes of accumulation and innovation. In the last few decades especially through the historical research on the technological evolution of industry, the understanding of the role of capital goods in the growth of the economy and in innovative processes has improved (see Rosenberg, 1963, 1982; Rosenberg and Mowery, 1998). The machine tool industry, in particular, has been seen in these analyses as a crucial mechanism in the spread of technological innovation in US industry: in the nineteenth century for the expansion of productive technology based on interchangeable components; at the beginning of the twentieth century for the advent of methods of mass production.

10. Certainly, different weights depended on the sector in which the firm belonged, and on the different degrees of involvement in formal and informal R&D activities, patents, trade in non-incorporated technology. In the mid-1960s, 60 per cent of the manufacturing firms that claimed to have innovated, reported 'investment in new machines and/or new processes' as their way of innovating (see Cacace, 1970). In the 1980s and 1990s, the purchase of innovative investment goods continued being the main channel of innovation in Italy (see Istat 1987, 1989, 1995). It is interesting to recall the increased and greater weight of R&D reported for the machinery and mechanical equipment industries in the early 1990s.

11. See Maddison (1995) and Istat (1950–72, 1973–98).

12. Italy had a significant spread of entrepreneurial 'spirits' but a relatively limited supply of managerial resources.

13. See Istat (1950–72, 1973–98). Moreover, up to the end of the 1960s, scientific studies and engineering at university were in decline both for undergraduates and graduates. Despite improvements, large gaps remained in the area of formal education. Even as late as 1977, little more than 40 per cent of those employed had finished middle school and the percentage of graduates in the working population remained comparatively low (see Vasta, 1999).

14. The 'Istituto Tecnico Industriale' was developed in the post-World War II

educational system as a five-year secondary school teaching technical-scientific subjects relevant for industrial technology development (mechanical engineering, electrical engineering, measures, fluid dynamics, automation, material technology and so forth). After graduating, school leavers could qualify as 'periti industriali' after a national exam. The number of 'Istituti Tecnici Industriali' increased from 89 (21 in Lombardia, 9 in Veneto, 8 in Piemonte, 7 in Emilia Romagna, the more endowed regions) in 1949, to 434 in 1969 (69 in Lombardia, 50 in Piemonte, 41 in Veneto, 32 in Emilia Romagna), and to 636 in 1979 (115 in Lombardia, 71 in Piemonte, 54 in Veneto, 39 in Emilia Romagna). In the course of the 1950s, the tendency emerged among Italian firms to use educated technicians – in addition to skilled heads of units coming from the ranks of the workers – to cover the chief technician (capo tecnico) functions in the production lines. Data sourced from Istat (1950–72, 1973–98) and the Crenos Databases Regio-IT 1951–93, Regio-IT 1960–96 (see Paci and Saba, 1998).

15. The figures for capital goods foreign trade refer to an aggregate flow relative to capital goods produced in various branches of mechanicals (class 7 in the SITC classification) and in the branch producing tools and precision instruments (861 SITC; elaboration on data sourced from Istat 1950–87). Also data from ISCO (1977), regarding trade in final and non-final investment goods, confirm the evolution of external trade showed in the graphs. For machine tools, we elaborated data from Ucimu-Istat. See 'Commission of enquiry and study into the machinery industry, *La produzione delle macchine utensili*, December 1950' in ASBI, Fondo 11, Serie 1.

16. There was a similar evolution in the relationship between domestic investment and the internal production of machine tools. Investment in machine tools accounts for a significant share (between 5 per cent and 10 per cent) of total industrial investment over the whole period 1950–80.

17. During the 1960s, Italy's exports gained ground in the 'specialized suppliers' sectors, just where firms producing capital goods were important. By the 1970s and 1980s, this progress reached a quite relevant quantitative and qualitative level, despite being concentrated in sector niches (see Gomellini and Pianta, 2007; developments until mid-2000 confirm this trend). The Italian share of world exports of machine tools doubled, passing from 2.5 per cent in 1955 to 5.4 per cent in 1965. Italian exports of machine tools, despite some dips, continued to increase their share of the international market between the 1970s and the 1990s, passing from 7.4 per cent in 1975 to 9.1 per cent in 1990 (ahead of the United States, while Japanese exports managed to gain a quarter of the world market, more or less the same as the German share; Mazzoleni, 1999).

18. Notably, the experimental centre UCIMU (Unione Costruttori Italiani Macchine Utensili) and the joint research institute RTM (Istituto per le ricerche di tecnologia meccanica e per l'automazione) of Fiat, Finmeccanica and Olivetti. In the mid-1960s, while the ratio of R&D to total sales in the Italian mechanical industry was modest, the flow of know-how from abroad was considerable.

19. After World War II, the US machine tool industry (technological and commercial leader from the middle of the nineteenth century, when it replaced British industry) opened a new path of technological innovation: the development of automated systems to control the movement of machine tools with high levels of precision (as a result of research carried out in the early 1950s at the Servomechanism Laboratory of MIT, with financing from the US Department of Defense). Numerically controlled machinery was produced and used in the United States essentially from the early 1960s and quickly reached an appreciable diffusion even among Italian firms. In the 1960s, some Italian firms (notably Olivetti and San Giorgio), who were active in the electronics field,

developed control systems for domestic machine tool producers (see Barbiellini Amidei, Goldstein and Spadoni, 2010). Wider diffusion of numerically controlled machine tools was reached in the mid-1970s worldwide (see Antonelli and Garofalo, 1978). It is estimated that in 1978 numerically controlled machinery accounted for 10 per cent of total Italian production compared to a little higher share for Germany and double that percentage for the United States and Japan (see Mazzoleni 1999).

20. Thanks to improvements in performance and the lower costs made possible by the introduction of control systems based on the new technology of the microprocessor and by specific localized innovations. In the subsequent years, the growing application of the innovations in microelectronics and information technology made available machinery characterized by increasingly flexible automation (typically, flexible automation systems and CAD-CAM systems). See Carlsson and Jacobsson (1991).

21. It is estimated that numerically controlled machines accounted for 38 per cent of all Italian machine tools production in 1988, compared to a similar share for the United States, a 50 per cent share for Germany and a share of almost 60 per cent for Japan (see Mazzoleni, 1999).

22. When and where pecuniary knowledge externalities matter, the total cost of external knowledge, including purchasing and governance costs (articulated in transaction, networking and absorption costs), is lower than its marginal productivity for prospective users. In these conditions, firms have an incentive to rely less on internal learning and more on external local knowledge pools.

23. The data confirm the empirical evidence which has emerged from numerous sector studies; consider, for example, the analysis of the role of textile machinery in the growth of the textile industry by Antonelli, Petit and Tahar (1992); Carlesi, Lanzara and Sbrana (1983) for furniture and paper industry; Bursi (1984) for ceramic industry.

24. This kind of State intervention was in sharp contrast to the US direct public subsidies to firms investing in research and development activities, associated with a strong public demand for knowledge-intensive goods and services and the complementary role of the academic system supported by public funding.

11. Knowledge exploitation strategies and the direction of technological change

11.1 INTRODUCTION

The distributed model of generation of technological knowledge had important consequences in terms of knowledge exploitation with the introduction of new production processes characterized by a strong capital intensity bias.

More specifically, the strong directionality of technological change being introduced in the Italian economic system, especially since the 1970s, can be considered the result of two complementary dynamics:

1. a typical Marx–Hicks process of meta-substitution between production factors implemented by the introduction of technological changes directed towards the intensive use of the most abundant and convenient production factor, that since the late 1960s has increasingly been capital (Acemoglou, 1998 and 2002);
2. the basic role of the strong interdependence between upstream and downstream sectors as a source of pecuniary knowledge externalities. In particular the vertical relations between upstream producers and downstream users of capital goods has magnified the directionality of technological change in the Italian economic growth process in favour of increasing capital intensity. As a consequence the introduction of process innovations based upon capital-intensive techniques became the prevalent form of innovation, especially in the downstream industries.

When the role of pecuniary externalities in knowledge exploitation is taken into account, the direction of technological change emerges as a crucial and strategic factor in increasing the chances of exploitation and appropriation of knowledge by embodying it in idiosyncratic production factors. Local factor markets are major external determinants in path-dependent introduction by firms of technological innovations. Because of composition effects, the productivity and cost-effectivity of a new technology reflect the match between the ratio of output elasticities of production factors and the ratio of their prices as determined by the characteristics of the local factor markets. Composition effects are the outcome of the sensitivity of output to the relative scale of employment of each single factor. The growth of total factor productivity derived from the introduction of a given biased technology is higher, the higher the output elasticity of the productive factor that is locally most abundant.

Composition effects act as sorting devices. For a given supply of new and rival technologies, with similar shift effects, composition effects act as powerful selection devices and, accordingly, the introduction and diffusion of technologies will be influenced by the local conditions in the factor markets. Labour-intensive technologies will spread faster in labour abundant countries, and capital-intensive technologies will be adopted faster in capital abundant countries. The adoption of new technologies that are characterized by high levels of output elasticity of labour, and potentially big bias effects, but small shift effects, might be delayed forever in capital-rich countries. This analysis is most important when the global economy is considered: in the global economy, in fact, firms based in highly heterogeneous local factor markets compete in quite homogeneous product markets.

Different agents, rooted in different regions, with different endowments and hence different conditions in their local factor markets, may react with similar levels of creativity to common changes in their current conditions, introducing markedly different new technologies in terms of factor intensity. This happens as a joint result of the effects of internal localized learning and the conditions of access to the local pools of collective knowledge, and of the selection mechanism stemming from powerful composition effects. Here, composition effects act as an inducement factor that explains both the direction of the introduction of new technologies and their selective adoption and diffusion (Antonelli, 2003).

The strong positive effects in terms of reduced production costs and increased knowledge appropriability stemming from the intensive use of idiosyncratic – either locally available or internally created – production factors, provide a clear incentive to select the direction of knowledge generation. Pecuniary externalities enable firms to better appropriate technological knowledge embodied in processes and products. The opportunities for localized knowledge appropriation provided by pecuniary externalities become a powerful mechanism to direct not only the introduction of new technologies but also the generation of new technological knowledge. A direct feedback emerges between knowledge exploitation and generation strategies.

Identifying the sources of the idiosyncratic production factors that are more convenient to use intensively becomes a powerful guideline and focusing mechanism directing the technology strategy of innovative firms. The result is the creation and exploitation of a broader distinctive competence set by firms. An innovation tool box that enables innovative firms to exploit strategically and dynamically their geographical and industrial localization.

11.2 EVIDENCE ON THE BIAS IN FAVOUR OF CAPITAL-INTENSIVE TECHNOLOGIES

The evolution of technological change in the Italian industrial system in the most part of the second half of the twentieth century was characterized by a strong directionality or *bias* in terms of changes in the technological conditions of production factors utilization. An analysis of the character of this technological change is, therefore, fundamental: first, the endogenous process of change in the marginal rate of technical substitution caused by the introduction of labour or capital saving technologies; second, the effects of the direction of technological change on the growth of TFP (on top of that on the factor markets).[1]

The simplest index of the direction of technological change was suggested by John Hicks: in the interpretative setting of an aggregate production function (Cobb–Douglas alike), with constant returns to scale, stable elasticity of substitution and acceptance of the properties of Eulero's theorem, the evolution of the distribution of returns among production factors is interpreted as an indicator of the direction of technological change, as the changes in factors' income

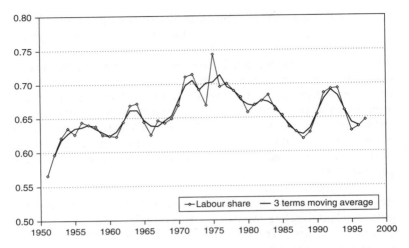

Figure 11.1   Labour share of value added: manufacturing industry

shares can be traced directly to the changes of the marginal productivity of the two basic factors of production.[2] Following this line of
reasoning, an increase in labour's income share, and, consequently, a
reduction in the share of returns going to capital, is interpreted as an
indicator of the introduction of new labour-intensive technologies,
which makes it advantageous to use proportionately more labour,
now more productive, and save capital. While from cases of an
increase in the share of returns going to capital instead, it is possible
to infer the introduction of new capital-intensive technologies. Only
when the factors' income shares are stable, and the product increases
more than could be explained by an increase in production factors,
would there be a case of neutral technological change, of an increase
of the efficiency of the productive processes without any change of
the relative efficiency of the factors.

Proceeding in this way it can be seen (Figure 11.1) that the
technological change, which characterized the evolution of the
Italian manufacturing system after World War II, was indeed non-
neutral. The share of returns going to labour increased significantly
for two decades, moved back after the mid-1970s: after a long
labour-intensive traverse, *capital-intensive* (labour saving) biased
technologies prevailed.[3] A sector level analysis is more informative,
offering, besides important confirmation, further interesting points

of interpretation: first, it confirmed that technological change was strongly directed in all sectors (see Figures 11.2 and 11.3); second, the technological bias assumed different characteristics in different sectors during the two main phases. The introduction of more capital-intensive technologies prevailed from the 1950s in the more traditional sectors, such as textiles, and wood and furniture (which had been characterized by higher than average shares of labour), and in the mechanical industry. It was, in particular, among modern sectors, such as chemicals, rubber and transportation equipment, that innovations had a labour-intensive bias. In the subsequent phase, after 1975, almost all sectors were directed on a *capital-intensive* technological path.

An analysis which considers both the particular process of expansion of the industrial base in Italy in the 1950s–60s and the endogenous nature of the direction of technological change, at a sector level, helps to explain the aggregate data. The direction of technological change is the result of an economic action set off by processes and dynamics that must be understood. In the 1950s and 1960s, most Italian manufacturing firms were on labour-intensive innovative paths which were based on learning processes linked to and structured around existing highly labour-intensive techniques.

Technological innovations were directed by the incentive to save on capital and employ a wide-ranging and abundant supply of inexpensive labour, with low levels of education but good levels of professional skills based on learning processes in quasi-craft productions.[4] With a factor endowment of relatively abundant labour and a relative scarcity of capital, it was convenient to introduce labour-intensive technologies, as it also was when the cost of labour started to increase rapidly (see Figures 11.4–11.6).[5] In fact, as the ample literature regarding induced technological change and more recent analysis on directed technological change helps to explain that, while the changes in factor costs (whether they be labour, capital or an intermediate input such as energy) must certainly be considered a main stimulus to the introduction of new technologies, the country/region factor endowment was driving the direction of technological change.[6] The pressure towards the introduction of labour-intensive technologies came to a halt only when this factor had become relatively expensive and 'scarce'.

The other main determinant of the labour-intensive direction of technological change was the technological opportunities defined

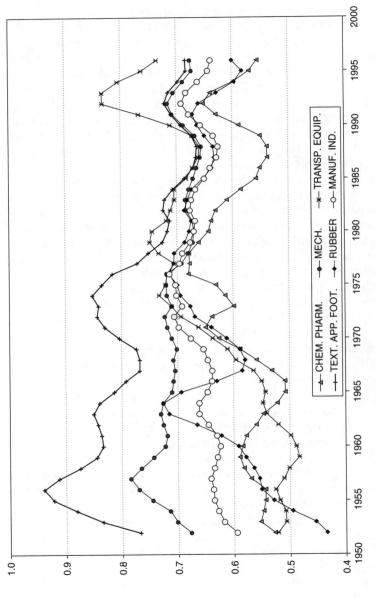

Figure 11.2 Labour share of value added: selected manufacturing sectors 1 (3 terms moving average)

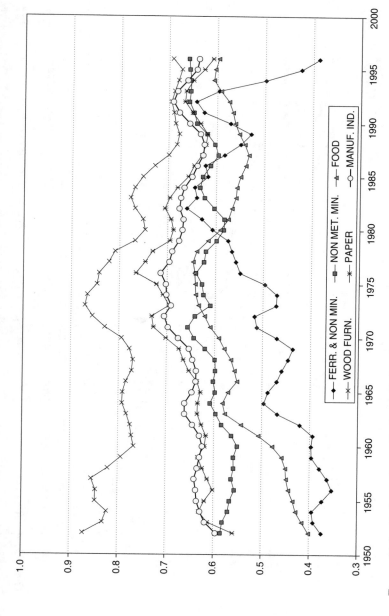

Figure 11.3 Labour share of value added: selected manufacturing sectors 2 (3 terms moving average)

145

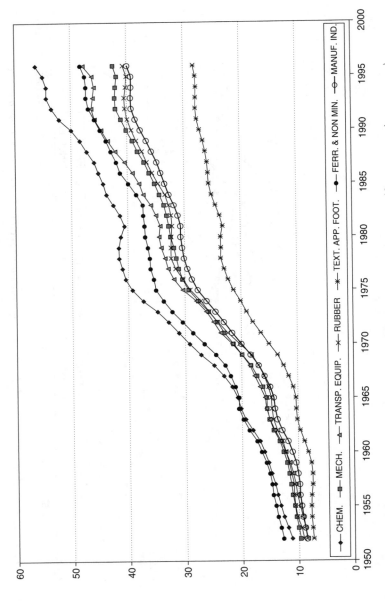

Figure 11.4 Real wage per unit of labour: selected manufacturing sectors (3 terms moving average)

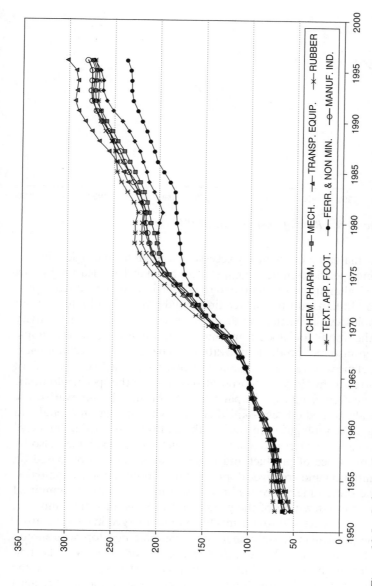

Figure 11.5 Indexes of real wages per unit of labour: selected manufacturing sectors (1965 = 100; 3 terms moving average)

Figure 11.6   Rate of unemployment (%): Italy

by the matching of the newly accessible foreign technologies and the existing specific technical competences and localized learning paths of the Italian firms, often limited to labour-intensive productive processes.[7] Italian industry, in fact, timely and profitably adopted foreign technologies, in particular, through an intense investment activity and the import of modern machinery, and due to relatively simple foreign-inspired product innovations. The available technological competences were fruitfully and systematically used so as to adapt imported technologies (incorporated or not) to the specific domestic economic environment, in particular favouring the innovative use of locally abundant semi-skilled labour, while saving on capital and energy. Technological innovation, thus, mostly assumed in 'modern' sectors a *labour-intensive* character, which can be explained also by the prevalence of product and organizational innovation based on the imitation and creative adoption of mass production technologies. At the same time, more traditional sectors were mostly committed to the mechanization of the production process, investing, initially, in mainly foreign affordable machinery (as emerged in Chapter 10).

The particular phase of national economic development should also be considered. In fact, during this period there was the first widespread national industrialization. Industry spread from the northwest triangle throughout the country, first, in the northeastern and central regions. The industrial base expanded radically through the creation and development (mostly on a limited scale) of several thousand new firms, especially in the traditional consumer goods sectors. This was a transformation process of a mainly agricultural economy into a mostly basic industrial economy, based on simple technology of low and sometimes very low capital intensity. It is, therefore, reasonable to assume that the data at the industry/sector level also reflects an aggregation effect resulting from the industrialization process.

The capital-intensive bias prevailing in the majority of sectors since the 1970s has, at least, two intertwined plausible explanations. First, it must be acknowledged that the new direction of technological change reflected the Italian economy's new endowment of factors. After two decades of rapid growth, the Italian economy's factor endowment was not unchanged: not only did labour costs increase significantly and conditions of employing labour become more rigid, but capital had, in the meantime, become relatively abundant. The accumulation of capital was, in fact, conspicuous and was such as to modify the relative advantage of using different production factors.[8] Moreover it was pulling in the same direction the strong intervention of industrial policy that selected the provision of public funds and loans at very low interest rates, as the main tool to favour the development of the Italian manufacturing industry: it increased significantly the speed at which new families of machinery spread.[9] When labour had become relatively expensive and 'scarce', the still strong growth of wages, while inducing innovations, further favoured the introduction of *capital-intensive* technologies conducive of substitution processes deeper than the options feasible in a given technical set. Firms were led to prefer workforce replacing investments, while drastically reducing the volume of investments devoted to increasing productive capacity.[10]

Second, the distinctive distributed innovation system, centred on the dynamic interdependence in vertical sectoral networks, was a crucial complementary mechanism. In fact, the full-scale functioning of the system of virtuous interactions between product innovations introduced by upstream machinery industries and process innovations introduced by downstream user sectors was an important driver (while an evolving result) of the newly prevailing strong capital-intensive innovation bias.

11.3   EFFECTS OF BIASED TECHNOLOGICAL CHANGE UPON TOTAL FACTOR PRODUCTIVITY

Our goal is to elaborate a comprehensive empirical measure of both the relative and absolute efficiency gains engendered: other than by the pure shift effects produced by the introduction of fully neutral technological change; or by the pure bias effect consequence of the introduction of fully biased technological changes, and the wide array of new directed technologies that consists of a change both in the level and the slope of the map of isoquants, with the consequent combination of bias and shift effects.

The direction of technological change, in as much that it modifies the slope of the map of isoquants through a change in the relationship between the output elasticity of the production factors, clearly affects the efficiency of productive processes in a markedly different way, in respect to the isoquants' movement towards the origin of a perfectly neutral technological change. Technological change always produces a mix of shift and bias effects on the production function: movements of the map of the isoquants towards the origin and modifications of the slope of the map of the isoquants. The directional effect may then add to or even subtract from the shift effect on TFP. Relative prices, or more precisely the relationship between the production factors price ratio (the slope of the isocosts) and the marginal rate of substitution (the slope of the isoquants), are therefore important in defining the growth in productivity, which is stimulated by the introduction of a new biased technology.[11]

To build a measure of the total effect of the features of technology on the efficiency of the production process we elaborate upon the so-called 'growth accounting' methodology. Output Y of each country i at time t, is produced from aggregate factor inputs, consisting of capital services (K) and labour services (L) proxied in this analysis by total full-time equivalent workers employed. ASHIFT is defined as the effect of the introduction of a pure Hicks-neutral technological change. Let us outline the main points in what follows.[12]

We specify in logarithm form a standard Cobb–Douglas production function and we apply the standard procedure to calculate the TFP, where the output elasticities of production factors are allowed to change over time, as it follows:

$$\ln ASHIFT = \ln Y(t, i) - \alpha(t, i) \ln K(t, i) - \beta(t, i) \ln L(t, i)$$
$$(11.1)$$

Where $\alpha_{i,t}$ and $\beta_{i,t}$ represent respectively the output elasticity of capital and labour for each country at each year, and $\alpha + \beta = 1$.

Next, following Euler's theorem as in Solow (1957), we assume that output elasticities equal the factors' shares in total income, as we consider constant returns to scale and perfect competition in both factor and product markets. In view of this, the output elasticity of labour is:

$$\beta(t, i) = w L(t, i) / Y(t, i) \qquad (11.2)$$

and hence:

$$\alpha(t, i) = 1 - \beta(t, i) \qquad (11.3)$$

The measure of *ASHIFT* obtained in this way, accounts for 'any kind of shift in the production function' (Solow, 1957: 312), and it might be considered a rough proxy of 'Technological Change' (Link, 1987). Using this, Solow intended to propose a way of 'segregating shifts of the production function from movements along it'. Solow is right if and when technological change is neutral and/or factors are equally abundant. Instead, the effects of biased technological innovations introduced in countries where factors are not equally abundant, are made up two elements. Besides the shift effect, one should also account for the bias effect, that is the direction of technological change.

Once we obtain the *ASHIFT* accounting for the shift in the production function, we can investigate the impact of the bias effect with a few passages. First of all, we get a measure of the TFP which accounts for the sum of both effects (for this reason we called it *ATOT*), by assuming output elasticities are unchanged with respect to the first year observed. At each moment in time the log of total-TFP is equal to the difference between the log of the output and the log of inputs weighted by their elasticities fixed at the first observed year:

$$\ln ATOT = \ln Y(t, i) - \alpha(t = 0, i) \ln K(t, i) - \beta(t = 0, i) \ln L(t, i)$$
$$(11.4)$$

Hence, we obtain the expected efficiency gains which would have been produced each year, after the increase in input levels, had the output elasticity of factors remained unchanged.

Next, we get the bias effect as the difference between the total effect of technological change ($ATOT$) and the shift effect ($ASHIFT$):

$$ABIAS = (ATOT - ASHIFT) \qquad (11.5)$$

Finally we may also measure (R), the relative bias efficiency index, as the ratio between the two indexes, that is, $ASHIFT$ (the Solow index) and the total TFP ($ATOT$) we introduced above:

$$R = ATOT / ASHIFT \qquad (11.6)$$

The indexes obtained from Equations (11.5) and (11.6) are straightforward and easy to interpret. Assuming that the slope of isocosts differs from unity, it is clear that when $ABIAS$ in a country is 0 and $R = 1$, technological change is typically neutral. When R in one country is above (below) one, then its technological activity is characterized by a positive (negative) directionality effect. When $ABIAS$ and R are large and positive, technological change is directed and has both a strong positive shift effect and a positive bias effect. In general terms, the direction of technological innovation, in as much as it facilitates a more intensive use of the most abundant (and less expensive) local resources, allows and enhances (adds to) the positive shift effects of technological change. Such a directional technology will be more efficient than a generic technology which intensively uses the production factors which are locally scarce and therefore more expensive. When $ABIAS$ is negative and $ASHIFT$ is positive, that is, $R < 1$, we grasp the case of a country that has introduced a superior technology with low levels of technological congruence. In this case, the unfavourable productivity effects of a directionality of technological innovation, either towards a more intensive use of the production factors which are locally most scarce and expensive, or towards a more intensive use of the production factors which are locally most abundant but technologically less congruent, allows and lessens (subtracts from) the positive shift effect of technological change.

$ABIAS$ was in fact calculated for the manufacturing industry for the two differently 'biased' periods 1951–75 and 1975–94. The results

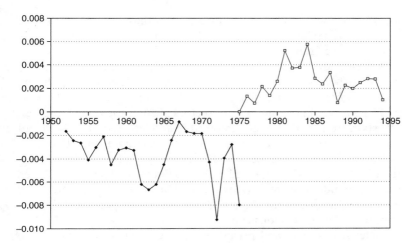

Figure 11.7   The effect of biased technological innovation on TFP growth: manufacturing industry

show that the evolution of the direction of technological change had significant and differentiated effects on the TFP growth of the Italian manufacturing industry (see Figure 11.7): the first traverse slowed down TFP dynamics, while the second speeded it up.

In the 1950s–60s labour-intensive directed technological innovation, in fact, rendered TFP growth lower than would have been, in theory, possible with a purely neutral technological change. This 'excessive' labour-intensive directionality may have been the necessary condition for a profitable adaptation of foreign technologies to local factor endowments; an adaptation conferring the benefit of a sustained, mainly 'imported', *SHIFT* TFP growth, at the 'price' of a negative-bias effect. A negative bias that began to be quite damaging, when in the early 1960s the price of the labour factor started to climb up steeply, after a decade of wage moderation. This excessive labour-intensive directionality may have reflected, in some industries, a relative narrowness in the span of technological knowledge available to the innovating firms, and its TFP impairing effect being therefore the result of a process of industrial modernization taking place on an inadequate and fragile technological base. It could be also assumed that, during this period, some other Italian firms were introducing innovations 'too intensive' in skilled labour, a scarce factor in the local endowment, pulled in that direction by the emerging worldwide 'skill-biased' technological change drift (a phenomenon increasingly evident in the United States).

A sector level analysis carried out using the same methodology offers further points of reflection (see Figures 11.8–11.10). During the first *labour-intensive* phase, technological *bias* subtracted points of TFP growth in the majority of sectors most of the time. However, transportation and rubber, among the modern sectors, stand out due to a positive (or less negative than the average) contribution of bias to the sector dynamics of TFP: perhaps the fruits of a success-ful adaptation of the imported technologies to the local semi-skilled labour-abundant factor endowment. The case of the traditional wood and furniture industry stands out due to the positive TFP con-tribution of its precocious capital-intensive bias.

Instead, in the second period, when a traverse that favoured an increase in the capital intensity of productive processes prevailed, the new direction of technological change enhanced TFP growth. This *capital-biased* innovation enabled firms to generate and adopt mechanical technologies, favouring a more productive/innovative use of available factors. Starting from 1975, the positive effect of capital-deepening on TFP growth was common to almost all the sectors. This positive effect was much more evident in the 'users' traditional sectors, particularly textiles and wood and furniture. Also, the *ABIAS* index for machinery reveals an interesting higher than average positive effect. Hence, sectoral data show how the TFP 'augmenting' introduction of *capital-intensive* technological innova-tions especially characterized the industries which were at the origin of the emergence of the system of vertical dynamic interdependence. As emerges from a *shift-share* analysis (see Table 11.1), it is signifi-cant that in the traditional sectors, in particular, the technological bias made a significant positive contribution to the manufacturing industry TFP performance (higher than their share of VA). The modern sectors producing machinery and intermediate products (mechanical and chemicals) followed a similar process of TFP 'augmenting' *capital-deepening* technological innovation, but on a more limited scale. Perhaps the differentiated TFP contribution of *bias* among modern sectors, which was more positive in machinery and lower than average in chemicals, indicates, starting from the mid-1980s, the difficulties and partial successes of the most modern component of manufacturing industry in participating at the frontier

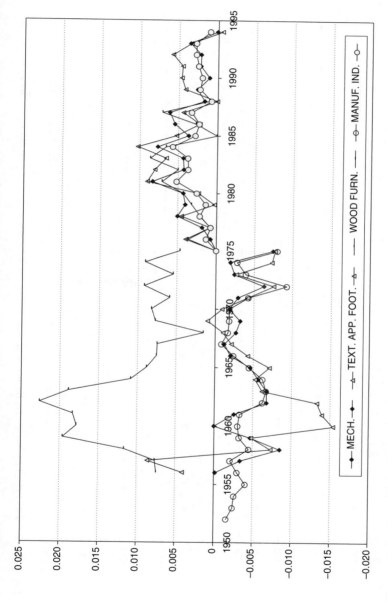

Figure 11.8   The effect of biased technological innovation on TFP growth: selected manufacturing sectors 1

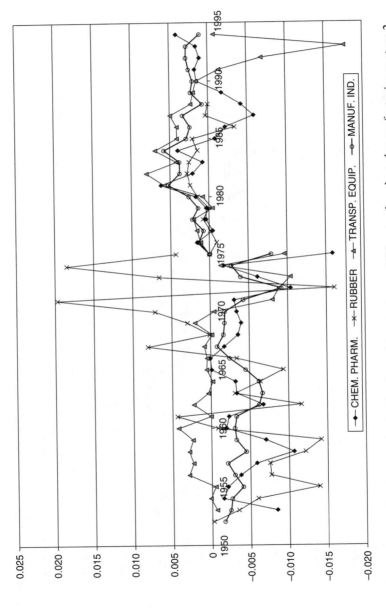

Figure 11.9   The effect of biased technological innovation on TFP growth: selected manufacturing sectors 2

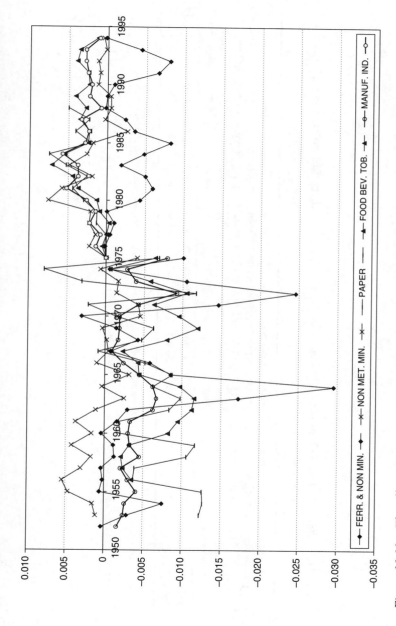

Figure 11.10 The effect of biased technological innovation on TFP growth: selected manufacturing sectors 3

Table 11.1 *Bias effect on TFP growth: shift-share analysis (% sectors contribution; average annual growth rates) – manufacturing industry*

	Bias effect on TFP modern sectors	Bias effect on TFP traditional sectors	Bias effect on TFP intermediate sectors	**Bias effect on TFP manuf. ind.**	**Modern sectors*** (%)	% points of avg. annual growth	VA share (avg.)	**Traditional sectors**** (%)	% points of avg. annual growth	VA share (avg.)	**Intermediate sectors**** (%)	% points of avg. annual growth	VA share (avg.)
1956–75	−0.34	−0.46	−0.50	**−0.40**	**31.29**	−0.13	38.7	**40.78**	−0.17	37.7	**27.9**	−0.12	23.6
1976–88	0.31	0.39	0.05	**0.28**	**50.9**	0.15	47.5	**45.6**	0.13	33.6	**3.5**	0.01	18.8

Notes: * chemical, mechanical, transp. equipment, rubber ** food, textile, wood *** ferrous min, non metal min, paper.

Source: Our calculations on data by Antonelli and Barbiellini Amidei (2007).

158

of 'skill-biased' technological change of this period, in directing the technological innovation processes in the most advantageous way.

On the whole, it is opportune to emphasize how, in this period, an authentic endogenous technological knowledge was actually developed due to the establishment and deepening of the process of vertical dynamic interdependence in Italian industry. The Italian manufacturing system appears to have been able to create and exploit new technological opportunities based on a close vertical interdependence between adopting traditional sectors and modern innovating sectors. Such technological options seem to lose part of their dynamic capacity after the 1990s.

NOTES

1. See Fellner (1961); David (2004).
2. The term 'technical change' defines the changes along the given isoquants (that result exclusively from processes of factorial substitution), while the term 'technological change' defines the changes of the map of the isoquants. A fundamental characteristic of 'technological change' is its direction, too often neglected with the tacit assumption of doubtful neutrality and the case of Italy confirms this completely. It should be remembered that there are various definitions of neutrality, but they can be traced back to two fundamental procedures. On one hand, according to Harrod, neutrality is defined in terms of the stability of the capital-output ratio, and on the other hand, according to Hicks, neutrality is defined in terms of the stability of the marginal rate of substitution (that is, substantially stable relative marginal efficiency of the production factors). The definition of neutrality elaborated by Hicks has the merit of being measured easily, and does not need assumptions, often demanding, regarding the evolution of relative factor prices.
3. Hicks (1965) defines the traverse as a movement from one growth equilibrium to another. In fact, the 1950–60s data suggest that the direction of technological change in Italian industry, as a whole, was, in this period, opposite to what was experienced after World War II in most industrialized countries with a bias towards more capital-intensive technologies, especially in the 1950s. In the mid-1990s, a new *labour-intensive* phase started, which was unconnected with important institutional developments in the Italian labour market.
4. See Antonelli and Barbiellini Amidei (2007).
5. The 1950s were characterized by a moderate growth in wages, starting from relatively low levels compared to international levels and basic models of industrial relations. The economic boom in the early 1960s caused the labour market to overheat due to the growth of demand for labour and the interrelated fall in the (low) percentage of working population (this was also because of the prevailing traditional social attitude towards the role of women and female workers in a situation where there were unexpected increases in wages pro-capita and urbanization; see Amatori, 1999). In 1962–63, the number of hours lost through strikes and the number of workers involved grew significantly, and appreciable wage increases were gained. Increased unemployment during the downturn in

1964–65 and the new south–north migratory flows eased pressure on wages and conflicts were reduced. The explosion of wage claims in the late-1960s led to the cost of labour (per employee and per product unit) increasing significantly, unexpectedly and uniformly in all sectors. This was due to the effect not only of big wage increases, but also of a reduction in working hours and working days and higher social contributions.

6. See Antonelli (2003). The Marx–Hicks hypothesis (Hicks, 1932), according to which technological change is both induced and directed by the growth of labour costs, was first questioned by the penetrating analysis of Salter and Samuelson, which demonstrated how in cases of increasing labour costs it is still advantageous to introduce new labour-intensive technology in a country where there is an abundance of labour (Samuelson, 1965; Salter, 1966). Variations in factor costs, therefore, determine the rate at which new technologies are introduced, while factor endowment explains their direction. When wages are very low because labour is abundant and, therefore, in absolute terms, the isocost has a particularly low slope, it is advantageous to introduce new production functions which use the more abundant factor, labour, intensively. Changes to the slope of the isocost due to increases in wages do not modify the relative advantage of generating and using *labour-intensive* technologies until a unitary slope is reached.

7. As firms are usually able to innovate only in a limited technological space defined by learning processes active in the close proximity of the techniques in use (Antonelli, 2003).

8. During the 1950s profit margins were high, and firms developed a greater capacity of self-financing in a situation of growing financial autonomy. The manufacturing industry during this period, in particular, enjoyed a high 'propensity to accumulation' (see Nardozzi, 1974; Bazzigaluppi and Gerosa, 1974; Barbiellini Amidei and Impenna, 1999). Throughout the 1950s, the gap between the levels of productivity and wages was rather wide and firms took advantage of the high profit margins: a favourable ratio between labour costs growth and productivity growth prevailed (lower than Italy's competitors) and this made it possible to combine some wage gains (starting from comparatively low levels) with sustained growth of profits, which facilitated the accumulation and financing of capital. In the 1950s, the Italian economy, still at modest levels of per capita income, had a high ratio of gross domestic savings (on average more than 25 per cent and only lower than Japan among the industrialized countries), although falling in relation to the increased share of dependent employment. The level of domestic savings remained comparatively high in the following decades (see Income, Savings and the Structure of Wealth of the Italian Family in 1966, appendix to the Bulletin of the Bank of Italy, 1967, number 4; Ando, Guiso and Visco, 1994). In the golden age years, the growth of private savings, in particular of families (also family firms) was significant. At the beginning of the 1950s, the distribution of income made a large share of domestic income available for direct investment in productive activities, income and wealth were, in fact, highly concentrated in the entrepreneurial classes, farm owners, and people in the 'liberal' professions. What is more, the high returns from industrial activity during the 1950s stimulated both the reinvestment of profits by the entrepreneurial classes, and the passage to business of members of the upper middle class and of the lower middle class (see Nardozzi, 1974). At the beginning of the 1960s, profit margins fell, partly due to increased labour costs; followed a slow-down in firms' self-financing and a fall in the propensity for accumulation (see Sylos Labini, 1967). The subsequent recovery of unit profits was cancelled out at the end of the 1960s by an appreciable increase in the share of income going to

labour. Firms' profit margins began to recover in the early 1970s, and continued to grow up to the 1980s; during the second half of the 1970s, the dynamics of real wages slowed down, the distribution of income moved in favour of profit. Investment activity was also stimulated by low or even negative real rates of interest; subsequently, in the 1980s, higher real rates of interest prevailed (Barca and Magnani, 1989). Overall the long-run profitability of firms remained quite high right up to the beginning of the 1990s (Rossi and Toniolo, 1996).

9. See Barbiellini Amidei and Impenna (1999).
10. See Cozzi (1979: 296); Caballero and Hammour (1997).
11. Analytically, it is not difficult to show that given an equation of costs including basic production factors and a typical Cobb–Douglas production function (such as: (1) $Y = L^{(b)} K^{(1-b)}$, and (2) $C = rK + wL$), a non-neutral technological innovation, modifying both the productivity of all factors and the intensity at which production factors are used, enhances total factor productivity more, the higher the ratio of the relative output elasticities and relative prices of the production factors (that is to say: (3) TFP = f $\{[b/(1 - b)]/(w/r)\}$, con f' > 0).
12. Such a method was perfected in Antonelli (2003) and applied in Antonelli and Quatraro (2010).

12. Knowledge generation and vertical dynamic interdependence within industrial filieres: econometric evidence on total factor productivity growth

12.1 INTRODUCTION

We now want to test the hypothesis that the Italian case was, for four decades after World War II, an example of a virtuous innovative system, developing and emphasizing the interdependence between innovative processes across manufacturing industries. The relevance of dynamics of sectoral relationships is a remarkable feature of Italian technological and structural change in the 1950–80s period. The hypothesis of the emergence of an original Italian innovation system can also reconcile the evidence of low levels of innovative activity, as measured by traditional indicators, such as R&D or patents, and high levels of total factor productivity, and try to solve the apparent Italian paradox. The interpretive model put forward can form the basis of an empirical investigation making it possible to draw attention to the plurality of innovative mechanisms operating in the Italian industrial system.

12.2 THE SECTORAL EVIDENCE

Looking across industrial sectors, the following hypotheses can be formulated:

1. In the whole industry, TFP increased as the result of the

introduction of technological (process and product) innovations induced by growth in aggregate demand and in wages;

2. Innovative activity and growth in the upstream sectors were stimulated by the combination of expansion of the derived demand for capital goods and intermediary inputs in the downstream sectors (Smith–Young–Kaldor demand pull innovation processes) and of the setting in motion of a process of localized technological change (learning by doing and by using, user–producer interactions);

3. At the same time, in the downstream traditional and durable goods sectors, the growth of TFP can also be 'explained' by TFP growth in the upstream sectors, due to both the classic spillover, trickle-down of technological externalities (knowledge as quasi-private good) and the specific pecuniary knowledge externalities (tied to the usage of dedicated capital and intermediary goods).

Our sectoral analysis is articulated in two steps. The first focuses on the systemic relationship at work by means of a circular model of interdependence. The second explores in more detail the role of specific determinants of total factor productivity growth.

Following the hypotheses and the interpretative framework elaborated, we put forward and test a system of equations with the aim of showing the strong role of sectoral interdependence in pushing the continual introduction of localized technological changes in Italian industry. We articulate the hypotheses that the growth of output of downstream industrial sectors specializing in the production of consumer goods, such as textiles and clothing, wood and furniture, transportation vehicles and appliances, was driven by the systematic increase of their total factor productivity. This is also true for the growth of output of the upstream industries, such as the mechanical engineering and chemical industries. In so doing, we stress the role of technological change in the growth of the Italian industrial system. The growth of total factor productivity of upstream sectors, specializing in the production of capital goods and advanced intermediary inputs, is demand pulled by the strong flow of derived demand exerted by the investments of the downstream sectors, which experienced a fast growth of output and market shares in the international markets during the second half of the twentieth century. The growth of output and market shares of the downstream industries was made possible by an increase in their efficiency and hence reduction in costs triggered by the increase of their total factor productivity, but the latter – here we put forward the hypothesis – was fed by the increase of upstream industries' TFP. The tight user–producer interactions were, in fact, beneficial to downstream industries that could take advantage of substantial pecuniary knowledge externalities generated by the upstream industries. When we recall that the derived demand for capital goods and intermediary products stemming from downstream industries pulled the growth of the output of upstream ones via the increase in their total factor productivity, we see that the loop is closed and the system of equations provides a plausible representation of the working of a system of innovation based upon the introduction of localized technological changes made possible by the pecuniary knowledge externalities generated within the system.

This approach to explaining technological change is far more articulated than the traditional post-Keynesian approach, because it combines the positive effects of investments embodying new technologies, with the support provided by the increase in the derived demand for capital goods, and the nested mechanisms for the generation and exploitation of technological knowledge feeding the introduction of technological innovations. The system grew because of the interaction between the demand pull exerted by downstream industries and the pecuniary externalities spilling from the upstream industries. Only the close user–producer relations along the inter-industrial filieres and within industrial districts, however, made it possible for the two dynamic processes to feed each other.

The argument elaborated so far can be summarized by the following system of four simultaneous equations:

$$\Delta \ln VA_{dt} = \lambda_I + \gamma_I \sum_{d \in D} \Delta \ln TFP_{dt} + \eta_{dt} \tag{12.1}$$

$$\Delta \ln TFP_{dt} = \alpha_I + \beta_I \sum_{u \in U} \Delta \ln TFP_{ut} + \varepsilon_{dt} \tag{12.2}$$

$$\Delta \ln TFP_{ut} = \alpha_{II} + \beta_{II} \sum_{d \in D} \Delta \ln (VA_{dt}) + \varepsilon_{ut} \tag{12.3}$$

$$\Delta \ln VA_{ut} = \lambda_{II} + \gamma_{II} \sum_{u \in U} \Delta \ln TFP_{ut} + \eta_{dt} \tag{12.4}$$

where $\Delta \ln VA_{dt}$ stands for the growth of value added (as proxy of output) of downstream sectors, $\Delta \ln VA_{ut}$ for the growth of value added of the upstream sectors, $\Delta \ln TFP_{dt}$ for the growth in total factor productivity of downstream sectors, $\Delta \ln TFP_{ut}$ for the increase in total factor productivity of upstream sectors.[1] The industries of textiles and clothing, food, transport equipment, wood and furniture, paper, rubber, ferrous and non-ferrous minerals, non metalliferous minerals, constitute the downstream sectors (D). The 'key' upstream sectors (U) are identified as the chemical and mechanical industries ($D \cup U = I$, where I is the overall set of manufacturing industries).

Considering the aims of the analysis, as well as the structure of the cross-sectional time-series data (characterized by a time range wider than the cross-sectional range), we adopted a SURE (Seemingly Unrelated Regression Equations) model. In fact, the latter model allows: (1) the appreciation of the behavioural differences of single sectors, in that it does not impose constraints of equality on the coefficients across sectors; (2) the testing of the relevance of innovation linkages between sectors and groups of sectors, in that it allows for the presence of not null contemporaneous covariance between the shocks hitting the different sectors.[2] The simultaneous estimation of the full system of equations, carried out for 10 manufacturing sectors, covers a period of more than three decades (1955–88).[3] The model has been estimated by using FGLS (Feasible Generalized Least Squares).[4]

The results are quite satisfactory (see Table 12.1). The system of equations yields significant results for several variables in all but two consumer goods sectors (the ferrous minerals and food sector). The results confirm the relevance of the tight aggregate systemic relationship within filieres between the industries of the Italian economic system: its keystone is the interplay between (1) the generation of technological knowledge supported by the flows of pecuniary externalities from upstream producers to downstream users, as demonstrated by the encouraging results of the test of Equation (12.2), and (2) the demand pull mechanism fuelled by the continual growth of the downstream sectors, which, with the consequent growth of their derived demand for capital and intermediary goods, pulled upstream firms to generate additional technological knowledge and introduced a continual flow of technological innovations, as documented by the results of the test of Equation (12.3). The system functioning

Table 12.1   Italian manufacturing industries TFP dynamics: SURE Analysis, 1955–1988; dependent variables: VA growth and TFP growth of downstream and upstream manufacturing industries; equations (12.1)–(12.4)

	Ferr. & non min.		Non met. min.		Chem. pharm.		Mech.		Transp. equip.	
Type of sector	d		d		u		u		d	
Equation	(12.1)	(12.2)	(12.1)	(12.2)	(12.4)	(12.3)	(12.4)	(12.3)	(12.1)	(12.2)
dependent variable	Δln VA	Δln TFP	Δln VA	Δln TFP	Δln VA	Δln TFP	Δln VA	Δln TFP	Δln VA	Δln TFP
Δln TFPd Ferrous	.814*** (0.03)		−.011 (0.03)						−.022 (0.02)	
Δln TFPd Non Met.	−.051 (0.07)		.903*** (0.06)						.072 (0.05)	
Δln TFPd Transp.	.115* (0.06)		.101* (0.05)						1.050*** (0.04)	
Δln TFPd Food	.011 (0.07)		−.023 (0.06)						−.024 (0.05)	
Δln TFPd Text.	.411*** (0.12)		.294*** (0.10)						.425*** (0.08)	
Δln TFPd Wood	−.174** (0.07)		−.088 (0.06)						−.202*** (0.05)	
Δln TFPd Paper	.032 (0.06)		−.004 (0.05)						−.067 (0.04)	
Δln TFPd Rubber	−.059 (0.05)		−.095** (0.04)						−0.22 (0.03)	
Δln TFPu Chem.		−.186 (0.23)		.060 (0.14)	.931*** (0.05)		.019 (0.03)			0.201 (0.18)
Δln TFPu Mech.		.463* (0.28)		.566*** (0.17)	.111* (0.06)		1.221*** (0.04)			.780*** (0.22)
Δln Vad Ferrous						−.256** (0.12)		.045 (0.05)		
Δln Vad Non Met.						−.383* (0.20)		.166* (0.09)		
Δln Vad Transp.						.074 (0.15)		.016 (0.07)		
Δln Vad Food						−.029 (0.19)		−345*** (0.09)		
Δln Vad Text.						.348 (0.33)		.247 (0.16)		
Δln Vad Wood						.179 (0.19)		.141 (0.09)		
Δln Vad Paper						.683*** (0.16)		.027 (0.07)		

	Food bev. tob.		Text. app. foot.		Wood furn.		Paper		Rubber	
	d		d		d		d		d	
	(12.1) $\Delta\ln$ VA	(12.2) $\Delta\ln$ TFP	(12.1) $\Delta\ln$ VA	(12.2) $\Delta\ln$ TFP	(12.1) $\Delta\ln$ VA	(12.2) $\Delta\ln$ TFP	(12.1) $\Delta\ln$ VA	(12.2) $\Delta\ln$ TFP	(12.1) $\Delta\ln$ VA	(12.2) $\Delta\ln$ TFP
	.005		.004		.019		−.001		−0.011	
	(0.02)		(0.03)		(0.03)		(0.02)		(0.03)	
	−.046		.038		−0.108*		−.035		−.060	
	(0.03)		(0.05)		(0.06)		(0.05)		(0.06)	
	.029		.016		−.047		.017		.052	
	(0.03)		(0.05)		(0.05)		(0.04)		(0.05)	
	.995***		−.010		−0.058		−.055		−.029	
	(0.03)		(0.06)		(0.06)		(0.05)		(0.06)	
	.234****		1.042***		.279***		.374***		.462***	
	(0.06)		(0.10)		(0.10)		(0.08)		(0.10)	
	−0.071*		−0.033		.935***		−0.150***		−.162***	
	(0.04)		(0.06)		(0.06)		(0.05)		(0.06)	
	−0.026		−0.013		.021		.967***		−.049	
	(0.03)		(0.05)		(0.05)		(0.04)		(0.05)	
	−0.045*		−0.038		.022		−.010		.979***	
	(0.02)		(0.04)		(0.04)		(0.03)		(0.04)	
		.033		.133*		.228*		.562***		−.263**
		(0.12)		(0.07)		(0.13)		(0.17)		(0.12)
		−.086		.381***		.313**		.754***		1.158***
		(0.14)		(0.09)		(0.15)		(0.21)		(0.15)

Table 12.1   (continued)

	Ferr. & non min.		Non met. Min.		Chem. pharm.		Mech.		Transp. equip.	
Type of sector	d		d		u		u		d	
Δln Vad Rubber						$-.389^{***}$ (0.13)	$.476^{***}$ (0.06)			
Constant	.013 (0.00)	.013 (0.02)	.016*** (0.00)	.005 (0.01)	.030*** (0.00)	.069*** (0.01)	.017*** (0.00)	−.005 (0.00)	.019*** (0.00)	−.012 (0.02)
R2	0.90	0.05	0.90	0.15	0.82	0.15	0.87	0.59	0.91	0.18
Prob>Chi²	676.9	3.11	520.1	10.6	336.9	31.8	649.2	129.4	1509.6	14.5

Independence: Breusch-Pagan = 675.06; Pr.: 0.0000

Notes:
N. observations =33
Std.-Errors in parenthesis.
***: significant at the 1% level, **: significant at the 5% level, *: significant at the 10% level.

has been able to support the extraordinary growth of the Italian industry not only in terms of output and labour productivity but also, and mainly, in terms of total factor productivity, as showed by the results of the test of the system of Equations (12.1)–(12.4).

In the second step of our sectoral analysis, in order to explore in more depth the innovative performance of manufacturing industries, we test (for the same 10 sectors, over the 1955–88 period, using FGLS) a SURE model in which the dependent variable is the growth of total factor productivity ($\Delta \ln TFP_{it}$) of the various upstream producer and downstream user sectors (as previously defined).

The following system of simultaneous equations hence holds $\forall i \in I$:

$$\Delta \ln TFP_{it} = \alpha_i + \beta_{1i}\Delta \ln (Kmach/L)_{it} + \beta_{2i}\Delta \ln (W/L)_{it}$$

$$+ \beta_{3i}\ln (W/L)_{it} + a\left[\beta_{4i} \sum_{d \in D, d \neq i} \Delta \ln (VA)_{dt}\right]$$

$$+ (1 - a)\left[\beta_{5i} \sum_{u \in U, u \neq i} \Delta \ln TFP_{ut}\right] + \beta_{6i}(Pat/VA)_{it} + \varepsilon_{it} \quad (12.5)$$

where $a = 1$ if $i \in U$, $a = 0$ if $i \in D$; $i \in I$.

To simplify, the general equation can be rewritten as a system of

Food bev. tob.		Text. app. foot.		Wood furn.		Paper		Rubber	
d		d		d		d		d	
.013***	.030**	.005	019**	−.000	.011	.014***	−.037*	.012**	.014
(0.00)	(0.01)	(0.00)	(0.00)	(0.00)	(0.01)	(0.00)	(0.02)	(0.00)	(0.01)
0.92	0.0	0.82	0.24	0.90	0.12	0.94	0.19	0.89	0.42
798.9	0.3	220.7	20.1	426.4	7.8	1238.8	24.6	720.8	55.8

two blocks of equations, with a distinct specification for the down-stream sectors ($a = 1$) on the one hand, and for upstream sectors ($a = 0$) on the other:

$$\Delta \ln TFP_{ut} = \alpha_u + \beta_{1u}\Delta \ln (Kmach/L)_{ut} + \beta_{2u}\Delta \ln (W/L)_{ut}$$

$$+ \beta_{3u} \ln (W/L)_{ut} + \beta_{4u}\sum_{d \in D}\Delta \ln (VA_{dt})$$

$$+ \beta_{6u}(Pat/VA)_{ut} + \varepsilon_{ut} \qquad (12.5a)$$

for each $u \in U$;

$$\Delta \ln TFP_{dt} = \alpha_d + \beta_{1d}\Delta \ln (Kmach/L)_{dt} + \beta_{2d}\Delta \ln (W/L)_{dt}$$

$$+ \beta_{3d} \ln (W/L)_{dt} + \beta_{5d}\sum_{u \in U}\Delta \ln TFP_{ut}$$

$$+ \beta_{6d}(Pat/VA)_{dt} + \varepsilon_{dt} \qquad (12.5b)$$

for each $d \in D$.

In both equations, the explicative variables are:

1. the rate of growth of machinery capital intensity, $\Delta \ln (Kmach/L)$, so as to capture the effect of new embodied technologies on innovative dynamics;
2. the rate of growth of wages per labour unit, $\Delta \ln (W/L)$, so as to measure the classic innovation induction of the labour cost dynamics;

3. the level of wages per labour unit in the sector, $\ln(W/L)$, so as to measure the effects of the relative levels of technical skills (quality of labour);
4. the ratio of the number of patents (granted to Italian firms by the USPTO) and the value added, Pat/VA, so as to measure the contribution of the output of innovative activity to the innovation performance of each sector.

The equation explaining TFP growth in the upstream key sectors (12.5a) also includes as an explicative variable:

(1) the growth in downstream sectors proxied by the rate of change of value added, $\Delta \ln VA_d$, in order to measure the inter-sector effect of demand pressure exerted by downstream firms for the introduction of innovations by firms in upstream industries.

On the other hand, in the downstream sectors' Equation (12.5b) we have:

(2) the growth of total factor productivity in the key upstream sectors, $\Delta \ln TFP_u$, in order to capture technological *spillovers*, as well as pecuniary knowledge externalities effects.

Where the α is the intercept, ε is the random error term and the β is the coefficient to be estimated. Different specifications of the model were considered.[5] Table 12.2 shows the results of the best specification, where in the equation for the upstream sectors' TFP we included as an explicative variable the VA growth of the two key (main and more intertwined) downstream sectors, transport equipment and textiles and clothing.[6] All the determinants listed above are included. The results of the regressions confirm the validity of the innovative model hypothesis, and reveal important differences across industries and, in particular, between the two groups of upstream and downstream industries.

The coefficient of the variable $\Delta \ln TFP_u$, proxy of the innovative contribution of technological *spillovers* and pecuniary externalities from upstream sector to downstream sector, was positive and significant in all but one user sector, for at least one of the two (chemicals or mechanicals) upstream producers. It is worth mentioning the positive contribution made by the innovative dynamics of the

Table 12.2 Italian manufacturing industries TFP dynamics: SURE, 1955–1988; dependent variable: TFP growth of manufacturing industries; equation (12.5)

	Ferr. & Non min.	Non met. min.	Chem. pharm.	Mech.	Transp. equip.	Food bev. tob.	Text. app. foot.	Wood furn.	Paper	Rubber
	d	d	u	u	d	d	d	d	d	d
$\Delta \ln K/L_i$	-0.526*	-0.162	1.187***	-0.473	0.285	-0.820***	0.248	-0.860***	-0.386	0.212
	(0.31)	(0.19)	(0.36)	(0.30)	(0.24)	(0.32)	(0.15)	(0.31)	(0.36)	(0.27)
$\Delta \ln W/L_i$	-0.616*	-0.095	-0.017	0.106	0.397*	0.470**	0.155*	0.282	0.322	-0.005
	(0.34)	(0.27)	(0.27)	(0.20)	(0.23)	(0.18)	(0.08)	(0.21)	(0.26)	(0.23)
$\ln W/L_i$	-0.066	-0.050	0.160*	0.153**	-0.102*	0.096**	-0.115***	0.024	0.101	0.097*
	(0.09)	(0.05)	(0.09)	(0.06)	(0.05)	(0.04)	(0.02)	(0.04)	(0.07)	(0.05)
$\Delta \ln$ TFPMech	0.565*	0.423**			0.918***	-0.034	0.360***	0.245	0.657***	0.944***
	(0.30)	(0.18)			(0.20)	(0.12)	(0.07)	(0.15)	(0.21)	(0.17)
$\Delta \ln$ TFPChem	0.041	0.020			0.090	-0.008	0.106	0.297**	0.342*	-0.227
	(0.22)	(0.14)			(0.17)	(0.13)	(0.07)	(0.13)	(0.18)	(0.15)
$\Delta \ln$ VATransp. Eq.			0.194	0.252***						
			(0.13)	(0.09)						
$\Delta \ln$ VAText. Cloth.			0.412	0.636***						
			(0.31)	(0.20)						
Pat/Vai	-45.991	-36.276	-1.682	-4.715	25.758**	59.633	-80.190	-10.798**	-18.441***	13.310**
	(39.73)	(27.75)	(1.07)	(4.02)	(12.59)	(42.93)	(51.05)	(5.16)	(6.09)	(5.33)

Table 12.2 (continued)

	Ferr. & Non min.	Non met. min.	Chem. pharm.	Mech.	Transp. equip.	Food bev. tob.	Text. app. foot.	Wood furn.	Paper	Rubber
Constant	0.163	0.121	−0.184	−0.155	0.035	−0.089	0.157***	0.064	−0.070	−0.178**
	(0.14)	(0.07)	(0.16)	(0.10)	(0.08)	(0.06)	(0.03)	(0.04)	(0.09)	(0.08)
R2	0.21	0.25	0.26	0.45	0.37	0.23	0.55	0.26	0.35	0.51
Prob>Chi²	11.0	9.9	18.1	45.7	33.6	13.0	60.7	16.9	27.8	38.9

Independence: Breusch–Pagan = 70.71; Pr.: 0.0085

Notes:
N. observations = 33
Std.-Errors in parenthesis.
***: significant at the 1% level, **: significant at the 5% level, *: significant at the 10% level.

172

mechanical industry to firms in the transport equipment, textiles and clothing, and rubber sectors. These results seem to corroborate the qualitative evidence provided in the last three decades by a rich set of sectoral studies (as shown in Chapter 8).

On the other hand, the key mechanical upstream sector appears to have benefited from the pull of the productive dynamics of the main users sectors, transport equipment and textiles industries ($\Delta \ln VA_d$).

Concerning the effect of new embodied technology, the intensity of machinery per unit of labour, has a positive and significant effect on the chemical industry's TFP dynamics; in two cases (food and wood industries) the variable's coefficient is negative and significant.[7]

The growth of the wage per labour unit has a positive and significant effect on the three main downstream industries' TFP (transport equipment, textiles and food), which may be interpreted as a productivity-enhancing induction effect of increasing labour costs.

The level of wage per labour unit exhibits a positive and significant coefficient in the key upstream sectors, chemicals and mechanical, and, among downstream ones, in the rubber industry and the food industry: it can be an indication of the contribution of skills and quality of labour to TFP dynamics in these sectors. Instead, in two other downstream sectors, transport equipment and textiles, the significant and negative coefficients may signal a progressive drying up of technological opportunities along labour-biased innovation paths.[8]

Finally, the patenting intensity variable (Pat/VA) not surprisingly, is positive and significant only in two modern downstream industries, transport equipment and rubber, populated by firms usually more structured than average. It is interesting that these two sectors were apparently able to combine the benefits of both the distributed innovation model (characterized by the complementarity between transactions in dedicated investment and intermediary goods and qualified user–producer interactions, based upon relevant pecuniary knowledge externalities, learning activities and external tacit knowledge) and the corporate innovation model (based on the R&D-centred generation and market-centred acquisition of codified knowledge, often embedded in patents).[9]

Econometric calculations on slightly different temporal windows (results not shown), with respect to the one under study here (1955–88), reveal that the workings of the intertwined system of *feedback* reached full maturity in the 1970s. The evolution of the system's architecture, until the late 1980s, was functional to its growth and enabled the relationship between the processes of learning-*by-doing* in the upstream sectors and the processes of learning-*by-using* in downstream sectors to be fruitfully interdependent. It is worth noting, however, that the 'innovative' linkages of the chemical sector with the other sectors became progressively weaker, signalling an evolution of the innovation system's architecture towards a 'poorer' (less functional) configuration.[10]

12.3   THE REGIONAL EVIDENCE

We also performed some econometric exercises on Italian regions' industrial sector productive and innovative structure. Adapting the sectoral model of the previous section, we are able to test across regions and macro-regions: (1) not only the role of upstream national capital goods producers in feeding the industry innovative performance, (2) but also the relevance of technical skills in the Italian innovative distributed system, adding a variable to capture the effect of the evolving availability at the regional level of educated technicians (variable only available at the spatial level).

Looking across Italian regions industry, a hypothesis can be formulated that:

1. On the whole, industry TFP developed in regions as a result of the introduction of technological innovations induced by domestic aggregate demand (Italian GDP) and growth of industrial wages at the regional level;
2. The TFP dynamics of the domestic mechanical industry, emerging in the sectoral testing as the crucial upstream innovative supplier, may have benefited the performance of the industrial sector in different regions, due to positive technological spillovers and pecuniary externalities on different manufacturing sectors within and across regions;
3. The availability of industrial technical skills at the regional level, may have empowered industry productive and innovative processes, allowing creative adoption of new technologies incorporated in capital goods and intermediary inputs, technological communication within and across industrial sectors (along industrial filieres), and sustaining processes of localized technological change.

Considering the aims of the analysis, as well as the structure of the data (again cross-sectional time-series data characterized by a time range wider than the cross-sectional range), we adopted a Panel data regression model, so as to: (1) take advantage of both the cross-sectional information reflected in the (mostly structural) differences between regions and the time-series (within) information reflected in the changes in regions over time, in testing the relevance of innovation linkages and the role of technical skills; (2) control for some types of omitted variables, both of the kind that differ between regions, but are constant over time (through fixed-effects estimation), and of those that vary over time, but are constant between regions (through random-effects estimation).[11]

Our benchmark regression equation for the 20 Italian regions (J), over the period 1961–94 (on which data are available), is then:[12]

$$\Delta \ln TFPInd_{jt} = \alpha_{jt} + \beta_1 \Delta \ln (K/L)Ind_{jt} + \beta_2 \Delta \ln (W/L)Ind_{jt}$$

$$+ \beta_3 \ln (THK/L)Ind_{jt} + \beta_4 \Delta \ln GdpIta_t$$

$$+ \beta_5 \Delta \ln TFPItaMech_t + \varepsilon_{jt} \qquad (12.6)$$

Table 12.3 shows the results for the whole Italian regions sample and for the two north-centre and southern Italy macro-regions.[13]

The ratio of students enrolled in 'Istituti Tecnici Industriali' (with a 4-year lag) on units of labour in industry ($THKjt/Ljt$) shows a positive and significant coefficient in the northern and centre Italy panel only, regions densely populated by industrial districts and characterized by the presence of localized manufacturing clusters centred on leading firms.[14] This result may be interpreted as an indication of the contribution of technical skills, provided by the educational system of the 'Istituti Tecnici Industriali', to TFP dynamics in the north-centre macro-region, through their role in processes of creative adoption and re-engineering, particularly useful in user–producer innovative interactions across sectors. Instead, in the southern macro-region and in the whole Italian regions panel, this variable is not significant.[15]

The variable $\Delta \ln$ TFP*ItaMech*, proxy of the innovative contribution of technological *spillovers* and pecuniary externalities from the domestic mechanical industry, has a positive and significant effect on industrial TFP for the whole Italian regions panel and for the two

Table 12.3   Italian regions industrial TFP dynamics: Panel analysis, 1961–1994; dependent variable: TFP growth of regional industry; equation (12.6)

	Italian Regions	North-centre Regions (1)	Southern Regions (2)
$\Delta \ln K/L$	−0.083**	0.050	−0.100
	(0.04)	(0.05)	(0.07)
$\Delta \ln W/L$	0.342***	0.283***	0.361***
	(0.06)	(0.06)	(0.11)
$\ln THKjt/Ljt$	0.135	1.189***	−0.262
	(0.10)	(0.21)	(0.23)
$\Delta \ln GDPIta$	0.318***	0.604***	0.194
	(0.12)	(0.13)	(0.26)
$\Delta \ln TFPItaMech$	0.272***	0.219***	0.289***
	(0.05)	(0.05)	(0.10)
Constant	−0.018***	−0.064***	0.004
	(0.00)	(0.01)	(0.01)
R2 (within)	0.2102	0.3332	0.1672
R2 (between)	0.2277	0.0529	0.2024
R2 (overall)	0.2103	0.2552	0.1672
N	680	408	272
Hausman	0.833	0.005	0.822
Method used	re	fe	re
Prob>F		0.000	
Prob>Chi2	0.000		0.000

Notes: Std.-Errors in parenthesis.
***: significant at the 1% level, **: significant at the 5% level, *: significant at the 10% level.
re: random-effects panel analysis, fe: fixed-effects panel analysis.
(1) It includes 12 north-centre Italian Regions, (2) It includes eight south Italian regions.

north-centre and south macro-regions. A positive result confirming the relevance of the virtuous distributed innovative system in feeding, for four decades after World War II, Italian industry innovation dynamics, in particular, in the north-centre macro-region.[16]

The growth of the wage per labour unit, $\Delta \ln(W/L)$, again has a positive and significant coefficient in all three regional panels, which may be interpreted as a positive innovation inducement effect of increasing labour costs.

Concerning the effect of new embodied technology, the intensity of total capital per unit of labour $\Delta\ln(K/L)$ is not significant in either the north-centre or in the southern macro-region, while it is negative and significant in the whole Italian regions panel.[17]

The Italian GDP growth, $\Delta\ln(\text{GDP}Ita)$, proxy of demand dynamics facing regional industries, also an expression of supra-regional (productivity) business cycles, shows a positive and significant coefficient in the north-centre panel, which may be interpreted as a positive demand induced effect on industrial TFP, but a not significant one in the southern macro-region. Interestingly, in Southern Italy both national and macro-region 'demand' variable (results of additional estimates not displayed) have a coefficient smaller and not significant across regions, conveying the impression of this part of the country being apart not as an autarchic macro-region, but more as a sum of 'isolated' regions.

On the whole, the empirical exercises show that the innovative process in the industrial system was stimulated by a factor cost induction process, both across sectors and regions (the growth of unit wages forced firms to innovate in order to offset growing costs of inputs per unit of output) and by a (more selective) process of incorporating new generations of technology, through high investment in capital equipment and increasing capital intensity of the production processes (which, as emerged from the TFP calculations of Chapter 9, already in itself and directly raised significantly labour productivity and nurtured output growth both across sectors and regions).

Further, a novel, distributed and polycentric, system of innovation emerged, based on processes of localized technological change, both in knowledge and regional space, in which the users–producers relationships played a central role augmented by regional co-localization within industrial districts. Of particular relevance and pervasiveness across sectors and north-centre regions, was the innovative contribution of pecuniary knowledge externalities spilling from domestic mechanical industry suppliers of dedicated capital goods and intermediary inputs. Here, the development of the technical skill endowment of the industrial labour force, also through the investment in secondary industrial technical education, played a significant role where (essentially in northern and centre Italian regions) it was employed in technological learning and communication processes. The demand pressures from the downstream sectors, combined with a system of inter-firm and inter-sector relationships, made it possible for firms in the upstream sectors to capitalize on tacit knowledge developed in the downstream sectors, combining it with internal learning processes. The strong economic incentives to match the specific demand of user sectors (heightened by persistent public incentives on investment in machinery), fuelled the introduction of product innovations by suppliers and process innovations by users. This helps to explain the significant industrial TFP dynamics for a long phase of the second half of the twentieth century in Italy.

NOTES

1. Where α and λ are the intercepts, ε and η are the random error terms, and β and γ are the coefficients to be estimated. The TFP series were obtained by calculations described in Chapter 9 on the basis of data (at constant prices) described there (see Antonelli and Barbiellini Amidei, 2007).
2. See Zellner (1962); Greene (1997); Moon and Perron (2008).
3. The variables used were built on the basis of data (at constant prices) described in detail in Antonelli and Barbiellini Amidei (2007).
4. FGLS gives consistent estimates, as does OLS (Ordinary Least Squares) equation by equation, but also gives more efficient estimates, since the equations are related and explanatory variables may differ in some respect in the different equations.
5. The regressions, in general, explain between one fifth and one half of the total variance. Alternative versions of the model in which some lagged variables had been inserted did not reveal any significant differences with regard to the crucial relationships, and the overall pattern of the results is confirmed. We also inserted variables expressing in different ways the determinants mentioned above. For example, in the case of W/L, we used as an alternative the wage per worker in each sector as a percentage of the average manufacturing wage per worker, $(W/L)_i / (W_{manuf}/L_{manuf})$: similar results were obtained.
6. These two industries alone accounted for 30 per cent of the manufacturing industry's total value added, on average, in the period.
7. Perhaps, this result is the manifestation of a capital deepening driven in these two sectors by a workforce downsizing, starting from relatively low capital/labour ratios.
8. These dynamics are confirmed at a regional level in Quatraro (2006).
9. The negative sign of the patent variable in the traditional wood and paper industries, populated by smaller firms, with scant international patenting activity, do not convey many economically meaningful results.
10. See Ricerche and Studi (1970), Zamagni (1991, 2010).
11. See Greene (1997).
12. A regional database was built on data (at constant prices) sourced from Antonelli and Barbiellini Amidei (2007), Crenos Databases Regio-IT 1951–93, Regio-IT 1960–96, Regio(cap)-IT 1970–94 (see Paci and Saba, 1998; Paci and Pusceddu, 2000), Svimez (1996), Prometeia (2003), Istat (1950–72, 1973–98).
13. We conducted estimates for our benchmark Equation (12.6), where $\varepsilon jt = uj + vjt$,

using both the fixed-effects and the random-effects models. For the whole Italian regions dataset and for the eight southern regions sample (Abruzzo, Molise, Campania, Puglia, Basilicata, Calabria, Sicilia, Sardegna), we display, in Table 12.3, the random effect estimation procedure results, since the Hausman test cannot reject the null hypothesis of no correlation between regressors and the unique errors v_{jt}; we display instead the fixed-effects (within group) estimation procedure results for the 12 north-centre regions (Val d'Aosta, Piemonte, Liguria, Lombardia, Veneto, Friuli Venezia Giulia, Trentino A.A., Emilia Romagna, Toscana, Umbria, Lazio, Marche), since the Hausman test rejects the null hypothesis of no correlation between regressors and the unique errors v_{jt}.

14. The equation (12.6) has also been estimated as a SURE model (using FGLS) testing the relationships for each 'single' region (results not displayed). Looking at SURE results concerning specific regions, we obtain for what pertains to the technical skills variable, positive and significant coefficients notably for Lombardia, Emilia Romagna, Toscana and Marche regions, the cradles of the Italian 'distretto'.

15. For southern Italy this result, perhaps, was also driven by a technical human capital drain, the result of intense internal (towards northern Italy) and foreign migration of young educated technicians, more than a shortage in the regional supply of educated technicians. We also acknowledge the potential endogeneity effect of expected future industrial TFP growth on families' choices about enrolment in technical schools across regions; we expect, however, a minor role of this effect in our sample.

16. Looking at SURE results concerning specific regions instead, for what pertains to the domestic mechanical industry TFP variable, we obtain positive and significant coefficients for almost all north and centre regions (notably for Piemonte, Veneto, Emilia Romagna, and the Central Adriatic Marche), while generally not significant coefficients among southern regions.

17. We do not have a long machinery capital time series at the regional industry level and thus we have to resort to total capital (including building and transport equipment). Looking at SURE results concerning specific regions, for what pertains to the total capital per unit of labour variable, we obtain mostly non-significant coefficients for both north-centre and southern regions, but still some both positive and negative significant ones in a few regions of the two macro-areas.

13. A distributed system of innovation: the Italian evidence in the second part of the twentieth century

This book elaborates the localized technological change approach and implements it with the notion of pecuniary knowledge externalities so as to appreciate the role of external factors in the generation and exploitation of technological knowledge. We have implemented a model, according to which firms pulled by increasing demand and wages, may introduce technological innovations that can increase total factor productivity only if, when and where external knowledge is available at costs that are below equilibrium. The model of localized technological change cum pecuniary knowledge externalities identifies the key conditions of the dynamics of technological change in the cost equation of the generation of technological knowledge and in the profit equation for its exploitation, affecting the output elasticity of inputs, but not their sum in the standard production function. In so doing, we have reversed the analytical core of the new growth theory and elaborated a frame that can account for the variety of specific contextual conditions that may or may not lead to the actual introduction of productivity enhancing technological innovations.

The research aimed to supply the basic analytical tools and the framework to provide a coherent interpretation of the excellent Italian long-term growth performance in the post-World War II era, highlighting the central role of the Italian distributed innovation system in sustaining fast rates of introduction of directed technological change.

The emergence, during the golden age era, and the full functioning until the early 1990s, of a distinctive distributed innovation system based both upon intensive specialization and division of labour within local manufacturing systems articulated in industrial districts and vertical dynamic interdependence within industrial filieres, was one of the decisive determinants of Italy's innovation capacity, both a cause and effect of Italy's remarkable growth process in the period and one of the more fertile effects of the intense process of structural transformation.

Our work has elaborated and applied a novel framework to analyse the post-war industrial development in Italy, characterized by the apparent puzzle of very low levels of expenditure on R&D and yet high TFP growth. The Italian growth process of the post-war period has its key specificity in the relation between the upstream sectors specializing in the supply of capital goods and advanced intermediate inputs and their downstream users (typically, low-tech producers of final goods). This was the main engine of productivity growth, and a causal factor in the strong directionality of technological change introduced in these years, strongly biased in favour of capital-intensive process innovations.

User–producer interactions were the source of major pecuniary knowledge externalities that played a key role both in the generation and in the exploitation of localized technological knowledge and in the introduction of localized technological changes. A recursive process between the continual expansion of the demand for Italian products in international markets, the increasing levels of investments and the derived demand for advanced capital goods sustained the continual introduction of technological innovations and substantiated a self sustaining process of positive feedbacks between the downstream demand pull transmitted upstream via the derived demand for capital goods and advanced intermediate inputs and the provision, by upstream manufacturers, to downstream users of a sequence of new vintages of advanced capital goods incorporating advanced technological knowledge. The creative reaction of upstream producers of capital goods, stirred by the downstream demand pull, fed the creative adoption of downstream users that were able to feed back to upstream manufacturers with crucial hints and technological communication about possible avenues for further improvements.

This process has been quite distinctive and peculiar to the Italian experience, in that it implemented a path of growth different to that followed by many industrialized countries. It relied on localized learning and bidirectional knowledge exchanges and interactions between components of the same system with the support of the parallel introduction of a major institutional and organizational innovation such as the industrial district which favoured the emergence and the effective working of a variety of intermediary markets, thus enabling advanced levels of specialization and enhanced division of labour between the upstream and the downstream sectors.

This theoretical interpretation, based upon a specific extension and elaboration of the localized technological change approach, is validated by a solid empirical evidence and is able to account for the high TFP growth.

The analysis is based on an original and dedicated dataset containing sectoral and regional series of TFP, capital intensity, wages per labour unit, R&D expenditures, patents granted in the United States, Technological Balance of Payments receipts and expenses for Italy over the 1950–90 period. Using both a SURE and a Panel model framework, the impact of user–producer interactions on the dynamic efficiency of the Italian industrial sector is investigated across industries and regions. The significant and distinctive features of Italian innovation dynamics in the post-World War II era are: (1) the emerging and functioning of a polycentric innovation system implemented by a distributed model of knowledge generation and exploitation based upon both horizontal dynamics of technological cooperation within industrial districts and vertical dynamic interdependence within industrial filieres; and (2) the strong directionality of technological change biased towards the introduction of capital-intensive process innovations.

The evidence for the emergence of an original distributed innovative system helps to solve the apparent Italian paradox of an economy characterized by a strong TFP growth and by the modest magnitude of the standard indicators of technological innovative activity intensity. This original distributed innovation system also helps to explain the four significant aspects of the Italian case: (1) the strong successful resilience of productive specialization in the traditional sectors; (2) the growth and consolidation of a relevant competitive international presence in related capital goods sectors; (3) the successful strong territorial productive concentration (districts) characterized by high levels of productive and innovative complementarity and interdependence; (4) the strong bias in favour of the introduction of capital-intensive process innovations.

The distributed model of organization of the polycentric and recombinant generation of technological knowledge that has emerged in the Italian experience, through the second part of the twentieth century, has been highly original and in many ways departed from the corporate model that had been first applied in the United States in the first part of the twentieth century and diffused in the rest of advanced industrialized countries in the second part of the century. The distributed model successfully experienced in Italy differs also from the so-called 'open innovation' model that emerged in the United States in the final part of the century.

The corporate model was based upon the pivotal role of the large corporation that was at the centre of the generation and exploitation of technological knowledge and introduction of technological change. The corporation performed large intramuros R&D activities aimed at feeding the systematic introduction of product innovations as a competitive tool in markets characterized by an intensive oligopolistic rivalry. These activities were supported by direct public subsidies to firms investing in R&D activities, strong public demand for knowledge-intensive goods and services and the complementary role of the academic system supported by public funding. The new open innovation model is more inclusive and systemic than the corporate model as it is increasingly based upon actual knowledge transactions between corporations and knowledge-intensive organizations and by the increasing role of high-tech start-up companies supported by new venture capitalism. The role of corporations in the performance of actual R&D activities is decreasing, but they are still central players in their funding and eventual exploitation in order to introduce technological innovations.

In the distributed model, instead, the generation of knowledge is primarily the result of a recombination of internal tacit knowledge, acquired by means of systematic learning processes and external knowledge, acquired by means of transactions, in the intermediary markets for capital and intermediate inputs, enhanced by knowledge user–producer interactions among small and highly specialized firms. Knowledge interactions cum transactions among downstream users and upstream producers of capital goods and advanced intermediary inputs played a pivotal role in the generation of technological knowledge and helped the progressive articulation of a distributed and polycentric model of knowledge generation, able to engender and disseminate substantial pecuniary knowledge externalities.

Pecuniary knowledge externalities were made possible by intensive interactions-cum-transactions in the new intermediary markets that were unfolding as a consequence of increasing levels of specialization and division of labour within industrial districts, complemented by technology sharing among firms within informal research consortia and technological platforms. Small, specialized firms and systematic vertical disintegration of the production processes are at the heart of this process. In this model the academic system plays a new pivotal role with the intensive participation of academic individuals as professional experts assisting small firms in the creative adoption and adaptation of the new technologies.

From this point of view, the technological change that characterized Italian economic growth was highly original because of the distributed model of knowledge generation, dissemination and exploitation that emerged. Technological change, based upon qualified vertical and horizontal interactions among firms, played a central role and it is indispensable to understanding the characteristics, the rhythms, the innate resilience but also the persistent fragilities of Italian economic growth during the second half of the twentieth century.

The model of localized technological change cum pecuniary knowledge externalities has proven able to provide a robust and integrated framework to understand the specific characteristics of the Italian way of generating technological knowledge and introducing innovation as key components and determinants of the remarkable growth of the Italian economy through the second part of the twentieth century.

From this viewpoint, the interpretative framework elaborated and implemented in this book can provide basic guidance for the interpretation of the role, in the recombinant generation of technological knowledge and in the introduction of technological innovations, of endogenous pecuniary knowledge externalities, generated within the system by knowledge interactions between upstream producers of capital goods and advanced intermediary inputs and downstream producers of consumer goods within inter-industrial filieres and industrial districts. In so doing, it provides a hint for the identification and appreciation of alternative models of knowledge generation and knowledge governance that do not follow the corporate model practiced in the United States in the first part of the twentieth century.

The characteristics of the Italian distributed model, as outlined and interpreted by the model of localized technological change cum pecuniary knowledge externalities, can provide useful guidance as a framework for elaborating the specific tools of an innovation policy in countries that are experiencing a process of rapid industrialization, based upon the building of a system of virtuous interdependence among industrial sectors of their economy.

References

Aage, T., Belussi, F. (2008), From fashion to design: creative networks in industrial districts, *Industry and Innovation*, **15**, 475–491.

Abramovitz, M. (1956), Resources and output trends in the US since 1870, *American Economic Review*, **46**, 5–23.

Abramovitz, M. (1989), *Thinking About Growth*, Cambridge, UK: Cambridge University Press.

Acemoglu, D. (1998), Why do new technologies complement skills? Directed technical change and inequality, *Quarterly Journal of Economics*, **113**, 1055–1089.

Acemoglu, D. (2002), Directed technical change, *Review of Economic Studies*, **69**, 781–810.

Aghion, P., Howitt, P. (1992), A model of growth through creative destruction, *Econometrica*, **60**, 323–351.

Aghion, P., Howitt, P. (1998), *Endogenous Growth Theory*, Cambridge, MA: MIT Press.

Aghion, P., Tirole, J. (1994), The management of innovation, *Quarterly Journal of Economics*, **CIX**, 1185–1209.

Amatori, F. (1999), *La grande impresa*, in Amatori, F., Bigazzi, D., Giannetti, R., Segreto, L. (eds), *Storia d'Italia. Annali*, vol. XV, *L'industria*, Einaudi, Torino.

Anderson, P.W., Arrow, K.J., Pines, D. (eds) (1988), *The Economy as an Evolving Complex System*, Redwood City, CA: Addison-Wesley.

Ando, A., Guiso, L., Visco, I. (eds) (1994), *Saving and the Accumulation of Wealth*, New York: Cambridge University Press.

Annunziato, P., Manfroni, P., Rosa, G. (1992), *La stima del capitale per settore e area geografica e alcuni indici di produttività*, Rome: Confindustria.

Antonelli, C. (1989), A failure-inducement model of research and development expenditures: Italian evidence from the early 1980s, *Journal of Economic Behaviour and Organization*, **12**, 159–180.

Antonelli, C. (1995), *The Economics of Localized Technological Change and Industrial Dynamics*, Boston, MA: Kluwer Academic Publisher.

Antonelli, C. (1999), *The Microdynamics of Technological Change*, London: Routledge.

Antonelli, C. (2001), *The Microeconomics of Technological Systems*, Oxford: Oxford University Press.

Antonelli, C. (2003), *The Economics of Innovation, New Technologies and Structural Change*, London: Routledge.

Antonelli, C. (2007), The system dynamics of collective knowledge: from gradualism and saltationism to punctuated change, *Journal of Economic Behavior and Organization*, **62**, 215–236.

Antonelli, C. (2008a), Pecuniary knowledge externalities and the emergence of directed technological change and innovation systems, *Industrial and Corporate Change*, **17**, 1049–1070.

Antonelli, C. (2008b), *Localized Technological Change: Towards the Economics of Complexity*, London: Routledge.

Antonelli, C. (2009), Localized appropriability: pecuniary externalities in knowledge exploitation, *Technology Analysis and Strategic Management*, **21**, 727–742.

Antonelli, C. (ed.) (2011a), *Handbook on the Economic Complexity of Technological Change*, Cheltenham, UK: Edward Elgar.

Antonelli, C. (2011b), Knowledge governance, pecuniary knowledge externalities and total factor productivity growth, WP Laboratorio di Economia dell'Innovazione Franco Monnigliano, Dipartimento di Economia "S. Cognetti de Martiis", Università di Torino & BRICK Working Papers, Collegio Carlo Alberto.

Antonelli, C., Barbiellini Amidei, F. (2007), Innovazione tecnologica e mutamento strutturale nell'industria italiana nel secondo dopoguerra, in Antonelli, C. et al. (eds), *Innovazione tecnologica e sviluppo industriale nel secondo dopoguerra*, Rome: Collana Storica della Banca d'Italia, Laterza, pp. 3–358.

Antonelli, C., Garofalo, G. (1978), La competitività italiana nel settore delle macchine utensili per la lavorazione dei metalli, in Alessandrini, P. (ed.), *Specializzazione e competitività internazionale dell'Italia*, Bologna: Il Mulino.

Antonelli, C., Marchionatti, R. (1998), Technological and organizational change in a process of industrial rejuvenation. The case of the Italian cotton textile industry, *Cambridge Journal of Economics*, **22**, 1–18.

Antonelli, C., Petit, P., Tahar, G. (1992), *The Economics of Industrial Modernization*, London: Academic Press.

Antonelli, C., Quatraro, F. (2010), The effects of biased technological change on total factor productivity. Empirical evidence from a sample of OECD countries, *Journal of Technology Transfer*, **35**, 361–383.

Antonelli, C., Teubal, M. (2010), Venture capital as a mechanism for knowledge governance, in Viale, R., Etzkowitz, H. (eds), *The Capitalization of Knowledge*, Cheltenham, UK: Edward Elgar, pp. 98–120.

Ark, B. van (1996), Sectoral growth accounting and structural change in post-war Europe, in Ark, B. Van, Crafts, N.F.R. (eds), *Quantitative Aspects of Post-war European Economic Growth*, Cambridge, UK: Cambridge University Press, pp. 84–165.

Ark, B. van, Crafts, N.F.R. (eds) (1996), *Quantitative Aspects of Post-war European Economic Growth*, Cambridge, UK: Cambridge University Press.

Arora, A., Fosfuri, A., Gambardella, A. (2001a), *Markets For Technology*, Cambridge, MA: MIT Press.

Arora, A., Fosfuri, A., Gambardella, A. (2001b), Specialized technology suppliers, international spillovers and investment: evidence from the chemical industry, *Journal of Development Economics*, **65**, 31–54.

Arrow, K.J. (1962a), Economic welfare and the allocation of resources for invention, in Nelson, R.R. (ed.), *The Rate and Direction of Inventive Activity: Economic and Social Factors*, Princeton, NJ: Princeton University Press for N.B.E.R., pp. 609–625.

Arrow, K.J. (1962b), The economic implications of learning by doing, *Review of Economic Studies*, **29**, 155–173.

Arrow, K.J. (1969), Classificatory notes on the production and transmission of technical knowledge, *American Economic Review*, **59**, 29–35.

Arrow, K.J. (1974), *The Limits of Organization*, New York: W.W. Norton.

Arthur, W.B., Durlauf, S.N., Lane, D.A. (eds) (1997), *The Economy as an Evolving Complex System II*, Redwood City, CA: Addison-Wesley.

Atkinson, A.B., Stiglitz, J.E. (1969), A new view of technological change, *Economic Journal*, **79**, 573–578.

Barbiellini Amidei, F., Goldstein, A., Spadoni, M. (2010), European acquisitions in the United States: re-examining Olivetti-Underwood fifty years later, Banca d'Italia Economic History Working Papers, no. 2.

Barbiellini Amidei, F., Impenna, C. (1999), Il mercato azionario e il finanziamento delle imprese negli anni Cinquanta, in F. Cotula (ed.), *Stabilità e sviluppo negli anni Cinquanta*. *Politica bancaria e struttura del sistema finanziario*, Roma-Bari: Collana storica della Banca d'Italia. Contributi, vol. VII.3, Laterza.

Barca, F. (ed.) (1997), *Storia del capitalismo italiano dal dopoguerra a oggi*, Rome: Donzelli.

Barca, F., Magnani, M. (1989), *L'industria fra capitale e lavoro*, Bologna: Il Mulino.

Bazzigaluppi, G., Gerosa, A. (1974), Profitti e processo di investimento: un'analisi disaggregata, *L'Industria*, **4**, 58–79.

Beaudry, C., Breschi, S. (2003), Are firms in clusters really more innovative?, *Economics of Innovation and New Technology*, **12**, 325–342.

Becattini, G. (1989), *Modelli locali di sviluppo*, Bologna: Il Mulino.

Belussi, F., Gottardi, G., Rullani, E. (eds) (2003), *The Technological Evolution of Industrial Districts*, Dordrecht: Kluwer.

Belussi, F., Pilotti, L. (2002), Knowledge creation, learning and innovation in Italian industrial districts, *Geographiska Annales*, **84B**, 125–139.

Bisogno, P. (ed.) (1988), *La politica scientifica in Italia negli ultimi 40 anni. Risorse, problemi, tendenze e raffronti internazionali*, Rome: CNR-ISRDS.

Boschma, R.A. (2005), Proximity and innovation: a critical assessment, *Regional Studies*, **39**, 61–74.

Boschma, R.A., Frenken, K. (2006), Why is economic geography not an evolutionary science? Towards an evolutionary economic geography, *Journal of Economic Geography*, **6**, 273–302.

Breschi, S., Malerba, F. (eds) (2005), *Clusters, Networks and Innovation*, Oxford, UK: Oxford University Press.

Bresnahan, T., Gambardella, A. (eds) (2004), *Building High-tech Clusters. Silicon Valley and Beyond*, Cambridge, UK: Cambridge University Press.

Bresnahan, T., Gambardella, A., Saxenian, A. (2001), Old economy inputs for new economy outputs: cluster formation in the new Silicon Valleys, *Industrial Corporate Change*, **10**, 835–860.

Broadberry, S.N. (1993), Manufacturing and the convergence hypothesis: what the long-run data show, *Journal of Economic History*, **53**, 531–558.

Broadberry, S.N. (1996), Convergence: what the historical record shows, in Ark, B. van, Crafts, N.F.R. (eds), *Quantitative Aspects of Post-War European Economic Growth*, Cambridge, UK: Cambridge University Press, pp. 327–347.

Brusco, S. (1982), The Emilian model: productive decentralization and social integration, *Cambridge Journal of Economics*, **6**, 167–184.

Bursi, T. (1984), *Il settore meccano-ceramico nel comprensorio della ceramica. Struttura e processi di crescita*, Milan: Franco Angeli.

Caballero, R.J., Hammour, M.L. (1997), Jobless growth: appropriability, factor substitution, and unemployment, NBER Working Paper Series, 6221.

Cacace, N. (1970), *Innovazione dei prodotti nell'industria italiana*, Milan: Franco Angeli.

Cacace, N., Gardin, P. (1968), *Produttività e divario tecnico*, Milan: Franco Angeli.

Cantwell, J. (2002), *The US Patent Database, 1950–1995*, mimeo.

Cantwell, J., Iammarino, S. (2003), *Multinational Corporations and European Regional Systems of Innovation*, London: Routledge.

Carlesi, A., Lanzara, R., Sbrana, R. (1983), *L'apertura dell'industria ai mercati internazionali. Tendenze e problemi nei settori del mobile, della carta e delle macchine per il legno*, Milan: Franco Angeli.

Carlsson, B., Jacobsson, S. (1991), What makes the automation industry strategic? *Economics of Innovation and New Technology*, **1**, 4.

Chandler, A.D. (1962), *Strategy and structure: Chapters in the History of the Industrial Enterprise*, Cambridge, MA: MIT Press.

Chandler, A.D. (1977), *The Visible Hand: The Managerial Revolution in American Business*, Cambridge, MA: The Belknap Press of Harvard University Press.

Chandler, A.D. (1990), *Scale and Scope: The Dynamics of Industrial Capitalism*, Cambridge, MA: The Belknap Press of Harvard University Press.

Chandler, A.D., Amatori, F., Hikino, T. (eds) (1999), *Big Business and the Wealth of Nations*, Cambridge, UK: Cambridge University Press.

Chesbrough, H. (2003), *Open Innovation. The New Imperative for Creating and Profiting From Technology*, Boston, MA: Harvard Business School Press.

Chesbrough, H., Vanhaverbeke, W., West, J. (2006), *Open*

Innovation: Researching a New Paradigm, Oxford, UK: Oxford University Press.

Christensen, L.R., Cummings, D., Jorgenson, D.W. (1980), Economic growth, 1947–1973: an international comparison, in Kendrick, J.W., Vaccara, B.N. (eds), *New Developments in Productivity Measurement and Analysis*, NBER Conference Report, Chicago, IL: University of Chicago Press.

Ciccone, A., Matsuyama, K. (1996), Start-up costs and pecuniary externalities as barriers to economic development, *Journal of Development Economics*, **49**, 33–59.

Ciocca, P., Toniolo, G. (eds) (1999), *Storia economica d'Italia*, vol. I, *Interpretazioni*; vol. II, *Annali*, Roma-Bari: Laterza.

Cohen, W.M., Levinthal, D.A. (1989), Innovation and learning: the two faces of R&D, *Economic Journal*, **99**, 569–596.

Cohen, W.M., Levinthal, D.A. (1990), Absorptive capacity: a new perspective on learning and innovation, *Administrative Science Quarterly*, **35**, 128–152.

Cozzi, T. (1979), *Teoria dello sviluppo economico*, Bologna: Il Mulino.

Crafts, N.F.R., Toniolo, G. (eds) (1996), *Economic Growth in Europe Since 1945*, Cambridge, UK: Cambridge University Press.

Crepon B., Duguet E., Mairesse J. (1998), Research, innovation and productivity: an econometric analysis at the firm level, *Economics of Innovation and New Technology*, **7**,115–158.

David, P.A. (1975), *Technical Choice Innovation and Economic Growth*, Cambridge, UK: Cambridge University Press.

David, P.A. (1993), Knowledge property and the system dynamics of technological change, *Proceedings of the World Bank Annual Conference on Development Economics*, Washington, DC: The World Bank.

David, P.A. (1994), Why are institutions the 'carriers of history'? Path dependence and the evolution of conventions, organizations and institutions, *Structural Change and Economic Dynamics*, **5**, 205–220.

David, P.A. (2001), Path dependence, its critics, and the quest for 'Historical Economics', in Garrouste, P., Ioannidis, S. (eds), *Evolution and Path Dependence in Economic Ideas: Past and Present*, Cheltenham, UK: Edward Elgar.

David, P.A. (2004), The tale of two traverses. Innovation and accumulation in the first two centuries of US economic growth, SIEPR Discussion Paper No. 03-24, Stanford University.

David, P.A. (2007), Path dependence: a foundational concept for historical social science, *Cliometrica. Journal of Historical Economics and Econometric History*, **1**, 91–114.

David, P.A., Foray, D., Dalle, J.M. (1995), Marshallian externalities and the emergence and spatial stability of technological enclaves, *Economics of Innovation and New Technology*, **6**, 147–182.

David, P.A., Rosenbloom, J.L. (1990), Marshallian factor market externalities and the dynamics of industrial localization, *Journal of Urban Economics*, **28**, 349–370.

D'Ignazio, A., Giovannetti, E. (2006), From exogenous to endogenous economic networks: internet applications, *Journal of Economic Survey*, **20**, 757–796.

Dollar, D., Wolff, E.N. (1988), Convergence of industry labor productivity among advanced economies, 1963–1982, *The Review of Economics and Statistics*, **70**, 4.

Dougherty, C. (1991), A comparison of productivity and economic growth in the G7 countries, Doctoral Thesis, Harvard University.

Durlauf, S.N. (2005), Complexity and empirical economics, *Economic Journal*, **115**, 225–243.

Durlauf, S., Johnson, P.A. (1992), Local versus global convergence across national economies, Working paper No. 3996 of the N.B.E.R., Cambridge.

Edquist, C. (ed.) (1997), *Systems of Innovation: Technologies, Institutions, and Organizations*, London: Pinter.

Fagerberg, J. (1987), A technology gap approach to why growth rates differ, *Research Policy*, **16**, 2–4.

Feldman, M.P. (1999), The new economics of innovation spillovers and agglomeration: a review of empirical studies, *Economics of Innovation and New Technology*, **8**, 5–26.

Fellner, W. (1961), Two propositions in the theory of induced innovation, *Economic Journal*, **71**, 305–308.

Foss, N. (1997), *Resources, Firms and Strategies. A Reader in the Resource-based Perspective*, Oxford, UK: Oxford University Press.

Foss, N.J. (1998), The resource-base perspective: an assessment and diagnosis of problems, *Scandinavian Journal of Management*, **15**, 1–15.

Freeman, C. (1991), Networks of innovators: a synthesis of research issues, *Research Policy*, **20**, 499–514.

Freeman, C. (1997), The 'national system of innovation' in historical perspective, in Archibugi, D., Michie, J. (eds), *Technology*

Globalization and Economic Performance, Cambridge, UK: Cambridge University Press, pp. 24–49.

Frenken, K. (2006), Technological innovation and complexity theory, *Economics of Innovation and New Technology*, **15**, 137–155.

Fuà, G. (1983), Industrializzazione nel Nord Est e nel Centro, in Fuà, G., Zacchia, C. (eds), *Industrializzazione senza fratture*, Bologna: Il Mulino.

Giannetti, R., Pastorelli, S. (2007), Il sistema nazionale di innovazione negli anni Cinquanta e Sessanta, in Antonelli, C. et al. (eds), *Innovazione tecnologica e sviluppo industriale nel secondo dopoguerra*, Rome: Collana Storica della Banca d'Italia, Laterza.

Golinelli, R. (1998), La ricostruzione dei dati di contabilità nazionale. Metodi e confronti, mimeo, Università di Bologna.

Gomellini, M., Pianta, M. (2007), Commercio con l'estero e tecnologia in Italia negli anni Cinquanta e Sessanta, in Antonelli, C. et al. (eds), *Innovazione tecnologica e sviluppo industriale nel secondo dopoguerra*, Rome: Collana Storica della Banca d'Italia, Laterza.

Greene, W.H. (1997), *Econometric Analysis*, Upper Saddle River, NJ: Prentice Hall.

Griffith, R., Redding, S., Van Reenen, J. (2003), R&D and absorptive capacity: theory and empirical evidence, *Scandinavian Journal of Economics*, **105**, 99–118.

Griliches, Z. (1979), Issues in assessing the contribution of research and development to productivity growth, *Bell Journal of Economics*, **10**, 92–116.

Griliches, Z. (1992), The search for R&D spillovers, *Scandinavian Journal of Economics*, **94**, 29–47.

Grossman, G.M., Helpman, E. (1994), Endogenous innovation in the theory of growth, *Journal of Economic Perspectives*, **8**, 23–44.

Guiso, L., Schivardi, F. (2007), Spillovers in industrial districts, *Economic Journal*, **117**, 68–93.

Hayek, F.A. (1945), The use of knowledge in society, *American Economic Review*, **35**, 519–530.

Hicks, J.R. (1932), *The Theory of Wages*, London: Macmillan.

ISCO (1977), *Analisi dell'interscambio commerciale con l'estero. 1952–1976*, Rome: ISCO.

Istat (1950–72), *Annuario statistico dell'istruzione italiana*, Rome: Istituto poligrafico dello Stato.

Istat (1950–87), *Statistica annuale del commercio con l'estero*, Rome: Istat.

Istat (1951–98), *Annuario statistico italiano*, Rome: Istat.

Istat (1973–98), *Annuario statistico dell'istruzione*, Rome: Istat.

Istat (1978–85), *Indagine statistica sulla ricerca scientifica*, in Bollettino mensile di statistica. Supplemento.

Istat (1987), *Indagine sulla diffusione della innovazione tecnologica nell'industria manifatturiera italiana*, Collana d'Informazione, Rome: Istat.

Istat (1989), *Indagine statistica sull'innovazione tecnologica nell'industria italiana*, Collana d'Informazione, Rome: Istat.

Istat (1995), *Indagine sull'innovazione tecnologica. Anni 1990–92*, Rome: Istat.

Jaffe, A.B. (1986), Technological opportunity and spillover of R&D: evidence from firms' patents, profits and market value, *American Economic Review*, **79**, 985–1001.

Jones, C.I. (2002), *Introduction to Economic Growth*, 2nd edition, New York: Norton.

Kaldor, N. (1972), The irrelevance of equilibrium economics, *Economic Journal*, **82**, 1237–1255.

Kaldor, N. (1981), The role of increasing returns technical progress and cumulative causation, *Economie Appliquée*, **34**, 593–617.

Kennedy, C. (1964), Induced bias and the theory of distribution, *Economic Journal*, **74**, 541–547.

Kleinknecht, A.H., van Montfort, K., Brouwer, E. (2002), The non-trivial choice between innovation indicators, *Economics of Innovation and New Technology*, **11**, 109–121.

Lane, D. (2002), Complexity and local interactions. Towards a theory of industrial districts, in Quadrio Curzio, A., Fortis, M. (eds), *Complexity and Industrial Clusters: Dynamics and Models in Theory and Practice*, Berlin: Springer Verlag, pp. 65–82.

Lane, D.A., Maxfield, R. (1997), Foresight complexity and strategy, in Arthur, W.B., Durlauf, S.N., Lane, D.A. (eds), *The Economy as an Evolving Complex System II*, Santa Fe, NM: Westview Press, pp. 169–198.

Lane, D. et al. (2009), *Complexity Perspectives in Innovation and Social Change*, Berlin: Springer.

Maddison, A. (1995), *Monitoring the World Economy, 1820–1992*, Paris: Development Centre of the Organisation for Economic Co-operation and Development.

Maddison, A. (1996), Macroeconomic accounts for European countries, in Ark, B. van, Crafts, N.F.R. (eds), *Quantitative*

Aspects of Post-war European Economic Growth, Cambridge, UK: Cambridge University Press, pp. 27–83.

Malerba, F. (1988), R&D growth in Italian industry in an international perspective, CESPRI Working Papers, No. 8, Università Commerciale L. Bocconi, Milan.

Malerba, F. (2005), Sectoral systems of innovation: a framework for linking innovation to the knowledge base, structure and dynamics of sectors, *Economics of Innovation and New Technology*, **14**, 63–82.

Malerba, F., Torrisi, S., Bussolati, C. (1996), L'evoluzione delle industrie ad alta tecnologia in Italia: entrata tempestiva, declino e opportunità di recupero, Bologna: Il Mulino.

Mansfield, E., Schwartz, M., Wagner, S. (1981), Imitation costs and patents: an empirical study, *Economic Journal*, **91**, 907–918.

March, J.C. (1991), Exploration and exploitation in organizing learning, *Organization Science*, **2**, 71–87.

Marshall, A. (1890 [1920]), *Principles of Economics*, 8th edition, London: Macmillan.

Martin, R.L. (1999), The new geographical turn in economics: some critical reflections, *Cambridge Journal of Economics*, **23**, 65–91.

Martin, R. (2007), The localization of industry, in Raffaelli, T., Becattini, G., Dardi, M. (eds), *The Elgar Companion to Alfred Marshall*, Cheltenham, UK: Edward Elgar, pp. 393–400.

Marx, K. (1867 [1976]), *Capital: A Critique of Political Economy*, Harmondsworth, UK: Penguin Books.

Matsuyama, K. (1995), Complementarities and cumulative processes in models of monopolistic competition, *Journal of Economic Literature*, **33**, 701–729.

Mazzoleni, R. (1999), Innovation in the machine tool industry: a historical perspective on the dynamics of comparative advantage, in Mowery, D.C., Nelson, R.R. (eds), *Sources of Industrial Leadership: Studies of Seven Industries*, Cambridge, UK: Cambridge University Press, pp. 169–216.

Meade, J.E. (1952), External economies and diseconomies in a competitive situation, *Economic Journal*, **62**, 54–67.

Milgrom, P., Roberts, J. (1995), Complementarities and fit. Strategy structure and organizational change in manufacturing, *Journal of Accounting and Economics*, **19**, 179–208.

Moon, H., Perron, B. (2008), Seemingly unrelated regressions, in *The New Palgrave Dictionary of Economics*, 2nd edition, Basingstoke, UK: Palgrave McMillan.

Nardozzi, G. (1974), Struttura industriale e accumulazione del capitale in Italia, *L'Industria*, 5–6.

O'Brien, P.K., Prados de La Escosura, L. (1992), Agricultural productivity and European industrialization, 1890–1980, *The Economic History Review*, **45**.

Nelson, R.R. (1959), The simple economics of basic scientific research, *Journal of Political Economy*, **67**, 297–306.

Nelson, R.R. (1982), The role of knowledge in R&D efficiency, *Quarterly Journal of Economics*, **97**, 453–470.

Nelson, R.R. (ed.) (1993), *National Systems of Innovation*, Oxford, UK: Oxford University Press.

Nelson, R.R., Winter S.G. (1982), *An Evolutionary Theory of Economic Change*, Cambridge, MA: The Belknap Press of Harvard University Press.

Onida, F. (1978), *Industria italiana e commercio internazionale*, Bologna: Il Mulino.

Onida, F., Malerba, F. (eds) (1990), *La ricerca scientifica*, Rome: SIPI.

Organisation for Economic Co-operation and Development (OECD) (2000), Main Science and Technology Indicators, STI-EAS Division, Paris.

Ostrom, E. (2010), Beyond markets and states: polycentric governance of complex economic systems, *American Economic Review*, **100**, 641–672.

Paci, R., Pusceddu, N. (2000), Stima dello stock di capitale nelle regioni italiane, *Rassegna Economica, Quaderni di Ricerca*, 97–118.

Paci, R., Saba, A. (1998), The empirics of regional economic growth in Italy 1951–93, *Rivista Internazionale di Scienze Economiche e Commerciali*, **45**, 515–542.

Paci, R., Sassu, A., Usai, S. (1997), International patenting and national technological specialization, *Technovation*, **17**, 25–38.

Parisi, M.L., Schiantarelli, F., Sembenelli, A. (2006), Productivity innovation and R&D: microevidence for Italy, *European Economic Review*, **50**, 2037–2061.

Parolini, C. (1991), Le imprese ad alta tecnologia, Milan: Franco Angeli.

Pastor-Satorras, R., Vespignani, A. (2004), *Evolution and Structure of the Internet*, Cambridge, UK: Cambridge University Press.

Patel, P., Pavitt, K. (1994), National innovation systems: why they are important and how they might be measured and compared, *Economics of Innovation and New Technology*, **3**, 77–95.

Patrucco, P.P. (2003), Institutional variety, networking and knowledge exchange: communication and innovation in the case of the Brianza technological district, *Regional Studies*, **37**, 159–172.

Patrucco, P.P. (2005), The emergence of technology systems: knowledge production and distribution in the case of the Emilian plastics district, *Cambridge Journal of Economics*, **29**, 37–56.

Patrucco, P.P. (2009), Collective knowledge production, costs and the dynamics of technological systems, *Economics of Innovation and New Technology*, **18**, 295–310.

Penrose, E.T. (1959 [1995]), *The Theory of the Growth of the Firm*, 1st and 3rd editions, Oxford, UK: Basil Blackwell (1959) and Oxford University Press (1995).

Prodi, R. (1966), *Modello di sviluppo di un settore in rapida crescita: L'industria della ceramica per l'edilizia*, Milan: Franco Angeli.

Prometeia (2003), Banca Dati Regionale, mimeo, Bologna, April.

Quatraro, F. (2006), Technological change and productivity growth in Italian regions, 1982–2001, *Région et Développement*, **24**.

Ricerche e Studi (R&S) (1970), *L'industria chimica*, Milan: Capriolo.

Romer, P.M. (1986), Increasing returns and long-run economic growth, *Journal of Political Economy*, **94**, 1002–1037.

Romer, P.M. (1990), Endogenous technological change, *Journal of Political Economy*, **98**, S71–102.

Rosenberg, N. (1963), Technical change in the machine tool industry: 1840–1910, *Journal of Economic History*, **23**, 4.

Rosenberg, N. (1982), *Inside the Black Box*, Cambridge, UK: Cambridge University Press.

Rosenberg, N., Mowery, D.C. (1998), *Paths of Innovation: Technological Change in 20th Century America*, Cambridge, UK: Cambridge University Press.

Rosenstein Rodan, P.N. (1943), Problems of industrialization of Eastern and Southern-Eastern Europe, *Economic Journal*, **53**, 202–211.

Rossi, N., Sorgato, A., Toniolo, G. (1993), I conti economici italiani: una ricostruzione statistica, 1890–1990, *Rivista di Storia economica*, **X**, 1.

Rossi, N., Toniolo, G. (1996), Italy, in Crafts, N.F.R., Toniolo, G. (eds), *Economic Growth in Europe Since 1945*, Cambridge, UK: Cambridge University Press.

Rossi, S. (2003), *La nuova economia. I fatti dietro il mito*, Bologna: Il Mulino.

Russo, M. (1985), Technical change and the industrial district: the role of interfirm relations in the growth and transformation of ceramic tile production in Italy, *Research Policy*, **14**, 329–343.

Russo, M. (2000), Complementary innovations and generative relationships: an ethnographic study, *Economics of Innovation and New Technology*, **9**, 517–557.

Ruttan, V.W. (1997), Induced innovation evolutionary theory and path dependence: sources of technical change, *Economic Journal*, **107**, 1520–1529.

Salter, W.E.G. (1966), *Productivity and Technical Change*, Cambridge, UK: Cambridge University Press.

Samuelson, P. (1965), A theory of induced innovation along Kennedy, Weiszacker lines, *Review of Economics and Statistics*, **47**, 343–356.

Scarda, A.M., Sirilli, G. (1982), Technology transfer and technological balance of payments, Quaderni CNR-ISRDS, No. 10.

Schmookler, J. (1966), *Invention and Economic Growth*, Cambridge, MA: Harvard University Press.

Schumpeter, J.A. (1911 [1934]), *The Theory of Economic Development*, Cambridge, MA: Harvard University Press.

Schumpeter, J.A. (1942), *Capitalism, Socialism and Democracy*, New York: Harper and Brothers.

Schumpeter, J.A. (1947), The creative response in economic history, *Journal of Economic History*, **7**, 149–159.

Scitovsky, T. (1954), Two concepts of external economies, *Journal of Political Economy*, **62**, 143–151.

Scott, A.J., Storper, M. (2007), Regions globalization development, *Regional Studies*, **41**, S191–S205.

Solow, R.M. (1957), Technical change and the aggregate production function, *Review of Economics and Statistics*, **39**, 312–320.

Svimez (1996), La politica per l'unificazione economica dell'ultimo cinquantennio e i problemi di oggi, Collana SVIMEZ, Bologna: Il Mulino, December.

Sylos Labini, P. (1967), Prezzi, distribuzione e investimenti in Italia dal 1951 al 1966: uno schema interpretativo, *Moneta e Credito*, **XX**, 79.

Sylos Labini, P. (1972), Investimenti, produttività e politica finanziaria, in Sylos Labini, P., *Sindacati, inflazione e produttività*, Roma-Bari: Laterza.

Teece, D. (1986), Profiting from technological innovation: implications for integration, collaboration, licensing and public policy, *Research Policy*, **15**, 285–305.

Teece, D.J. (1998), Capturing value from knowledge assets: the new economy, markets for know-how and intangible assets, *California Management Review*, **40**, 55–79.

Teece, D.J. (2000), *Managing Intellectual Capital*, Oxford, UK: Oxford University Press.

United States Patent and Trademark Office (USPTO) (2001), *Utility Patents in the TAF Database – PATSIC file*, CD-ROM.

Vasta, M. (1999), *Capitale umano e ricerca scientifica e tecnologica*, in Amatori, F., Bigazzi, D., Giannetti, R., Segreto, L. (eds), *Storia d'Italia. Annali*, vol. XV, *L'industria*, Torino: Einaudi.

Verspagen, B. (1996), Technology indicators and economic growth in the European area: some empirical evidence, in Ark, B. van, Crafts, N.F.R. (eds), *Quantitative Aspects of Post-war European Economic Growth*, Cambridge, UK: Cambridge University Press, pp. 215–243.

Viner, J. (1931), Costs curves and supply curve, *Zeitschrift für Nationalökonomie*, **3**, 23–46.

Von Hippel, E. (1988), *The Sources of Innovation*, Oxford, UK: Oxford University Press.

Von Hippel, E. (2005), *Democratizing Innovation*, Cambridge, MA: MIT Press.

Weitzman, M.L. (1996), Hybridizing growth theory, *American Economic Review*, **86**, 207–212.

Weitzman, M.L. (1998), Recombinant growth, *Quarterly Journal of Economics*, **113**, 331–360.

Williamson, O.E. (1996), *The Mechanisms of Governance*, New York: Oxford University Press.

Wolff, E.N. (1985), Industrial composition, interindustry effects, and the US productivity slowdown, *Review of Economics and Statistics*, **67**, 2.

Wolff, E.N. (1991), Capital formation and productivity convergence over the long term, *American Economic Review*, **81**, 3.

Young, A.A. (1928), Increasing returns and economic progress, *Economic Journal*, **38**, 527–542.

Zamagni, V. (1990), *Dalla periferia al centro. La seconda rinascita economica dell'Italia, 1861–1990*, Bologna: Il Mulino.

Zamagni, V. (1991), L'industria chimica in Italia dalle origini agli anni '50, in Amatori, F., Bezza, B. (eds), *Montecatini 1888–1966. Capitoli di storia di una grande impresa*, Bologna: Il Mulino.

Zamagni, V. (2010), *L'industria chimica italiana e l'IMI*, Bologna: Il Mulino.

Zeitlin, J., Herrigel, G. (eds) (1999), *Americanization and its Limits: Reworking US Technology and Management in Postwar Europe and Japan*, Oxford, UK: Oxford University Press.

Zellner, A. (1962), An efficient method of estimating seemingly unrelated regressions and tests for aggregation bias, *Journal of the American Statistical Association*, **57**, 298.

Index

academic system knowledge 4, 31, 32, 87, 183
adaptive reactions 10, 13, 42, 51, 129, 133
  see also creative adoption; foreign technology adaptation
agricultural sector 115, 124, 125
Antonelli, C. 5, 12, 16, 17, 24, 25, 26, 28, 31, 35, 37, 40, 44, 58, 76, 80, 90, 115, 116, 117, 118, 119, 121, 122, 123, 135, 136, 138, 140, 158, 159, 160, 161, 178
Arora, A. 23, 26
Arrow, K.J. 15, 19, 20, 31, 58–9, 88
Atkinson, A.B. 15–16
automated numerically controlled machinery 125–6, 127, 129–30, 131
automotive industry 99, 100, 101

Barbiellini Amidei, F. 115, 116, 117, 118, 119, 121, 122, 123, 135, 138, 158, 159, 160, 161, 178
Becattini, G. 85–6
Belussi, F. 79–80, 81–2
biased technological change *see* directed technological change
bounded rationality 52–3
Bresnahan, T. 24, 25
bundling of knowledge 34, 36, 56, 57

capital 52, 90, 125, 126, 130, 150, 151
capital abundance 140, 142, 149
capital goods 37, 77, 111–12, 125–6, 127–30, 131–2, 133, 134, 135, 174
  see also machinery

capital goods markets
  Italian distributed model 75, 77, 81, 84, 85, 86, 88, 89, 90, 181, 182
  knowledge generation and vertical dynamic interdependence 163, 164, 165, 174, 177
  localized knowledge exploitation and appropriation 37
capital goods prices 130
capital goods sectors
  Italian distributed model 75, 81, 84, 85, 86, 89, 90, 181, 182
  knowledge generation and vertical dynamic interdependence 163, 164, 165, 174, 177
  localized knowledge exploitation and appropriation 37
capital-intensive sectors 116, 117, 118, 119, 120
  see also ferrous and non-ferrous metals industry; non-metalliferous minerals industry
capital-intensive technologies
  capital supply 140, 142
  Italian distributed model 181, 182
  knowledge exploitation strategies and direction of technological change 139, 141–9, 154–9
  knowledge generation and vertical dynamic interdependence 168, 169, 171–2, 173, 175, 176, 177

structural change and systemic
interdependence in Italy 125,
127, 130, 133
capital–labour substitution 12, 38,
139, 142, 149, 150
capital productivity 142
capital scarcity 143
central Italy 88, 93, 97–8, 103, 106,
114, 115, 116, 128, 133, 149
see also north-central Italy
ceramics industry 78–9, 83–4, 89,
130, 132
Chandler, A.D. 29, 34, 135
chemical industry
Italian distributed model 80–81,
86
knowledge exploitation
strategies and direction of
technological change 143,
144, 146–7, 154, 156, 158,
159
knowledge generation and vertical
dynamic interdependence
163, 165, 166, 168, 170, 171,
172, 173, 174
measures of innovative activity in
Italy 99, 100, 101, 103, 106,
107, 108, 116–18, 119, 120
structural change and systemic
interdependence in Italy 126,
134
Ciccone, A. 23
clothing industry *see* textiles and
clothing industries
clustering 20, 46, 58–67, 87, 175
see also firm density; industrial
districts
codified knowledge 27, 28–9, 30, 32,
87, 110, 111, 173
cognitive distance 32
Cohen, W.M. 21, 25, 30
communication channels 5, 13–14,
26, 42, 44, 46, 47, 81, 174, 177,
181
see also knowledge
communication costs;
knowledge interactions

competences 15, 16, 17, 27, 30, 36,
37, 53, 141, 148
see also human capital; qualified
labour; skilled labour; skills;
technical skills
complementary assets 34, 35
complementary knowledge *see*
knowledge complementarity
complementary niche markets 78,
79, 80, 84, 86
complex systems 44, 55, 75–6, 82,
88
composition effects 116, 140
consumer goods sector
Italian distributed model 79–80,
83–4, 85, 86, 88, 89
knowledge exploitation
strategies and direction of
technological change 149
knowledge generation
and vertical dynamic
interdependence 163
structural change and systemic
interdependence in Italy
125–6, 130–31, 132, 134
contractual relationships 4, 30, 31,
81, 82, 87
corporate model of localized
technological knowledge
generation 3, 28, 29, 87, 173,
183
creative adoption 5–6, 111, 112,
129–30, 135, 148, 154, 174,
175, 181, 184
creative reactions
Italian distributed model 5–6, 76,
85, 89–90, 181
localized technological change
10–14, 17, 18, 42
model of localized technological
change 51, 67
pecuniary knowledge externalities
24

David, P.A. 24, 26, 38, 46, 48, 159
demand 5–6, 11, 12, 17, 22–3, 52,
174, 175, 176, 177

see also demand pull; derived
demand
demand pull
Italian distributed model 76, 77,
78, 85, 89, 181
knowledge generation
and vertical dynamic
interdependence 163, 164,
165, 170–73, 177–8
structural change and systemic
interdependence in Italy 124,
130–31, 134, 135
technological innovation 12
derived demand
Italian distributed model 77, 78,
83, 88–9, 181
knowledge generation
and vertical dynamic
interdependence 163, 164,
165
model of localized technological
change 60
pecuniary knowledge externalities
47, 60
structural change and systemic
interdependence in Italy
134
design industry 79–80, 109, 110
directed technological change 36–8,
39, 40, 43, 65–6, 68–9, 90, 125,
181
see also intentional decision-
making; knowledge
exploitation strategies and
direction of technological
change
distributed model of localized
technological knowledge
generation 24–30, 87
see also Italian distributed model
division of labour
Italian distributed model 5, 78,
80, 83, 85–6, 89, 181, 182,
184
pecuniary externalities 22–3
structural change and systemic
interdependence in Italy 130

downstream sectors 163–5, 166–73,
177–8
see also consumer goods sector
Durlauf, S.N. 44, 76
dynamic processes 38, 41, 44, 76,
79, 80, 84, 88

economic disequilibrium 10–14, 17,
42, 51, 53, 67
economic growth 1, 4, 22–3,
113–14, 168, 174, 175, 176,
177, 184
educational level 126–7, 132, 143,
174
see also human capital; skilled
labour; technical secondary
education
efficiency
external knowledge in localized
knowledge generation 44–5
Italian distributed model 85–6,
89
knowledge exploitation
strategies and direction of
technological change 150–53
knowledge generation
and vertical dynamic
interdependence 163, 164
localized knowledge exploitation
and appropriation 36, 39
localized technological
change and Total Factor
Productivity 112–14
model of localized technological
change 53
structural change and systemic
interdependence in Italy 133
electrical and electronic equipment
industries 93, 99, 100, 101, 103,
106, 107, 108
Emilia-Romagna, Italy 80–81, 93,
97–8, 99, 103, 106, 114
endogenous processes
communication networks 44
external knowledge 12–14, 41–2,
67
externalities 41

idiosyncratic production factors
    83
national innovation systems 88
pecuniary knowledge externalities
    13, 38, 41, 184
technological change 3, 12, 38,
    134, 143, 159
entry barriers 34, 36, 39–40, 45,
    64, 65
European markets 5–6
European Patent Office 103, 106
exclusivity 34, 35, 39, 59, 61
exports 129, 130
external codified knowledge 27, 28,
    29, 30, 32, 87, 110, 111, 173
external knowledge
    corporate model 87
    distributed model of localized
        technological knowledge
        generation 26–30, 87
    innovation systems 13–14, 41
    Italian distributed model 3–4, 5,
        29, 79, 82, 90, 183
    knowledge governance costs
        30–32
    knowledge interactions 41
    localized technological change
        12–13, 111
    localized technological knowledge
        generation 15, 17, 18
    model of localized technological
        change 51–2, 53, 54, 55, 67,
        68
    as a public/quasi-public good
        19–20
    see also external codified
        knowledge; external
        knowledge costs; external
        tacit knowledge; pecuniary
        knowledge externalities
external knowledge costs 53, 54–6,
    57, 60, 61, 62, 63, 64, 65, 67
external tacit knowledge 27, 28, 29,
    30, 87, 173, 178
externalities 41, 49
    see also external knowledge;
        pecuniary knowledge

externalities; technological
    externalities

fashion industry 79–80
feedback 14, 37, 42, 77, 78, 83, 140,
    173
    see also innovation cascades;
        positive feedback
ferrous and non-ferrous metals
    industry
    knowledge exploitation
        strategies and direction of
        technological change 145,
        146, 147, 157, 158
    knowledge generation
        and vertical dynamic
        interdependence 165, 166,
        168, 171, 172
    measures of innovative activity in
        Italy 116, 117, 118, 119
filieres
    Italian distributed model 4, 5, 76,
        77, 78, 79–82, 83, 84, 85, 86,
        182, 184
    pecuniary externalities 22–3
    pecuniary knowledge externalities
        44
    structural change and systemic
        interdependence in Italy 130,
        131, 134, 135
    see also knowledge generation
        and vertical dynamic
        interdependence
firm density 41, 46–8, 58–67
    see also clustering; geographical
        proximity; industrial
        districts
firm size 85–6
    see also large firms; medium-sized
        firms; small firms
firms *see* filieres; firm density; firm
    size; incumbent firms; learning
    firms; myopic firms; new firms;
    resource-based theory of the
    firm; State owned enterprises
    (SOEs)
flexible production factors 52

food industry
  Italian distributed model 83–4, 89
  knowledge exploitation
    strategies and direction of
    technological change 145,
    157, 158
  knowledge generation
    and vertical dynamic
    interdependence 165, 167,
    169, 171, 172, 173
  measures of innovative activity
    in Italy 107, 116, 117, 118,
    119, 120
  structural change and systemic
    interdependence in Italy 132
foreign non-incorporated
  technology acquisitions *see*
  Technological Balance of
  Payments (TBP)
foreign patent activity 102, 103–5
foreign technology adaptation 82,
  125, 127, 131, 132, 133, 135,
  153
foreign technology imports 127,
  129, 132, 148
  see also Technological Balance of
  Payments (TBP)
Fosfuri, A. 23, 26
France 95–6, 104, 109, 110, 113,
  114
Freeman, C. 26, 31, 90
furniture industry *see* wood and
  furniture industries

Gambardella, A. 23, 24, 25, 26
GDP 93, 94, 95, 113, 174, 176, 177,
  275
generic technological knowledge
  20–21
generic technology 45
geographical proximity 31, 32, 41,
  77, 80, 85
  see also clustering; firm density;
  industrial districts
Germany 95–6, 102, 103, 104, 106,
  109, 110, 113, 114
Griliches production function 56–8

Hayek, F.A, 25–6
Hicks, J.R. 12, 139, 141, 150, 159,
  160
high-tech industries 4, 99, 118, 183
human capital 70, 126–7, 128
  see also competences; qualified
  labour; skilled labour; skills;
  technical skills

idiosyncratic production factor
  prices 47, 48
idiosyncratic production factors
  and innovation systems 43–4
  Italian distributed model 80, 83,
  86, 90
  knowledge exploitation
    strategies and direction of
    technological change 140,
    141
  localized knowledge exploitation
    and appropriation 35–6, 38,
    39–40, 43, 59
  localized technological knowledge
    generation 17, 18, 69
  specific technological knowledge
    20
idiosyncratic technology 45, 46,
  77
imitation 19, 34, 132–3, 148
imitation barriers 34, 36, 39–40, 45,
  59, 64, 65, 69
incumbent firms 34, 45
industrial districts
  distributed model 87
  Italian distributed model 4, 5, 76,
  77, 78, 79–81, 82, 83, 85–6,
  88–9, 181, 182, 184
  knowledge generation
    and vertical dynamic
    interdependence 175
industrialization 148–9
innovation cascades 70, 77, 83, 84
innovation systems 13–14, 21, 22,
  41–9, 58–67, 70
  see also Italian distributed
    innovation system; national
    innovation systems

intellectual property 4–5, 59, 61,
69, 71
intentional decision-making
complementary knowledge in
innovation systems 44
Italian distributed model 76
knowledge communication 31
localized knowledge exploitation
and appropriation 35, 36–8,
39
localized technological knowledge
generation 16–17, 18
pecuniary knowledge externalities
23, 24
technological paths in innovation
systems 48
see also directed technological
change
inter-industry knowledge
interactions 4, 77, 78, 79,
80–81, 83, 184
intermediary goods 110, 111–12,
135, 174
intermediary goods markets
Italian distributed model 4, 5,
80, 81, 84, 85, 86, 88, 89, 90,
181, 182, 183
knowledge generation
and vertical dynamic
interdependence 163, 164,
165, 173, 174, 177
pecuniary externalities 23
intermediary goods sectors
knowledge exploitation
strategies and direction of
technological change 154,
158
measures of innovative activity
in Italy 99, 116, 117, 118,
119, 120
structural change and systemic
interdependence in Italy 126,
134
see also ferrous and non-ferrous
metals industry; non-
metalliferous minerals
industry; paper industry

internal codified knowledge 28, 29,
30
internal knowledge 13, 26, 27–9, 30,
32, 37, 53, 54, 55
internal knowledge costs 54
internal tacit knowledge 3, 28, 29,
30, 183
international markets 5–6, 85, 88,
163, 181
intra-industry knowledge
interactions 4, 77, 78, 79,
80–81, 83, 184
invention/inventors 19, 20, 34, 35
investment
Italian distributed model 77, 78,
84–5, 89, 181
knowledge exploitation
strategies and direction of
technological change 148,
149
knowledge generation
and vertical dynamic
interdependence 163, 164,
173, 178
structural change and systemic
interdependence in Italy 124,
125–30, 132
irreversibility of production factors
11, 12, 51–3
Istituti Tecnici Industriali 127, 131,
175, 176
Italian distributed innovation
system 6, 87–90, 132–5, 180–85
Italian distributed model
described 3–4, 5–6, 29, 75–90
case study evidence 78–82,
84–6
national innovation systems 6,
87–90, 132–5, 180–85

Japan 95–6, 102, 103, 104, 109, 110,
113, 114

Kaldor, N. 12, 23, 78, 89, 163
know-how 4, 110, 131
knowledge absorption costs 27, 54
knowledge accumulation 3, 25–6,

68, 81, 86, 87, 108, 132, 133, 134–5
knowledge appropriability 20
see also localized knowledge appropriability
knowledge communication costs 13, 30, 54
knowledge complementarity
distributed model of localized technological knowledge generation 25–6
external knowledge in innovation systems 43, 44, 45, 46, 48, 49
internal and external knowledge 26, 27, 29
Italian distributed model 29, 77, 81, 83, 86, 186
knowledge communication 31
localized knowledge exploitation and appropriation 37
localized technological knowledge generation 15
model of localized technological change 53, 58, 59, 67–8, 69
pecuniary knowledge externalities 48, 49
specific and generic technological knowledge 20
knowledge districts 83
knowledge exploitation *see* knowledge exploitation strategies and direction of technological change; localized knowledge exploitation
knowledge exploitation strategies and direction of technological change
effects of biased technological change on Total Factor Productivity 150–59
evidence for bias in favour of capital-intensive technologies 141–9
introduction 139–41
knowledge exploration 21, 29–30, 32, 35, 44

knowledge externalities *see* external knowledge; pecuniary knowledge externalities
knowledge generation 27–30
see also knowledge generation and vertical dynamic interdependence; localized knowledge generation
knowledge generation and vertical dynamic interdependence
regional evidence 174–8
sectoral evidence 162–74
knowledge generation function 53–6
knowledge governance costs 25, 26–7, 30–32, 43, 44, 47–8, 54–5, 57, 67, 69
knowledge indivisibility 25–6, 29, 42–3, 68
knowledge inputs 21, 26–9, 60, 68
knowledge integration 27, 28, 29, 31, 34, 35
knowledge-intensive organization 4–5, 32, 83, 183
knowledge interactions
distributed model 26, 28, 87
external knowledge 30–31, 41, 42
Italian distributed model 4, 5, 76, 77, 182
localized knowledge exploitation and appropriation 37
model of localized technological change 55, 59, 62–4, 67
networking 31
technological knowledge generation 28, 30
see also communication channels; inter-industry knowledge interactions; intra-industry knowledge interactions; knowledge communication costs; user–producer interactions
knowledge non-exhaustibility 21, 25, 54, 58
knowledge outputs 21, 26, 60, 68
knowledge outsourcing 4, 31, 32
knowledge prices 41, 60

knowledge rents 36, 39, 40, 61, 62, 65
knowledge substitutability 29
knowledge supply 60, 65
knowledge transactions 28, 30, 55, 67, 87

labour abundance 132, 140, 142, 143, 148, 154
labour cost increases
  Italian distributed model 76
  knowledge exploitation
    strategies and direction of technological change 143, 146–7, 149, 153
  knowledge generation
    and vertical dynamic interdependence 173, 174, 176
  model of localized technological change 52
  structural change and systemic interdependence in Italy 130, 133
  and technological innovation 12
  see also wage per labour unit
labour cost reductions 86
labour-intensive technologies 140, 142, 143, 148, 153–4, 155–8
labour markets 85–6
labour mobility 59, 87
labour productivity 113, 124, 142, 168, 177
labour relations 85–6, 87, 124, 133
labour scarcity 124, 130, 133, 143, 149, 153–4
labour supply 52, 124, 125, 150, 151
  see also capital–labour substitution; division of labour; human capital; labour abundance; labour markets; labour scarcity; labour value added share; qualified labour; skilled labour; unemployment
labour value added share 142, 144–5

Lane, D.A. 42, 76, 79, 82
large firms 3, 4, 34, 86, 87, 133, 134, 183
Lazio, Italy 93, 97–8, 99, 103, 106
learning
  composition effects 140
  distributed model 87
  and external knowledge in innovation systems 44
  Italian distributed model 3, 4, 29, 76–7, 79, 89, 182, 183
  knowledge exploitation
    strategies and direction of technological change 143, 148
  knowledge generation
    and vertical dynamic interdependence 163, 173, 174, 177
  knowledge governance costs 32
  localized knowledge exploitation and appropriation 35
  localized technological change 111
  localized technological knowledge generation 15–16, 17, 18
  structural change and systemic interdependence in Italy 132, 134, 135
  Technological Balance of Payments in Italy 110
  technological innovation 11, 12, 13
  technological knowledge generation 27, 28, 29, 30
  see also academic system knowledge; learning firms; valorization of learning
learning firms 37, 75
Levinthal, D.A. 21, 25, 30
licences 30, 109, 110, 131, 133
Liguria, Italy 93, 97–8, 99, 106
local pools of knowledge
  composition effects 140
  distributed model of localized technological knowledge generation 27, 28

external knowledge in innovation
systems 44–5, 46
Italian distributed model 3, 77,
82, 84, 86, 90
model of localized technological
change 53, 58, 59–60, 61–2,
64, 65, 66–7, 69
pecuniary knowledge externalities
47, 48, 58, 59–60, 61–2, 64,
65, 66–7
structural change and systemic
interdependence in Italy 133
local product markets 18
local production factor abundance
external knowledge in innovation
systems 43
Italian distributed model 77, 80,
83, 86
localized knowledge exploitation
and appropriation 36, 43,
46, 59
localized technological knowledge
generation 16
model of localized technological
change 59, 64, 65, 66, 69
structural change and systemic
interdependence in Italy 135
local production factor markets 18,
140
see also capital goods markets;
intermediary goods markets;
labour markets
local resource endowments 69–70
localized knowledge appropriability
34–40, 43, 59–60, 61, 66, 69,
77, 141
localized knowledge appropriability
reduction 59, 60, 61, 62, 63,
64, 65
localized knowledge exploitation
complementary knowledge in
innovation systems 44
external knowledge in innovation
systems 43
idiosyncratic technology and
locally abundant production
factors 46

Italian distributed model 79, 80,
84, 86, 90
localized knowledge
appropriability 34–40
localized technological knowledge
generation 17
model of localized technological
change 64–5
production costs 45
localized knowledge exploration
44
localized knowledge generation
external knowledge in innovation
systems 44–5, 46
knowledge exploitation
strategies and direction of
technological change 141
localized technological innovation
15–18
model of localized technological
change 53–6, 67, 68–9
specific and generic technological
knowledge complementarity
20
localized paths of technological
change 69–70
localized technological change
10–14, 17, 18, 24, 42, 111–21,
180–81, 184–5
see also model of localized
technological change
Lombardia, Italy 93, 97–8, 99, 106,
114

machine tools industry 83–4, 99,
101, 130, 131
machinery 125–6, 127, 129–30, 131,
148, 149, 154, 159
machinery capital intensity 168,
169, 171–2, 173, 177, 178
machinery industry
Italian distributed model 4, 78,
80–81, 83–4, 85
knowledge exploitation
strategies and direction of
technological change 154,
159

measures of innovative activity in
    Italy 99, 100, 103, 105, 106,
    107, 110
structural change and systemic
    interdependence in Italy 127,
    129–30, 131–2
manufacturing industries
Italian distributed model 79–80,
    83–4, 85, 86, 88, 89
knowledge exploitation
    strategies and direction of
    technological change 142–9,
    152–9
knowledge generation
    and vertical dynamic
    interdependence 163,
    165–74, 175–8
measures of innovative activity
    in Italy 93, 99, 100, 101, 113,
    114, 115, 116–20
structural change and systemic
    interdependence in Italy
    124–6, 127, 130–32, 133–4
see also automotive industry;
    ceramics industry; chemical
    industry; design industry;
    electrical and electronic
    equipment industries;
    fashion industry; ferrous and
    non-ferrous metals industry;
    food industry; high-tech
    industries; mechanical
    engineering industry; non-
    metalliferous minerals
    industry; paper industry;
    plastics industry; precision
    instruments industry;
    rubber industry; textiles
    and clothing industries;
    transportation equipment
    industry; wood and furniture
    industries
March, J.C. 34, 37
Marche, Italy 98–9, 103, 106, 114
Marchionatti, R. 80
Marshall, A. 9, 20, 21–2, 41, 50
Marx, K. 12, 136, 139, 160

mass production 124, 148
Matsuyama, K. 23, 44
Maxfield, R. 79
measures of innovative activity in
    Italy
localized technological
    change and Total Factor
    Productivity (TFP) 1–2,
    111–20
patents 102–8, 109, 110, 111, 112
R&D expenditures 1, 93–101,
    111, 112
Technological Balance of
    Payments (TBP) 108–11
mechanical engineering industry
Italian distributed model 78, 80,
    86, 88, 89
knowledge exploitation
    strategies and direction of
    technological change 143,
    144, 146–7, 154, 155, 158
knowledge generation
    and vertical dynamic
    interdependence 163, 165,
    166, 168, 170, 171, 172, 173,
    174, 175–6, 177
measures of innovative activity in
    Italy 99, 100, 101, 103, 106,
    107, 108, 116–18, 119, 120
structural change and systemic
    interdependence in Italy 131,
    134
see also machine tools industry;
    machinery industry; robotics
    industry
medium-sized firms 85, 134
metals 107
see also ferrous and non-ferrous
    metals industry
minerals *see* ferrous and non-
    ferrous metals industry; non-
    metalliferous minerals industry
model of localized technological
    change
basic model 51–3
conclusions 67–71
dynamic interplay between

positive and negative pecuniary knowledge externalities 58–67
Griliches production function 56–8
knowledge generation function 53–6
modern sectors
knowledge exploitation strategies and direction of technological change 143, 148, 154, 158, 159
structural change and systemic interdependence in Italy 133–4
Total Factor Productivity 116–18, 119, 120
see also chemical industry; high-tech industries; mechanical engineering industry; rubber industry; transportation equipment industry
monopolistic prices 59, 61, 65–6
myopic firms 52–3

national innovation systems 6, 26, 87–90, 132–5, 180–85
negative pecuniary externalities 22
negative pecuniary knowledge externalities 47–8, 58–60, 61–2, 63, 64, 65–6
Nelson, R.R. 19, 25, 38, 53, 55, 90
net pecuniary knowledge externalities 60–64, 65–6
Netherlands 105, 113
networking costs 27, 30, 54
networks 11, 13–14, 31, 76
new biased technologies 36, 69, 150
new firms 34, 62–4, 65, 133, 149
see also new knowledge-intensive firms; new specialized firms
new growth theory 19–21, 70, 180
new knowledge-intensive firms 79
new specialized firms 4, 5, 80, 81, 86, 88–9
new technological knowledge 13, 53, 54, 55, 56, 57, 61

see also localized knowledge generation
nodes 46, 47
non-metalliferous minerals industry 116, 117, 119, 145, 157, 158, 165, 166, 168, 171
non-rivalry of knowledge exchange and use 59
north Italy 88–9, 93, 97–8, 99, 103, 106
north-central Italy 175–6, 177–8
northeast Italy 88, 93, 97–8, 99, 103, 106, 114, 115, 116, 128, 133, 148–9
northwest Italy 88–9, 93, 97–8, 99, 103, 106, 114, 115, 116, 128, 133

open innovation model 4–5, 183
opportunity costs 120
optimum cluster size 41, 48
optimum knowledge pool size 61, 66–7
organized structures, Italian distributed model 76
output 60, 61, 150–51
output growth 1, 71, 163–4, 168, 177

paper industry
knowledge exploitation strategies and direction of technological change 145, 157, 158
knowledge generation and vertical dynamic interdependence 165, 167, 169, 171, 172
measures of innovative activity in Italy 116, 117, 118, 119, 120
structural change and systemic interdependence in Italy 130
Parisi, M.L. 84–5, 112
past dependence 45, 48, 88
patents
corporate model 87

as external knowledge 30
Italian distributed model 79
knowledge generation
    and vertical dynamic
        interdependence 168, 169,
        170, 171–2, 173
measures of innovative activity
    in Italy 102–8, 109, 110, 111,
    112
structural change and systemic
    interdependence in Italy 131,
    133
path dependence 17, 38, 43, 45, 48,
    55, 69–70, 88, 140
Patrucco, P.P. 29, 80–81, 86
pecuniary externalities 22–3
pecuniary knowledge externalities
    adaptive reactions 13
    distributed model of localized
        technological knowledge
        generation 25, 27
    environmental contexts 32
    external knowledge in innovation
        systems 43, 44
    and innovation systems 21, 22,
        41, 42–3, 46–7, 70
    Italian distributed model 76, 77,
        81, 82–3, 86, 89–90, 183–4,
        185
    knowledge complementarity 48,
        49
    knowledge exploitation
        strategies and direction of
        technological change 139–40,
        141
    knowledge generation
        and vertical dynamic
            interdependence 163, 164,
            165, 170, 173, 174, 175–6
    localized knowledge exploitation
        and appropriation 35, 36,
        38–9
    localized technological knowledge
        generation 21, 22
    model of localized technological
        change 54–6, 57–67,
        69

positive and negative effects of
    firm density 46–8, 58–67
relevance 23–4
structural change and systemic
    interdependence in Italy 131,
    134, 135
synchronic knowledge
    indivisibility 27, 68
versus technological externalities
    68
see also negative pecuniary
    knowledge externalities;
    net pecuniary knowledge
    externalities; positive
    pecuniary knowledge
    externalities
Penrose, E.T. 16
perfect competition 59, 61
Piemonte, Italy 93, 97–8, 99, 103,
    106, 114
plastics industry 80–81, 101, 130
polycentric character 29, 55, 76–7,
    86, 177, 182, 183
positive feedback 46, 56, 58, 85, 88,
    181
positive pecuniary externalities 22
positive pecuniary knowledge
    externalities 47–8, 55–6, 60, 61,
    62–4, 65
precision instruments industry 100,
    106, 107, 132
private sector 93, 96, 115, 133
process innovations 78, 79, 84–5,
    89, 139, 149, 163, 178, 181, 182
Prodi, R. 78
product innovations 84–5, 89,
    132–3, 134, 148, 149, 163, 178
product prices 45, 48, 59, 61–2, 64,
    65–6
production cost increases 53
production cost reduction
    external knowledge in innovation
        systems 43, 45
    Italian distributed model 77
    knowledge exploitation
        strategies and direction of
        technological change 140–41

knowledge generation
and vertical dynamic
interdependence 164
localized knowledge exploitation
and appropriation 36, 39, 43
model of localized technological
change 62, 63, 66, 69
production costs 45
production factor costs 143
production factor intensive use
external knowledge in innovation
systems 43, 45
Italian distributed model 77, 80,
83, 86
knowledge exploitation
strategies and direction of
technological change 141
localized knowledge exploitation
and appropriation 35–6, 37,
· 38, 39–40, 43
localized technological knowledge
generation 15, 16
model of localized technological
change 64, 65, 66, 69
production factor prices 11, 12, 17,
22, 23, 38, 39, 150
production factor substitution 12,
38, 139, 142, 149, 150
production factors 20, 57, 58
see also capital; capital goods
markets; idiosyncratic
production factors;
intermediary goods markets;
labour markets; labour
supply; local production
factor abundance;
production factor intensive
use; production factor
prices; production factor
substitution
production functions 56–8, 141–2,
150–53
productivity 140, 150, 168, 181
see also capital productivity;
labour productivity; output
growth; Total Factor
Productivity (TFP)

profitability valuation 37–8
proximity 79–80
see also cognitive distance;
geographical proximity;
relational proximity
public funding 93, 133, 183
public goods 19–20
public research institutes 32, 87

qualified labour 30, 59, 127
see also competences; human
capital; skilled labour;
technical skills

R&D
corporate model 3, 87, 173, 183
Italian distributed model 83,
84–5
model of localized technological
change 53
structural change and systemic
interdependence in Italy 131,
133
technological knowledge
generation 27, 28, 29, 30
R&D expenditures 1, 77, 93–101,
111, 112
reciprocity 30, 82, 83–4
recombination processes 5, 15, 21,
26, 29, 31, 110, 111, 183, 184
recursive processes 41–2, 181
regions of Italy *see* central Italy;
Emilia-Romagna, Italy;
Lazio, Italy; Liguria, Italy;
Lombardia, Italy; Marche,
Italy; north Italy; north-
central Italy; northeast Italy;
northwest Italy; Piemonte,
Italy; Sassuolo, Italy; south
Italy; Toscana, Italy; Veneto,
Italy
relational proximity 77, 80
relationships 30
see also knowledge interactions;
networks; reciprocity;
relational proximity; user–
producer interactions

repeated interactions/transactions 5, 31, 59, 81
research centres 26, 30, 32, 87, 131
resistance to change 17
resource-based theory of the firm 16, 70
revenues 62, 63, 65, 66
rivalry of knowledge exchange 59
robotics industry 101
rubber industry
  corporate model of localized technological knowledge generation 173
  knowledge exploitation strategies and direction of technological change 143, 144, 146–7, 154, 156, 158
  knowledge generation and vertical dynamic interdependence 165, 167, 169, 171, 172, 173
  measures of innovative activity in Italy 100, 101, 107, 116–18, 119, 120
Russo, M. 78–9

Sassuolo, Italy 78–9
Schumpeter, J.A. 9, 10–11, 17, 34, 46, 59
Scitovsky, T. 22, 33
search 13, 24, 30, 31, 34, 35, 36, 44, 46
search costs 13
sectors
  knowledge exploitation strategies and direction of technological change 142–3, 154
  knowledge generation and vertical dynamic interdependence 162–74
  measures of innovative activity 93, 99–101, 103, 106–8, 113, 115, 116–20
  see also agricultural sector; capital goods sectors; capital-intensive sectors; consumer goods sector; downstream sectors; intermediary goods sectors; manufacturing industries; modern sectors; private sector; traditional sectors; upstream sectors
selective strategies 18, 35, 38, 40, 46, 140–41
semi-skilled labour 132, 135, 148, 154
skilled labour 13, 83, 87, 127, 132, 153–4, 159
skills 27, 69–70
  see also competences; human capital; skilled labour; technical skills
small firms
  external knowledge 15
  Italian distributed model 3, 4, 5, 81–2, 83, 86, 101, 183, 184
  structural change and systemic interdependence in Italy 133, 134
Solow, R.M. 122, 123, 151, 152
south Italy 88, 93, 97–8, 99, 103, 106, 114–15, 116, 128, 175–6, 177
South Korea 102, 105
southeast Italy 88, 115
southwest Italy 115
Spain 95, 105
specialization
  external knowledge in innovation systems 43
  Italian distributed model 4, 5, 78, 80, 81, 83, 84, 85–6, 88, 89, 101, 106–7, 181, 182, 183, 184
  measures of innovative activity in Italy 101, 106–7, 109–10, 116
  pecuniary externalities 22–3, 38
  structural change and systemic interdependence in Italy 130, 131, 135
specific technological knowledge 20
State owned enterprises (SOEs) 133, 134

Stiglitz, J.E. 15–16
structural change 86
structural change and systemic
    interdependence in Italy
    1950s–1960s 124–5, 126–31,
        132–3, 134, 141, 142, 153–4
    1970s–1980s 125–6, 127, 128,
        129, 131–2, 133–5, 141, 142,
        154, 159
    1990s 125, 126, 127, 128, 129,
        135, 141
Sweden 105
Switzerland 104
synchronic knowledge integration
    25–6, 27, 68

tacit knowledge
    distributed model 87
    Italian distributed model 5, 81, 86
    localized knowledge exploitation
        and appropriation 37
    localized technological knowledge
        generation 15, 17
    technological innovation 12
    technological knowledge
        generation 27, 28–9, 30
technical assistance 109, 110, 131
technical secondary education 127,
    128, 131, 175, 176, 177
technical skills 143, 148, 168, 169,
    170, 171–2, 173, 174, 175–6,
    177
Technological Balance of Payments
    (TBP) 108–11, 131
technological externalities 22, 68,
    163, 170, 174, 175–6
technological innovation 10–11,
    34–40
technological knowledge 20–21, 58
technological paths 38, 43, 45, 48
technological systems 80–81
Teece, D.J. 29, 34, 35
textiles and clothing industries
    Italian distributed model 80,
        83–4, 88, 89
    knowledge exploitation
        strategies and direction of

technological change 143,
    144, 146–7, 155, 158
knowledge generation
    and vertical dynamic
        interdependence 163, 165,
        167, 169, 170, 171, 172, 173
measures of innovative activity in
    Italy 116, 117, 118, 119, 120
structural change and systemic
    interdependence in Italy 126,
        130, 132
Toscana, Italy 93, 97–8, 99, 103, 106
Total Factor Productivity (TFP)
    external knowledge spillovers
        20–21, 70
    Italian distributed model 4, 6, 77,
        84, 89–90, 182
    knowledge exploitation
        strategies and direction of
        technological change 140,
        150–59
    knowledge generation
        and vertical dynamic
            interdependence 162–3,
            164–5, 166–73, 174, 175–8
    measures of innovative activity in
        Italy 1–2, 111–21
    model of localized technological
        change 53, 57–8, 61, 62, 66
    structural change and systemic
        interdependence in Italy 132,
        135
traditional sectors
    Italian distributed model 4, 83–4,
        88–9
    knowledge exploitation
        strategies and direction of
        technological change 143,
        148, 149, 154, 157, 158
    measures of innovative activity in
        Italy 101, 108, 116, 117, 118,
        119, 120
    structural change and systemic
        interdependence in Italy
        125–6, 131, 133, 134
    see also consumer goods sector;
        food industry; textiles and

clothing industries; wood
and furniture industries
traditional technologies 110
transaction-based interactions 5,
82, 182, 183
transaction costs 13, 27, 30, 81
transportation equipment industry
corporate model of localized
technological knowledge
generation 173
knowledge exploitation
strategies and direction of
technological change 143,
144, 146–7, 154, 156
knowledge generation
and vertical dynamic
interdependence 163, 165,
166, 168, 170, 171, 172, 173
measures of innovative activity in
Italy 93, 100, 101, 106, 107,
116–18, 119
structural change and systemic
interdependence in Italy 132
trust 30, 32, 82

UK 95–6, 104, 113, 114
unemployment 12
universities *see* academic system
knowledge
upstream sectors 163, 164–5,
166–73, 174, 177, 178
see also capital goods sectors;
intermediary goods sectors
USA 95–6, 102, 103–5, 113, 114,
133, 183
user–producer interactions
distributed model 87
external knowledge 31
Italian distributed model 4, 5,
76, 77, 78, 79–81, 82, 83, 84,
85, 86, 88, 89, 90, 181, 182,
183, 184
knowledge exploitation
strategies and direction of
technological change 139
knowledge generation
and vertical dynamic

interdependence 164, 173,
177
structural change and systemic
interdependence in Italy 131,
134, 135
USPTO 102, 103, 104–5, 107

valorization of learning
distributed model 87
Italian distributed model 3, 82, 85
localized knowledge exploitation
and appropriation 36, 37
localized technological knowledge
generation 15
model of localized technological
change 53
structural change and systemic
interdependence in Italy 133
Technological Balance of
Payments in Italy 111
value added (VA) share
knowledge exploitation
strategies and direction of
technological change 158
knowledge generation
and vertical dynamic
interdependence 164–5,
166–8, 169, 170, 171–2, 173
measures of innovative activity
in Italy 114–15, 116, 118–20,
158
Veneto, Italy 98–9, 103, 106, 114
vertical transmission mechanisms
22–3, 31, 149, 182
see also knowledge generation
and vertical dynamic
interdependence

wage per labour unit
Italian distributed model 76, 86,
182
knowledge exploitation
strategies and direction of
technological change 143,
146–7
knowledge generation
and vertical dynamic

interdependence 168,
169–70, 171–2, 173, 175,
176, 177
model of localized technological
change 52
structural change and systemic
interdependence in Italy 124,
126, 130, 132, 133
technological innovation 12
see also labour cost increases;
labour cost reductions
wage reductions 86
Weitzman, M.L. 21, 26, 29, 53,
55
Williamson, O.E. 30
Winter, S.G. 38

wood and furniture industries
Italian distributed model 83–4, 89
knowledge exploitation
strategies and direction of
technological change 143,
145, 154, 155, 158
knowledge generation
and vertical dynamic
interdependence 163, 165,
167, 169, 171, 172, 173
measures of innovative activity in
Italy 116, 117, 118, 119,
120
structural change and systemic
interdependence in Italy 130,
132